THE OXFORD HISTORY OF MUSIC
VOL. II

THE
POLYPHONIC PERIOD OF MUSIC
PART II

THE OXFORD
HISTORY OF MUSIC
VOL. II

THE POLYPHONIC PERIOD
PART II
METHOD OF MUSICAL ART
1400–*c.* 1600

BY

H. E. WOOLDRIDGE, M.A.
LATE SLADE PROFESSOR OF FINE ART IN THE
UNIVERSITY OF OXFORD

SECOND EDITION
REVISED BY
PERCY C. BUCK
KING EDWARD PROFESSOR OF
MUSIC IN THE UNIVERSITY OF
LONDON

NEW YORK
COOPER SQUARE PUBLISHERS, INC.
1973

Revised edition Published 1929 by Oxford University Press
Reprinted by Permission of Oxford University Press
Published 1973 by Cooper Square Publishers, Inc.
59 Fourth Avenue, New York, New York 10003
International Standard Book Number 0-8154-0470-0
Library of Congress Catalog Card Number 72-97072

Printed in the United States of America

PREFACE TO THE FIRST EDITION

WHEN preparing the first volume of this work I was permitted by the kindness of the keeper of the Laurentian Library at Florence to have a considerable number of pages of the *Antiphonarium Mediceum* photographed, and was thereby enabled not only to study its methods at leisure, but also to exhibit some interesting examples in facsimile. I had hoped to obtain similar material for the present volume, and to give illustrations of another very remarkable work in the same Library, commonly known as the Squarcialupi MS., containing compositions by Landini and his school, but permission to make photographs was in this case, I regret to say, not accorded. For my examples from this work, therefore, and from some others in Florence, I am indebted to the courtesy of a student of the MS., Mr. J. Wolf, and of Messrs. Breitkopf and Haertel, who published a number of that gentleman's transcriptions in the quarterly Journal of the *Internationale Musikgesellschaft*. The examples of the work of Machault I owe to the kindness of the authorities of the Bibliothèque Nationale in Paris, who allowed all necessary photographs to be made.

I desire also to thank Mr. Godfrey Arkwright for permission to print an extract from his edition of Tye's six-part Mass *Euge bone*, Mr. J. R. Stainer and Miss Stainer for leave to use their published facsimiles and transcriptions of MSS. in the Bodleian Library, Miss Stainer for most kindly scoring many examples from printed part-books, and Mrs. H. E. Wooldridge for translating large portions of important German works for my use.

H. E. WOOLDRIDGE.

51162

PREFACE TO THE SECOND EDITION

THE *Oxford History of Music*, which was published in 1901, consisted of six volumes, of which the first and second were written by the late Professor Wooldridge. It is now found necessary to issue a new edition of these two volumes, and it is but seemly, in the case of a scholar of such high standing, to explain why they are not merely reprinted in their original form.

The purpose of the *Oxford History* was to give, in reasonable perspective, the story of the whole growth of the Art of Music; and in the first two volumes that story was to be brought down to the great climax with which the sixteenth century closed. It has, however, been a common criticism of this first volume that, masterly as it admittedly is, it plunges too rapidly into those developments of European music which ultimately led to the great polyphonists. The story of music is a long one, and the texture of modern music is composed of strands which lead back to immemorial ages. And by the scholar, the student, and the amateur alike some account of these earlier stages, fuller than that offered by Professor Wooldridge, is now felt to be desirable.

It has been decided, therefore, to add to the *Oxford History of Music* an Introductory Volume, in which the work of the earlier pioneers in the Art of Music is dealt with by authoritative scholars. This new volume contains essays on Greek music, Jewish music, Plain-song, Treatises on music, Notation, Folk-song, Troubadors, Folk music, and other kindred subjects; thus covering in detail the ground of the first three chapters of the original first volume.

The endeavour has been made throughout to preserve

intact, as far as possible, the results of Professor Wooldridge's scholarship in his own words. But certain small portions have been omitted (together with many examples, or portions of examples) and occasionally a small interpolation has been made, or a new example added, in order either to elucidate the text or to include results of a later research. Further, in vol. ii Professor Wooldridge's accounts of the Spanish School (including Vittoria) and Palestrina have been revised and augmented by Mr. J. B. Trend and the Reverend Dom Anselm Hughes, O.S.B., respectively, and two new chapters have been added: *Song*, by Mr. J. A. Westrup, and *Instrumental Music*, by Mr. Gerald M. Cooper.

P. C. BUCK.

1932.

CONTENTS

CHAPTER I

FORMATION OF SCHOOLS

CHAPTER II

THE NETHERLAND SCHOOL (p. 88)

CHAPTER III

CHAPTER IV

THE PERFECTION OF THE METHOD (p. 197)

CHAPTER V

SONG

CHAPTER VI

INSTRUMENTAL MUSIC (p. 375)

FORMATION OF SCHOOLS

ENGLAND

THE earliest rise of an English School of composition, properly so called, may be traced probably to the first quarter of the fifteenth century. The specimens of earlier date which we have examined occur in scattered MSS., and are themselves few in number, isolated, and nameless, affording no suggestion of any close association of workers, or of that busy emulous activity of individuals united in promoting the gradual evolution of a common ideal, which constitute the life and progress of a school. But at the period at which we have now arrived, we become aware of collections of compositions, suggesting from their number, similarity, and relative importance, the work of a true school. We also obtain glimpses of the school itself, which is partly seen as existing through the influence and technical ability of one man, and partly also as belonging to a class which arose from the institution of Royal and princely 'Chapels', musical establishments created in imitation of the Papal choir, which were now beginning to be formed in all the principal courts of Europe.

The benefits to the art which were derived from the existence of these privileged bodies of musicians were fully recognized in their own day. Indeed, Johannes Tinctoris, the Flemish theorist, writing in 1477, attributes all the great improvements apparent in music in his time directly or indirectly to the institution of Chapels, since, as he says, the advantages connected with the position of a singer in a Chapel Royal—the honour and glory, and the liberal emoluments—were such as caused this distinction to be much sought after, 'so that many able men were stirred up to a closer study of the art, in order both to obtain an appointment and to do well in it. Whence,' he adds, 'it comes that in the present age the science of our music has received so wonderful an enlargement that it might seem to be a new art.' From this it would seem that the ordinary Colleges of singers attached to Cathedrals, often poorly paid and subject to clerical influence, could not be compared, in respect of musical impulse and originality, with the Royal Chapels, which formed part of the King's household establishment and were answerable to the sovereign alone; and indeed it is easy to see that these associations of carefully chosen workers, recognized as authorities, invited to provide the music which they were themselves to sing, stimulated in composition by the hope not only of Royal commendation and reward but also of public recognition and approval, must have been in all cases wonderful centres of artistic progress, hotbeds of composition, daily putting forth finer and still finer productions.

The principal sources from which contemporary examples of English fifteenth-century music may be obtained are three in number. The first is a volume forming part of the Selden collection of MSS. in the Bodleian Library in Oxford, containing fifty-three examples of the work of the period, composed probably between 1415 and 1455; the second is a large choir-book containing one hundred and thirty-eight compositions, dating from about 1430 to 1480, now in the library of St. Edmund's (Catholic) College, at Old Hall, near Ware, in Hertfordshire; the third is to be found in certain MSS. at Vienna (formerly at Trent), Modena, and Bologna, in which are preserved some English productions of this time, in character not altogether unlike those in the Old Hall MSS., but containing also important differences. Besides these, the Douce and Ashmole collections in the Bodleian, and a volume in the Cambridge University Library containing a mutilated Mass, afford examples which also are deserving of attention.

The examples in the Douce and Ashmole MSS. being somewhat earlier in date than those of the larger collections, we may refer to them now before passing on. They are of considerable interest, since they exhibit, besides examples of the current form, traces of two distinct methods, inherited from the previous century, neither of which was destined to survive in the form in which we here see them. One is the French method which was illustrated in some of our examples of Machault's secular work, which consists in a repetition of part of the music to a fresh text, with an *ouvert* for the first time and a *clos* at the end of the second. In the Douce MS. 381, are three examples of this shortened *Ballade* form—*Ie have so longe kepe schepe*, *My cares comen ever anew*, and *I rede thou be*; these exemplify a certain kind of French influence, not difficult to understand, which seems to have been exerted upon English music for a time, but which was clearly not great or extensive, since no other examples of it apart from these three are known to exist. The second method is that of a continuous *faulx bourdon*, a mode of treatment which, notwithstanding its popularity as a form of extempore discant, was never, as we shall see, tolerated in serious composition.

Since we shall not return to these MSS., a little song (*Alas departynge*), which illustrates very effectively the current method of two-part writing before the middle of the century, may be given now from Ashmole, 191. Here we perceive at once the evidence of a considerable advance. Both parts are perfectly melodious and delightful to sing, yet the kind of melody employed is distinctly contrapuntal and polyphonic in character, containing many phrases, in both parts, which will be found still in use by the treble and tenor voices in some of the best compositions of the following century. The composer has been liberal in his use of thirds and sixths, yet with judgement, so that the ear is charmed, not satiated as in the previous example.

ALAS DEPARTYNGE.

Song for two voices.

Bodl. Lib.
MSS. Ashmole, 191, fol. 194-5.

About 1445.

The music contained in the Selden MS. is miscellaneous in character. The greater part of the volume consists of sacred songs in two parts, chiefly relating to the Saviour's nativity, of a kind already familiar to us from our former examples, *Quene of Evene, Iesu Cristes milde moder*, and others already given in the present work. In these songs the bold and facile style of the text affords excellent opportunities for the display of the characteristic English qualities in the music, and we recognize at once the great gifts of metrical melody, and the energetic yet suave expression, which have distinguished our native composers at all times. The rest of the MS. is composed of works of higher technical aim—such, for instance, as the interesting *Deo Gracias Anglia*, or celebration of the victory of Agincourt, for two solo voices and three-part chorus;—and we find also copies of a few works of still greater musical importance, existing in other collections, given here without the composers' names; indeed, with one exception, names are withheld throughout the volume. It should also be said that the collection includes two secular pieces of some value. One is a song in praise of agriculture; the other is a drinking song, *Tappster, Dryngker*, in a style somewhat suggestive of the later 'Catch', in which the personages would seem to be farmers met together upon a market day. Of these two pieces there is little to be said, except that they are in no way inferior technically to the sacred pieces. They are, however, the work of composers who were still apparently content with the old bareness of sound, which sometimes, indeed, occurs in a most strident manner when, as it would seem, there could be no possible necessity for its appearance. An instance of this may be found at the words 'Avale the stake', in the drinking song.

In the *Deo Gracias*, which here follows, the melody is quite admirable, and again we find the descant also pleasing in itself; but again, also, the combination is often unsatisfactory, producing, as usual at this time, sometimes bare harmony, and sometimes aimless and arbitrary discord like that of Machault and the Italians. Moreover, the application of the rules of *Musica Ficta* much weakens the fine melody, which is in the severest form of the first ecclesiastical mode.

Deo Gracias Anglia.

Bodl. Lib.
Selden MSS., B. 26, fol. 17ᵛ.

Before 1421.

[Duo]

De - o gra - ci - as . . An - - gli - - a red - de pro vic - - to - - - - - - ri - a. Owre Kynge went forth to Nor - man - dy, with grace . . and might . . . of chy - val - ry; Ther God for

hym . . wrought merve - - lus - ly, wher -

- fore Eng - londe may calle and

cry; De - o gra - - - - - - ci - as.

Chorus.

De - o gra - ci - as An - - - -

- - gli - - a red - de pro

vic - - to - - - ri - a.

The limits of our space forbid any further exhibition of the
contents of this MS., but it may be said that the specimens
given fairly represent the different kinds of subject to be found
in it, and the special methods employed in dealing with them.
With respect to the authorship of the music, or of any part of
it, nothing can be suggested at present, since the MS. gives no
clue to this, nor to the place of origin. On the other hand, we
may perhaps venture to say that there can be little doubt that
the collection represents one aspect, interesting from its variety,
of a newly forming English school; for the agreement in respect
of method is so evident in each branch of composition, and the
steps by which progress was advanced are so marked, that a
consideration of these fifty-odd pieces as the work of composers who were entirely independent or isolated, seems impossible. That an English school actually existed during the first
half of the fifteenth century, and that it had already reached
a relatively high degree of excellence in its productions before
the year 1450, is clear from a poem—*Le Champion des Dames*,
by Martin le Franc—composed certainly between 1436 and
1444, in which the special superiority of the leaders of the
contemporary French school, Guillaume Dufay and Binchois,
as compared with the men of the older generation, Tapissier,
Carmen, Cesaris, is said to arise from their adoption of English
methods:—

'Et ont pris de la contenance
Angloise, et ensuivy Dunstable.'

The Old Hall MS.[1] is somewhat later in date than that which we have just examined, and is of great importance, both on account of the large number of compositions, all purely ecclesiastical, which are contained in it, and also from the fact that the authors' names are given apparently whenever possible. By far the largest part of the volume is devoted to settings of the ordinary of the Mass, not grouped, however, in their natural order, but so that all the portions of one kind are together; thus the volume begins, for instance, with thirty-six settings of the *Gloria*, and these are followed by many others dealing with the *Credo, Sanctus*, &c., while the greater part of the remaining space is occupied by antiphons, motets, and hymns, chiefly in honour of the Blessed Virgin. Especially noticeable among these are two motets, in which the texts of the two upper parts consist of prayers to the Virgin and St. George on behalf of King Henry VI. The prayer to the Virgin, adopted in the upper voice of the motet in which the invocation of St. George occurs, is already known (without the special prayer for the king which has been inserted), and appears in at least one collection of Latin hymns, but the prayer to St. George, in the middle voice of the motet, is unique, and apparently peculiar to some foundation dedicated to the Saint. After requests for the sovereign—'Be thou present in the councils of Henry our King, sustain him against his enemies, put on the shield, bend the bow, bring him succour'—the singers continue: 'Glorious hope of the English people, hear the petitions of thy servants now singing unto thee; may we, through thee, *our patron*, obtain the gift of peace in the land of the living[2].' This, and the fact

---

[1] For an account of this MS. see Mr. W. B. Squire's article in the Journal of the *Internationalen Musikgesellschaft*, 1900–1, p. 342. A critical edition of this MS., with a rendering in modern notation, is about to be published by the Plainsong and Mediaeval Music Society, 1929.

[2] Miles fortis custos plebis
sis Henrici nostri regis
presens ad consilium.

that two of the principal composers in this MS. were prebend and canon respectively of St. George's, Windsor, would seem to suggest that foundation as the place of origin of this fine collection.

The names of the composers, given in the MS., are as follows: Cooke, Aleyn, Sturgeon, Damett, Burell, Gyttering, Tyes, Excetre, Lyonel or Leonel, Pycard, Rowlard, Queldryk, Gervays, ffonteyns, Oliver or Olyver, Chirbury or Chyrbury, Typp, Forest, Swynford, Pennard, Lambe, Mayshuet or (?) Mayshurst; and last, though not least—for his work is excellent—'Roy Henry' himself, whose name stands at the head of two settings of portions of the ordinary of the Mass, the *Gloria* and the *Sanctus* [1].

It is difficult, in considering this MS., entirely to disregard a supposition which presents itself to the mind, namely that these composers, with whose work that of the king himself is associated, may possibly have constituted the Royal Chapel, or a part of it. It is true that we know very little concerning this earliest period of the history of the Chapel. It is known of course that Henry V, though a great patron of minstrelsy, also possessed a Chapel—*plena cantoribus ampla capella*, a contemporary poem calls it—and that he sent orders from France, during his second expedition, that it should come to keep the Easter of 1418 with him at Rouen; moreover, some of its

> Contra hostes apprehende
> arma scutum, archum tende,
>   sibi fer auxilium.
> Gloriosa spes Anglorum,
> audi vota famulorum
>   tibi nunc canencium.
> Per te nostrum ut patronum
> consequamur pacis donum
>   in terra vivencium.

[1] The discovery of Henry's work as a composer of music of the highest class was of course unexpected, but is not surprising, if we consider that the king had been brought up from childhood under the immediate care of Beaufort, Bishop of Winchester, and moreover that he was always not only of a studious and retiring disposition but also exceedingly devout.

members may perhaps be recognized in William Thorley, chaplain, Walter Wodehall, organist of St. Paul's, William Dyolet, Richard Laudewarnake, Thomas Wodeford, and Gerald Hesyll, clerks and singers, who received money from the Exchequer for their expenses in going to France.[1] This is all that can be said at present concerning the Chapel of Henry V, and with respect to that of his son we know nothing beyond the probable fact of its existence. It may be that the long minority of Henry VI, followed by the constant troubles which depressed his life, may have prevented the formation of a complete musical establishment, but that something of the kind existed during this time, possibly at St. George's, seems not unlikely, if we consider the special prayers for the king which are to be found in this collection; remembering also that Thomas Damett, the prebend of Windsor, and composer of the motet invoking the help of St. George, already mentioned, is described in a patent of this reign as 'one of the chaplains of the *Royal Chapel* '.

But however this may be, we undoubtedly possess, in the music of the Old Hall MS., a collection which exhibits all the qualities necessary to the creation of that supreme authority which belongs to a Chapel Royal; for it is clear, even from the imperfect examination of the MS. which is all that has yet been possible, that in number, variety, and consistent application of the traditional technique, this series of compositions cannot have been excelled by any contemporary collection. Not all its specimens, however, are absolutely agreed in point of style, a fact which is to be accounted for probably by the considerable period of time which is covered by the MS.; so that while we here find preserved works which must undoubtedly have been among those exhibiting the novelties, referred to by writers of the time, which excited the admiration of foreign composers, we find also a far greater number, probably by the

[1] See *History of English Music*, by H. Davey, London, without date.

more ancient men, in which the older methods are still persistently apparent.

Thus, at first sight, the English music of the fifteenth century, as here represented, reveals, as compared with that of the fourteenth, very few points of difference. We observe in both the same incapability to imagine the main subject as apart from a *cantus prius factus*, and the same reliance upon plainsong or popular melody, or something written in imitation of these; we observe also the same timidity and absence of resource in the methods of opening the composition; we are struck by the same irrational use of discord, which is employed, apparently, sometimes with a view to expression and sometimes from sheer inability to preserve any kind of melody if concordance were always necessary; the same superstitious avoidance of the third in the close; and finally the same apparent insensibility to the need of harmonic propriety in groups of sounds. But we may at the same time perceive, upon closer observation, a growing tendency in some composers towards the abolition of crude discord, and in many cases even an absolute preference for pure concord throughout; by these composers also the interval of the third is more often used with the fifth in closes not final, and sometimes indeed supplies its place. In other respects, such as the basis of the composition and the methods of opening, there is much that is interesting, though more as attempt than as achievement. The points of imitation in the two following examples may appear stiff; but they indicate a deliberate intention to control the texture of the music, and the note to the second Gloria: 'Hic sunt duo cantus in uno triplo unus post alium fugando sex temporibus', shows an awakening form-consciousness.

Old Hall MS. fol. 23 b.   Pycard.

More often the·voices open with a plain counterpoint, almost entirely note under note, which is sustained for some little time; sometimes even the opening passage is in pure *faulx bourdon*; but the method perhaps most in favour is that in which the unison and octave, or unison octave and fifth, is heard as the first sound, and then, while two of the voices continue to hold their notes firmly, the remaining part is heard rising or falling, as the case may be, to the third; and this method is as old as Machault, in whose *Agnus Dei* (p. 245 of the first volume) it may be seen, slightly ornamented. The effect of the third, appearing in this manner, and completing the chord, is so remarkably pleasing, and so welcome to the ear, that the entire abstention from the use of that interval in direct combination with the fifth, which still continued among the general body of composers at this time, can only be taken as proof of an extraordinary respect for established rules, and a most devout belief in their efficacy, on the part of musicians.

It would be impossible to exhibit here all the methods contained in this valuable MS., which should be made the subject of a special investigation, but we may give the opening of Damett's motet in which the prayer to St. George occurs, and a *Sanctus* and *Osanna* by the king himself. The king's compositions are extremely interesting for their own sake, and are often original and beautiful in their effects. In his music the struggle towards continuous beauty of pure sound—a struggle in which the artist is sorely hindered both by the severity of the tradition and by the poverty of the inherited material—is perhaps more obvious than in that of almost any composer of this MS., among those whose works have been examined.

MOTET.

SALVATORIS MATER.

Great Mode Perfect, Small Mode Imperfect, Time Perfect.

Old Hall MS., fol. 89^b.   Thomas Damett.

¹ D C B in origin 1.

tem - plum De - i, por - tus . . ma - - -

An - - - - - - - - gli - am, ip -

- ris, ad quam . re - i cur - - runt

- sum . te - - - que com - men-

Ma - - - - ri - - -

cum fi - du - ci - a: sum - mi . re - gis spon -

- - - da - - re . . va - le - a - mus .

- - - - - - - - - - ae . . .

- sa dig - - na cunc - tis . . . &c.

et lau - - da - - re, ... &c.

&c.

SANCTUS.

- oth. Ple - ni sunt . coe - li et ter - ra

glo - ri - a tu - - a. O - - - -

- - - - - - san - na in . . . ex -

- cel - - - - - - - - - - - - sis.

Following upon our consideration of the Selden and Old
Hall MSS., a third source, already mentioned, from which
examples of the English work of this period may be obtained,
remains to be examined—the collections, that is to say, which
are contained in certain codices in libraries at Trent (now at
Vienna [1]), at Modena [2] and at Bologna [3]. The English compositions which are found in these collections are of unusual
historical value, since they would seem to indicate the existence
of a small and perhaps select school of English composers,
distinct from that represented by the Selden and Old Hall MSS.,
a school the names of whose members are recorded for the most
part in foreign MSS., whose reputation was chiefly among foreign
writers and composers, and whose work was in all probability
carried on abroad. Among the members of this school were
Dunstable—its acknowledged leader—Power, Gervays, Forest,
Benet, Bedingham, Stanley, Stove, Merkham, Alain. Of these
composers, Power, as it would seem, was also largely recognized
in this country, for the Old Hall MS. contains twenty-one
compositions with his name; two ascribed to Forest, one to
Gervays, and one to Alain are also given in the same MS., but
the remaining members, including Dunstable, were apparently
unknown to the scribe. Two contemporary copies, indeed,
of authentic works by Dunstable are known to exist in this
country, one in the Old Hall MS. and one in the Selden collection, but both are given as anonymous.

It has already been pointed out that the compositions of that
part of the English school whose activity is recorded in the Old
Hall MS. reveal very noticeable varieties of style, and a considerable inequality of merit, and it may now be said that in the
works of the foreign branch we perceive, on the other hand,
great similarity of treatment, and a kind of deliberation and

[1] Translations by Guido Adler and Oswald Koller are published as part
of the series of *Denkmäler der Tonkunst in Österreich*, by Artaria & Co.,
Vienna.   [2] Bibl. Estense, Cod. VI, H, 15.
[3] Liceo Musicale, Cod. 87.

regularity in the manner of proceeding which suggest, certainly
more than those in the English libraries, the idea of a school
led by one man, and reproducing, according to the ability of
individual members, the methods of a chief. And it is no
doubt to this solidarity that we may attribute the fact that the
members of the school were able, in the midst of foreign influences, to preserve, so distinctly as we see that they did, the
native English character in their works, and that they succeeded
even in imposing their methods upon the musicians by whom
they were surrounded. They had brought with them indeed
from this country a method founded upon the specially English
development of the principles of *faulx bourdon* recorded by
Guilelmus Monachus, a method which was totally new, and
extremely surprising to the French and Italians. Instead of
the dry and aimless writing of the individual parts to which
they were accustomed, the foreign musicians now for the first
time perceived the possibility of a continuous flow of suave
sound, rising and falling in waves of melody, divided into
manageable phrases, and harmonized almost entirely in the
mellifluous imperfect consonances; not cloying the ear, but by
a constant interchange of thirds and sixths refreshing it and
exciting its interest. In listening to music such as this the
practitioners of the outworn methods of Machault and Landini
may well have been both delighted and envious.

> 'Tu as bien les Anglois ouy
> Jouer à la Court de Bourgongne,
> N'as pas, certainement ouy
> Fut il jamais telle besongne:
> J'ay veu Binchois avoir vergongne
> Et soy taire emprès leur rebelles
> Et du Fay despite et frongne
> Qu'il n'a mélodie si belle [1].'

And although this was spoken of instrumental music, yet the
examples which follow show that it might equally well apply to
music of the highest class.

[1] *Le Champion des Dames*, Martin le Franc.

CRUX FIDELIS.

Modena, Bibl. Estense, i. 98.   John Dunstable.

ta - - - - - - - - - lem

pro - - - - - - fert . . . . .

. . . . . fron - - - - - - -

. de flo - - - - - - -

re

ger

mi

ne.   &c.

&c.

&c.

AVE REGINA.
First Part.

Bodl. Lib. MSS. Selden, B. 26, fol. 16ᵛ.   Leonel Power.

AGNUS DEI.

In this composition a duet for two single voices follows, constituting the second *Agnus* and *Miserere*, after which the third repetition of the words is taken by the full chorus.

These specimens are fairly typical of the work of Power and Benet, but with regard to Dunstable it may be said that while the example gives an excellent idea of the extreme purity and suavity of his music, it exhibits him in only one aspect, and that in other compositions he is sometimes both more formal and more learned than in this. He was indeed the first of English composers to create works, of any considerable extent, controlled throughout by some coherent scheme founded upon purely technical resources and apart from or beside the plain-song. This great advance is well illustrated, for instance, in a fine motet, *Veni Sancte Spiritus*—too long, unfortunately, to be given here—in which the element of unity is supplied by a tenor in long notes, repeating twice, while the necessary variety is obtained from the upper parts, which descant in a different measure at each resumption of the subject. Thus, at its first utterance, the tenor, in the great mood imperfect, is accompanied by the upper parts in time perfect with the minor prolation; at its repetition in the same mood, the counterpoint is in time imperfect with the minor prolation, while at its final appearance it is itself diminished, and the whole concludes in the measure with which the upper parts began, that is, in time perfect with the minor prolation. It is very possible that this method, by means of which the idea of a distinct organic whole is not unsuccessfully conveyed to the mind, may have originated with Dunstable, and this indeed might have been in itself sufficient to establish his fame; but, since it is to be met with also in the works of his foreign contemporaries, the question of priority must remain unsettled until our knowledge with respect to the exact chronological order of musical events at this time is considerably extended.

Besides attempts, such as this, towards the creation of a musical form suitable to the resources of music as they were then understood, mere learned puzzles sometimes occur in the work of Dunstable, uninteresting in themselves, but showing a great mastery of the means at his command, and in this matter also he may have been an originator. Such a puzzle, for instance, is prefixed to another motet upon the text *Veni Sancte Spiritus*, in the foreign MSS., which bears the direction—'*Et dicitur primo directe, 2° subverte lineam, 3° reverte remittendo tertiam partem et capies dyapenthe, si vis habere tenorem*'; two others also are found in a MS. of Henry VIII's time; of these one is still undeciphered, but the other has yielded to modern investigation. The latter composition is fortunately so short that it may be given here entire [1].

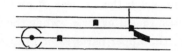

A dorio tenor hic ascendens esse videtur
Quater per genera tetrachordum repetetur.

Brit. Mus. Add. MS. 31922.   J. Dunstable.

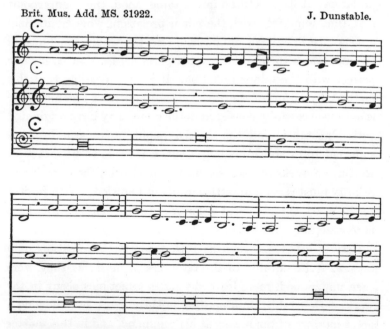

[1] This was deciphered by Mr. J. R. Stainer, and is published in *Early Bodleian Music*, vol. ii.

On the other hand Dunstable's work is sometimes apparently in a lighter vein. A song, for instance, set by him to French words, *Puisque m'amour*, has been preserved in the Trent MSS.; the only noticeable difference, however, which it displays, as compared with his motets, is that it is comparatively short, and that it contains two points of imitation, which appear and reappear alternately and frequently throughout the work. The song *O Rosa Bella*, also, apparently very popular abroad, and often adopted as the theme of compositions of various kinds, from the Mass downwards, is thought to have been set by him in three parts; the particular composition, however, with which his name is identified, has been ascribed to him as it would seem upon very slender evidence, since only one of the seven existing copies of this setting (that in the Vatican Library) bears the name of Dunstable, while the remaining six—two at Paris, one at Pavia, one at Dijon, and two at Vienna (from Trent)—are anonymous.

But whether treating serious or lighter subjects, the music of Dunstable—its actual texture, that is to say—remained, like that of all his contemporaries, exactly the same, always and throughout. In beauty, in sweetness and purity of sound— qualities derived chiefly from the specially English development of the *faulx bourdon* descant—it by far exceeded that of the foreign schools, to whom indeed, as they themselves confessed, it came as a revelation, and the prospect of a new art; but its texture was equally with that of the foreign music lacking in respect of variety, and was not at all adaptable to the special sentiment of the words. The eminence therefore of Dunstable, and also of his colleague Power—as compared with their followers—consisted not so much in a finer and more expressive style than theirs, as in more effective varieties of plan and contrivance in the presentation of this somewhat monotonously beautiful material; in methods, that is, such as we have already

noticed, in the repeating tenor or ground, in varieties of proportion in the measure, in the arrangement of the voices—now
grouping, now separating them—and so on.

Dunstable is considered generally, not only as a distinguished
English musician, but as the leader of the native school. And
English he was by birth, and distinguished by his talents; but
as regards his leadership of the native school, this must now
appear as more than doubtful in the sense in which the saying
has hitherto been understood; that is to say, it is now probable
that he was never at the head of an undivided body of composers
in this country. For in considering the English school of this
period it would seem to be desirable, if we may venture to
formulate any final conclusion at all from the scanty material
at our disposal, that we should perceive, rather more clearly
than hitherto, the existence of two branches. One of these,
represented almost exclusively in foreign codices, was established abroad, as it would seem, during the first quarter of the
fifteenth century—probably soon after Agincourt, in the years
during which so much of France became for a time English
ground—while the other, whose work is seen chiefly in the
Selden and Old Hall MSS., continued the native tradition in
this country. The method of the English composers whose
works are found abroad is remarkable chiefly for its renunciation
of arbitrary discords. These, though always forbidden since
1400 by the learned treatise-writers, had been abundantly sanctioned in practice by Machault and Landini, and were continued
by those who came after, not necessarily entirely from choice,
but partly because the methods of avoiding them were not
apparent until they were revealed in the florid *faulx bourdon*
descant. These methods, though at once eagerly embraced by
the foreign schools, for whom they became the basis of the great
evolutionary movement of the latter half of the century, were
probably not understood, possibly not perfectly known, and

certainly not fruitful among the greater part of the composers of the native school in England. The inclination towards complete concordance is visible indeed in some of the compositions in the Old Hall MSS., so far as these have been examined, but the decided tendency of the English branch is towards the continuance of arbitrary discord; indeed, this tendency remained as a characteristic and a reproach in the native English methods even until the middle of the following century, when composers were still to be found—Pygott, the master of Wolsey's Chapel, among them—who employed them without shame [1].

If then we may be allowed to assume the existence in the fifteenth century of two distinct branches of the English school, one practising abroad and the other at home, it is with the members of the advancing foreign branch that Dunstable must be associated, since his work, similar to theirs in technique, exists also practically entirely in foreign collections [2]. The benefits therefore which his genius conferred upon the art of music were bestowed apparently in an alien school, nor indeed do we gather, either from anything that is known of his life, or from the disposition of his remaining works, that (except perhaps in his earliest years) he ever practised in this country. Born about 1390, and educated presumably among the makers of the music described by Guilelmus Monachus, he was evidently firmly established abroad and recognized as the benefactor of foreign music between 1436 and 1444, the period during which Martin le Franc wrote his eulogistic verses. But as regards England, not only is there no obvious trace of his influence here,

[1] See Morley's examples, *Plain and Easy Introduction*, &c., p. 137 (Reprint).

[2] Mr. H. Davey has already suggested the supposition of Dunstable's prolonged absence from this country in his *History of English Music* (no date). The fact that music by Leonel Power is to be found both in the foreign collections and, in considerable quantity, in the Old Hall MS. also, might be explained upon the hypothesis of the composer's return to this country, to practise here.

either during his life or after his death—until indeed it was
exerted in this country in the shape of Flemish teaching—but
it would be difficult even to show proof that from the time of
his departure from this country until his return to die or to be
buried here, his name was so much as known in the land of
his birth.

France and the Gallo-Belgic Provinces.

The tradition established by Machault in France continued
apparently from the time of his death, about 1370, onwards
through the first quarter of the fifteenth century, with but little
alteration. In the second quarter, however, that is to say about
1435, we become aware of the existence of a considerable movement, the premonitory indication of change, displayed chiefly
in a large and important increase in the number of composers;
and this not only in France, but also and more especially in
the neighbouring territories of Burgundy, which now included
Belgium and the rest of the Low Countries.

Two circumstances may have contributed to create this
movement. On the one hand, we may remember that Belgian
singers were now already beginning to be employed together
with the French in the Papal choir, and that the passing to and
fro of possible candidates, and of others attracted by the new
conditions in Rome, would naturally become the occasion of a
constant interchange and circulation of musical ideas throughout Western Europe; on the other hand, we may recognize the
existence of important bodies of local musicians, both in the
principal cathedrals and in the chapel of Philip the Good, by
whom a new impulse, if once communicated to them, would be
systematically continued and developed.

The first distinct sign of movement is to be found, so far as
we know at present, in a collection, consisting chiefly of songs,
sacred and secular, now in the Bodleian Library in Oxford, and

marked *MSS. Canonici, misc.* 213[1]. The pieces constituting this collection were brought together apparently not later than 1436, and were for the most part composed during the ten years immediately preceding that date; but the MS. also contains works which may have been produced as early as the beginning of the second decade of the century. The collection, moreover, is connected with the practice of the later fourteenth century by its inclusion of works by J. Césaris and Zacharias the Italian Papal singer; while it also belongs, to a certain extent, to the period which was now to follow, from the very considerable number of compositions by Dufay and Binchois which are contained in it.

The work in fact represents a period of transition, in preparation for the great change which was imminent. The actual methods of composition are indeed still but little altered from the fourteenth-century practice, but the old harshness is often partially reduced, and the attempt towards fullness and impressiveness of sound is more frequent than before; the real nature, however, of the impending change, which was not to arise naturally out of the suggestions of the material itself, was still far from being discerned, since the authors of these songs had not as yet apparently encountered the English musicians, from whom they were to receive the sweet and pure methods of the free *faulx bourdon* descant. This we may gather not only from the character of their music, but also from the fact that among the sixty composers whose names are to be found in this collection we meet with Frenchmen, Belgians, and Italians, but no Englishman. It is noticeable that the collection was continued apparently up to the very eve of the foreign recognition of Dunstable and his followers; for accepting the year 1436,

---

[1] A critical account of part of this MS. by the late Sir John Stainer, with extracts translated by Mr. J. R. F. Stainer and Miss Stainer, and an introduction by the late E. W. B. Nicholson, Bodley's Librarian, was published in 1898 (Novello).

upon the authority of the late E. W. B. Nicholson, Bodley's Librarian, as the latest date of any composition in the book, and the limits 1436–44 which Mr. Stainer gives for the date of Martin le Franc's poem *Le Champion des Dames*, it is clear that the important events to which the French author refers as contemporary [1] must have been imminent when this MS. was finished.

Chief among the contributors to this collection are the members of the Papal choir—Dufay, Brassart, Arnold de Lantins, Malbeque, Fontaine, Grenon, Hasprois, Liberth, Loqueville, Binchois (second Rector of the Duke of Burgundy's Chapel), Ciconia, Hugo de Lantins, &c. The names of Tapissier, Carmen, and Cesaris, just mentioned in our note, occur in the MS.; and in order to show the kind of accomplishments which *ébahirent tout Paris* examples of Carmen, Cesaris, and Binchois are now given, together with a comparatively early work by Dufay, dated 1425, three years before his first appointment to the Papal choir. In all these examples the dry melody, and the arbitrary discords which sometimes render whole passages unintelligible, are to be found; they are indeed characteristic of the entire collection, and probably no specimen that might be shown could be said to be entirely free from them.

The work of Cesaris given as our example is remarkable chiefly for its cacophony, not altogether surprising indeed in a pupil of Machault; that of Carmen, however, is interesting from its fugal form, which may be considered as of the Italian species, for it will be noticed that the statement of the subject is accom-

[1] 'Tapissier, Carmen, Cesaris, / N'a pas long temps (si) bien chantèrent / Qu'ilz esbahirent tout Paris / Et tous ceulz qui les fréquentèrent: / Mais oncques jour ne dechantèrent / En mélodie de tel chois, / Ce m'ont dit qui les escoutèrent, / Que Guillaume du Fay et Binchois. / Car ilz ont nouvelle pratique / De faire frisque concordance / En haulte et en basse musique, / En fainte, en pause, et en muance, / Et ont pris de la contenance / Angloise, et ensuivy Dunstable; / Pourquoy merveilleuse plaissance / Rend leur chant joyeulx et notable.'

panied by a non-fugal passage, as in the madrigal by Zacharias
(see vol. i, p. 268), but here in two parts. The song by Binchois
is remarkable for its clearly instrumental opening; indeed we
may even perhaps suppose, from the appearance of a similar
treatment at the end of the first line of text, that the instrumental accompaniment doubled the voices throughout.

MON SEUL VOLOIR.

Bodl. Lib., MSS. Canonici,
    misc. 213, fol. 122ᵃ.   J. Cesaris.

Mon

Cer-

seul . . vo - loir . . ma sou - ve - rayne   joy -

- tes . . m'a - mour . . . c'est ma vye et ma

tient,   Quan- dire . une . . . . au - tre . .

- tir.

je . . ne vau - - droy - - - - - - - -

- - - - - - e . . . .

Fugue.

PONTIFICI DECORI.

Bodl. Lib., MSS. Canonici,
misc. 213, fol. 26ᵛ.

Iohannes Carmen.

¹ Words printed as in original throughout.

- lant et se - cu - li fes - ta fi - bris . lax - is e -

- gre - gi - a . . . . &c.

&c.

&c.

Bodl. Lib., MSS. Canonici,
misc. 213, fol. 56ᵛ.   TRISTRE PLAISIR.

Binchois.

Tris - tre plai - sir . . et dou - lou - reuse

joi - e, ... As-pre . doul -

ceur, re-con-fort en - nuy - eulx, Ris en plou-rant, .

sou - ve - nir . ob - li - eux . . M'ac - com-pang-

-nent . . com-bien que seu - le soy - - - e.

In 1436 Dufay was appointed Canon of Cambrai, and resigned his post in the Pope's choir in the year following; shortly afterwards he became also Canon of Mons and Prebendary of Bruges. He fixed his residence at Cambrai, where as a boy he had been a chorister, and notwithstanding some journeys, remained there during his life.

From the time of his settling at Cambrai probably may be dated the beginning of his second style of composition. In this style, in which he continued while he lived, we find nothing of the former methods remaining; no more dryness in the melody nor intolerable harshness of arbitrary discord are to be heard, but we perceive a new conception of music altogether, similar to that with which we have become acquainted already in the works of Dunstable and his followers. We recognize, unmistakably, the suave and flowing melody in the separate parts, the pure harmony of the whole, the agreeable phrasing, the propriety in the sequence of the combined sounds, which we noticed as characteristic of the compositions of our own countrymen in the foreign collections during this period. From 1446 onwards, probably, Dufay was engaged upon the work of completing the applicability of this new art to all kinds of composition, but especially, as it would seem, for the benefit of his own church of Cambrai. In 1453 his munificence in this respect was acknowledged by the Chapter, while between 1459 and 1470, which was the year of his death, 'Masses, Antiphons, Hymns, and Magnificats' were produced by him, and copied into the choirbooks of the cathedral, apparently continuously.

Compositions in all these forms, here mentioned from the records of payment to the copyist, are now to be found in the various codices containing works of this period at Vienna (from Trent), Modena, and Bologna, and at Rome in the archives of St. Peter's and of the Papal Chapel; and from these sources we may gather some idea of the methods now employed in the treatment of these principal features of the divine worship.

The Mass is of course, for Dufay as for others, the subject of the greatest care, thought, and effort in composing. His methods here, it may be said, are upon the whole adopted apparently from Dunstable; but while he constantly employs the device, also frequent with Dunstable, of different measures proceeding together, we also find a far greater use of the canon, both long and short, in his work than in that of his model. The English, indeed, as has been said, made at this time little or no use of the canon in serious music, while in the schools from which Dufay's first method was derived it was already common, though lightly considered; but it is evident that Dufay now perceives in it a certain importance, and although he never allows the subject of the canon to stand alone, that is to say without an extraneous accompaniment, he is so much impressed by this importance that he uses canon frequently and as a leading device. Often also he combines it with the older proportional devices, as in the *Gloria* and *Credo* of the Mass *Se la face ay pale*, in both of which the theme appears first as a short canon or imitation in the two upper parts, in perfect time, and afterwards in long notes for the tenor in the minor mode perfect, the higher voices continuing in their original measure. In the Hymns and Magnificats, on the other hand, no devices appear; a moderately floreated counterpoint to the subject, which is itself also from time to time somewhat broken, is all that the composer allows, and in the harmony the simple sounds of the old *faulx bourdon*, which was always considered appropriate to the Psalms and Hymns of the office, are frequently perceived. In all these forms, however, beautiful as is often the result of the methods employed, the primary and fundamental dependence of the composition upon a given theme, not in itself intended to be musically effective, is a source of weakness; the sustaining

II   H

framework is not obvious, nor even seen as fulfilling an aesthetic purpose, and the stream of exquisite sound, therefore—which, notwithstanding the frequent bare octaves and fifths, is the principal characteristic of the music of this period—is not more satisfying than an address in some mellifluous unknown tongue would be. But the means, of course, which were to supply the needed strength had not yet appeared. There was no perception as yet of the idea of rational harmonic progression as in itself sufficient to satisfy the hearer, nor of the still greater power of those apparently trifling devices, canon and imitation, which can create inexhaustible schemes of musical thought of the most profound and ever-varying interest.

MASS.

Se la face ay pale.

KYRIE.

Sistine Chapel Lib., 14, 25[1].
Trient MSS., Cod. 88.

G. Dufay.

[1] Printed by Rochlitz, *Sammlung vorzüglicher Gesangstücke* &c., 1838–40: 3 vols.

CENT MILLE ESCUS.

Paris, Bibliothèque Nationale.   Ascribed to Dufay.

Cent   mille es - cus . . . . .

Cent   mille   es - cus . . .

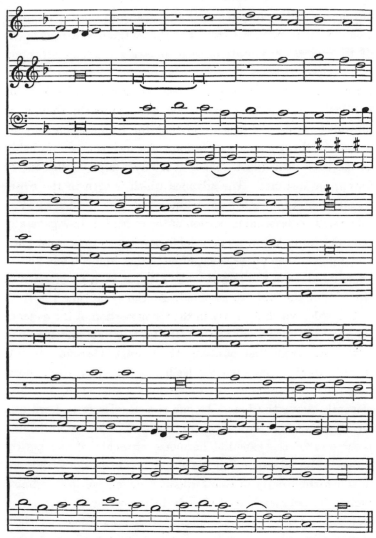

The song *Cent mille escus*, just given, is generally ascribed
without question, upon the authority of a MS. in the Bibl.
Nationale at Paris, to Dufay. It contains, however, important
features which are absent from the methods of this composer,
so far as we know them. The opening, indeed, in which a point

of fugue is still accompanied by an extraneous accompaniment, would seem to be in his style, but the methodical arrangement of the points of imitation, each following immediately upon a full close, belongs to a somewhat later period, while the closes themselves reveal so great an advance beyond his habitual methods of construction and approach, that it is difficult to resist the conclusion that the composition may be a work of the younger generation, of some member probably of the later transitional school of Dufay's pupils—Busnois, or Caron, for instance. The advance which is seen in the closes is indeed of the utmost importance and may be described as follows. The descending portion of the cadence is now generally removed from its former invariable position in the lowest part, and is given to an upper voice, often to that immediately above, while its place in the lowest voice is taken by a progression of the fifth of the scale to the final. At the same time the sixth of the scale, which formerly in the rising portion of the cadence interposed immediately between the leading note and the final, now retires from that position; the passage, therefore, is now directly to the final from the leading note, which itself moreover usually appears as the resolution of a suspended fourth or eleventh above the bass. At one step therefore, and without any apparent transitional process, we find ourselves in definite possession of the essential harmonic elements of the perfect cadence, the subsequent theme of so many exquisite variations, in which the beauty of counterpoint is developed to its utmost limits. Sometimes indeed already in the works of Dufay and Binchois, as also in the examples of Guilelmus Monachus, these elements have appeared for a moment, tentatively and often incompletely introduced, but in every case they have again disappeared beneath the habitual forms, at once resumed; here, however, it is clear that they occupy an assured position, and are repeated again and again with absolute confidence in their entire fitness for their purpose.

Another important point of resemblance to the later school
visible in this work is also to be seen in the closes, in the conduct
of the lowest part, at bars 21, 22 and 30, 31 of our illustration;
here the bass is silent at the moment of the close, leaving the
harmony to be completed by the upper parts, and, while these
are holding the final note, he himself strikes out the beginning
of a new passage of imitation. This method is of great value
as a means of rhetorical effect, and was continued throughout
the polyphonic period. Its appearance, together with that of
the new cadence, occurring in *Cent mille escus,* may be profitably
compared with that in the subjoined passages from songs by
Busnois and Caron.

A complete example of the work of Busnois, which gives
good proof of the steady development of canon during the
generation which succeeded Dufay, is next given. It will be
noticed that not only is the opening subject used throughout,
but inversion is often attempted, and the concluding passage
even begins with a kind of *stretto.*

JE SUIS VENUT.

II I

Mention was made above of the existence of a transitional school arising among the younger pupils of Dufay and Binchois, and to this school Busnois and Caron were said to belong; we may now refer to two other pupils, Basiron and Obrecht, who together with J. Regis are usually thought to complete the number of its members. This school was not especially remarkable for a general identity of aim, but rather, as in most periods of transition, each man is seen as developing those among the newly received ideas which are most interesting to himself. Certain preferences, however, are certainly shared in the present case in common, though in varying degrees, by the members; by all, for instance, the improvement of canon and imitation, both in themselves as a contrapuntal device and also in their more rhetorical aspect, was attempted. Formerly, it will be remembered, the treatment of canon was almost entirely ineffective; either the composer wrote a long and somewhat purposeless passage of fugue in two of the upper parts, or he seized a passing and casual opportunity to imitate when it presented itself, and repeated the formula twice or thrice before abandoning it. Now, however, we perceive that the attention of composers has been arrested by the possibilities of methodical treatment which are contained in this device; the conduct of the point is now seen as demanding a certain measure of contrivance and forethought, in order that the hearer's attention may be not only aroused by its appearance but also rewarded by its development. The imitation, therefore, which was formerly confined to two of the voices, now often appears in all the parts, and the point is no longer answered only at the unison or octave but also at the fifth. The imitative subject itself also is presented in a short but striking musical sentence, and is made capable of appearing in more than one relation to its answer. In all these respects the merit of the example just given from the work of Busnois is conspicuous. The work of Basiron also is interesting, not only from its single point of imitation admirably treated in four parts, but also for the tendency which it reveals towards the use of massive plain chords, which may be observed in the beginning of his *Osanna*, here following. We see in this perhaps a somewhat early use of a grandiose effect; but the construction of chords was among the first discoveries of the school; it developed quickly, and before the end of the century masters such as Josquin and Brumel had arrived at a degree of perfection in its treatment which was only limited by the nature of the materials at their disposal.

In the motet by Obrecht, which has also been included among our examples—*Parce Domine*—there is no reference to an earlier period; we are conscious indeed, on the contrary, of a great advance in power and solidity of effect, and of an easy mastery of the material which suggests the full maturity of the composer's talent; its characteristics, in fact, are such in all respects as would favour its ascription to the latter years of Obrecht's life, years which he passed in Antwerp as the Maestro di Capella of the Cathedral.

MASS : DE FRANZA.

OSANNA.

Missarum diversorum auctorum liber primus.
Venice : Petrucci, 1508.

Philippus Basiron.

MOTET.

PARCE DOMINE.

From Glareanus,
Dodecachordon,
Basle, 1547, p. 260.

Jacob Obrecht.

It will be observed that the noble melancholy which is the
characteristic quality of this beautiful composition is largely due
to the fact that it is written in the Aeolian mode. Indeed
Glareanus himself gives the motet in his great work as a perfect
example of the management of that mode, especially as regards
the lowest part:—*Basis pulcherrime hunc habet modum,* he says.
And certainly the treatment of this voice is most admirable; the
sentiment of the whole is expressed in its broad sad phrases,
alternating with periods of silence, each phrase proceeding to
some appropriate close.

Upon the death of Dufay, in 1474, the leadership of the
Gallo-Belgic or Netherland school passed to the greatest of his
surviving followers, Johannes Okeghem, then between forty and
fifty years old, and at the head of the Royal Chapel in Paris.
By some this master is thought to have been the pupil of the man
whom he succeeded; but by others, and with more probability,
his education is ascribed to Binchois, at Antwerp. Be this, how-

ever, as it may, he is in fact the true successor of both these composers, for in his work, more than in that of any other members of the school, the chief constructive means of their technique—apart from the *cantus firmus*, and as seen in their proportional devices, and in their frequent canonic imitation—are continued and developed.

By what means, or through what channels, the influence of Okeghem was brought to bear upon the main body of the contemporary composers, or how a man, who was for thirty years at least high in office in the French royal musical establishment, could communicate his methods and his enthusiasm to the relatively distant and scattered members of the school of the Netherlands, does not appear; but since many of his pupils exist for us only in name, and their histories and circumstances are as yet quite undiscovered, we may perhaps suppose that more of them than we know were, like Josquin Desprès, with him in the French Royal Chapel.

But though the influence of the master was great and widely extended, Okeghem was probably not at first followed unanimously, or acclaimed as leader without a dissentient voice. In the Netherlands themselves, for instance, the small transitional school, consisting of Busnois, Basiron, Regis, Caron, and Obrecht, whose work we have just examined, is supposed to have at first remained independent, some of its members continuing the traditions of Dufay with but little change, and others modifying them in a manner different from that of Okeghem; but it is also admitted that this school was eventually merged in the larger one, that a fusion of aims, of which the work of Josquin is the great visible sign, was effected, and that all thenceforward pursued upon the whole the same objects.

The special object of the work of Okeghem may be said to have been the development of the latent formal resources of the music of his time. These were of several kinds, but the most important were of course canon or fugue, and the proportional devices of augmentation and diminution. Both of these means are well exhibited, in combination, in a short movement from the composer's *Missa Prolationum*, printed by Sebald Heyden in his *Ars Canendi*; in this extremely intricate work we may perceive two concurrent canons, for high and low voices respectively, and also, in the lower voice of each canon, an augmentation of the subject. In the lower canon the augmentation is continued for a short time only, since otherwise the voice in which it appears would soon have been carried too far from its leader; and probably this fact alone has prevented the completion of this extremely difficult device. Notwithstanding the hardness of the task which the author has imposed upon himself the melodies of the separate voices have not appreciably suffered. It cannot of course be said that they possess the freedom and flow of sound which would have arisen naturally in an untrammelled composition, but there is no apparent sign of yielding, on the part of the writer, to superior force, nor any obvious awkwardness demanding allowance or excuse. And this in itself is a proof of great mastery.

Apart from the difficulties which Okeghem created for himself in treating forms already existing, he invented others—for so we may perhaps understand the account given by Glareanus—of a kind either unknown or at least very unusual. He was fond, Glareanus says, of constructing '*Catholica*' in music, that is to say, melodies which might be sung in any mode at the discretion of the singers, 'yet so,' says the author somewhat darkly, 'that the ratio of the harmony and of the consonances be nevertheless observed.' The first example of this kind of music given by Glareanus is the well-known fugue for three voices, in the fourth above, at the distance of a perfect breve—a work of so much importance that, notwithstanding the fact that it has been often printed, it is given in part below.[1] The

[1] Since both Hawkins and Burney have printed this canon, it is unfortunately necessary to point out that their translations are wrong. Hawkins

signature is derived from the original canon, where it appears as a figure giving a choice apparently either of two flats or two sharps. The signature of two flats, which is generally adopted, would indicate, in the modal point of view, a twice transposed Aeolian, and this gives a good result; that the composition is not equally satisfactory, however, in all modes may be seen from a reference, for example, to the ninth bar of our translation, where, supposing the signature to be removed and the Mixolydian mode to be exhibited, great difficulties must occur, difficulties which the rules of *musica ficta*, either by ♭ or ♯, would be powerless to remove.

CANON.

Three in one, in the fourth above.

From Glareanus;
Dodecachordon, p. 454.   Iohannes Okeghem.

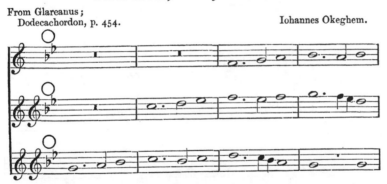

was first led astray by his own supposition of an error in the direction given by Glareanus—*Fuga trium vocum in epidiatessaron (nam sic nunc loquuntur) post perfectum tempus.* 'Epidiatessaron'—meaning, he says, a fourth *below* —proves impossible in translation, while 'epidiapente,' or a fifth *below*, gives a solution which he adopts; but this was of course only acceptable as an inversion of the proper interval, the fourth *above*, shown in our translation. Moreover, apart from this misconception, Hawkins has rendered his solution quite useless by presenting it in imperfect time, a measure which he has adopted notwithstanding the circle which stands at the beginning of the canon. Burney avoids this mistake, and has even printed a note upon the subject, aimed at Hawkins; he falls, however, himself into the same error as his predecessor with respect to the canonic interval, which he also believes to be the fifth below the subject.

It has not been considered necessary to quote any further examples of the music of Okeghem, since the specimen that we have given may be thought sufficiently to display its character and general aims. The difficulties, invented in order to be overcome, are throughout his work—so far as we know it— apparently of much the same nature as those just exhibited, while as regards the relative facility with which the task is accomplished, and the degree of pleasure to be derived from the actual sounds evolved in its execution, examination reveals little variation among the individual compositions, whether sacred or secular. The standard of beauty attained by Okeghem, how- ever, in his work, though sufficiently high, as has been said, if we consider the circumstances of its production, is not con- stantly or even often equal to that attained by Dunstable, in whose compositions the individual voices were governed by no other consideration than that of simple contrapuntal relation to each other and to the *cantus*.

But even if the immediate results obtained by Okeghem, in his unremitting pursuit of canon and its kindred devices, had been less pleasing than they are actually seen to be, the work performed by him would none the less have been beneficial, and indeed necessary for music. In any case it had become inevit- able. Canon, brought actually into use by the musicians of the fourteenth century, had long lain in an undeveloped and stagnant condition; and though, in the hands of Dufay, who received it from the Italians, it had begun to assume a more living aspect, and though greater beauty and a certain harmonic propriety were now infused into it, its old typical form, consist- ing of long prosing passages for two voices, in which one duti- fully repeats, sometimes at an almost unrecognizable distance, every note uttered by the other, still continued. But in the general awakening and reformation of musical means which

came at the close of the fifteenth century, it was inevitable that
the true nature of canon as a constructive agent, apart from all
other considerations, should be perceived. The device therefore
became now, as we have seen, the subject of experiment; the
old reply by one voice, at a long distance, to a subject supported
by accompaniment, was abandoned, the imitation was brought
closer and closer to the unaccompanied subject, more and more
replies were derived, by imitation, from one proposition, proportional devices were mingled with the canonic, and so on; in
short, the investigation of the possibilities of canon became the
chief work of the time, and attracted universal attention. Considering then that the line of general effort lay in this direction,
it is evident that until the theory of fugue or canon had been
settled, until the limits of its use had been reached and it had
taken its place as a regular and recognized musical means, no
general progress was possible; for the device having been now
perceived in its true nature, a new method for its application,
based upon newly discovered principles, was also required. And
it is in this sense that the unremitting study of the phenomena
of canon, which it fell to the lot of Okeghem to undertake, was
said to be necessary; that it was, moreover, beneficial must
appear not only in the wonderful enlargement of the technical
means of music which was its immediate result, but also from a
consideration of the enormous efforts of contrapuntal ingenuity
involved in the success of these complicated canonic construc-
tions; for the mastery which was the result of this immense
labour, transmitted by Okeghem to his pupils, and by them to
their successors, made all the work that was to come comparatively easy.

The pupil in whose work the fact of this transmission of
Okeghem's mastery is most conspicuous is, of course, Josquin
Desprès. Indeed, as regards the methods of fugue or canon,

this composer may probably be said to have carried their subtleties even beyond the point to which they had attained when he received them, if that were possible; and the comparative ease with which he must have performed the most difficult operations of this kind, as a consequence of receiving the appropriate methods and useful rules complete from their inventor, appears from a comparison of the quantity of his productions in this kind, which was very great, with that of the inventor himself, who though enjoying a far longer life than that which fell to the lot of his pupil, brought out, according to all the accounts, relatively little of any kind.

The greater part of Josquin's learning and invention in these recondite forms of composition is exhibited in his numerous settings of the ordinary of the Mass—a subject considered indeed by all composers of the time as an appropriate occasion for the display of every kind of formal ingenuity; and in these settings canonic and proportional devices, now in one voice and now in another, are throughout unceasing. Thus, remembering that thirty-two Masses by Josquin still exist, in print or MS., we may form some idea of his activity in this field.

Our first example of the composer's work is the *Sanctus* from one of his Masses upon the melody *L'homme armé*.[1]

---

[1] Dr. Burney's analytical notes upon this Mass may be considered of sufficient interest to be given here. They occur at p. 494 of his History, vol. ii. 'In every movement of Josquin's Mass,' he says, 'some part or other, but generally the tenor, is singing the tune in different notes and measures; sometimes in augmentation, and sometimes in diminution. In the *Kyrie*, or first movement, the tenor has the first part of the tune which the superius, or upper part, had led off; in the next movement, or *Christe*, it has the second part. In the third, fourth and sixth movements, the tenor has the subject tune in different and difficult notations, and in the fifth and seventh the same part sings it in *retro*, or, as it is called in the musical technica of the times, *cancrizans*.

'In the *Sanctus*, the soprano leads off the subject on D, moving in breves and semibreves, accompanied by the counter tenor in a free and airy

MASS.

L'homme armé.

SANCTUS.

Liber primus missae Josquin.
Fossembrone: Petrucci, 1516.

Josquin Desprès.

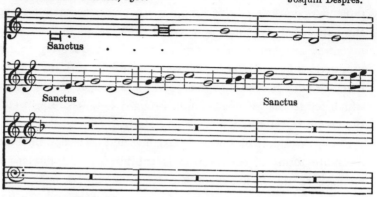

melody; and, after six bars, the tenor sings the theme in F, and in augmentation: when the first part is finished, the bass leads off a new subject of close imitation between itself, the counter tenor, and the soprano; and while the tenor is singing the second part of the tune, the intelligent musician will see several ingenious contrivances in the other three parts.

'The *Osanna* has many curious contrivances in *moto contrario*, double counterpoint, &c., in three parts; while a fourth is still singing *L'homme armé.*

'In the two next movements, *Benedictus qui venit*, and *In nomine*, by a curious species of contrivance, *Duos* are formed by two parts singing the same intervals in different measures; that is, while one performs the melody in semibreves, the other sings it in minims, and *e contra.*

'The next movement, *Agnus Dei*, in four parts, is an exercise for time, as the proportions in all the parts are different. After this, there is a second movement, to the same words, where three parts, in different measures, are drawn out of one:—*tria in unum.*

'The next, and last, movement is a third *Agnus Dei*, à 4, in which the superius, or upper part, performs the tune in longs and breves, with this direction, *clama ne cesses*; which implies perpetual singing, without keeping any of the rests that may occur, and allowing only for the time of the notes. The other three parts are in close fugue, during the whole movement, and often in canon, the tissue of which is carried on with wonderful art and ingenuity.'

A description of any other of Josquin's Masses would probably differ but little from this.

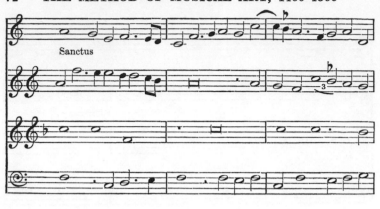

Sanctus

dominus

deus

saba

II   L

It is difficult, no doubt, in considering the remarkable character
of the work just exemplified, to imagine the exact point of view
in which Josquin himself regarded these ingenious contrivances.
That they astonished the world, and were expected of him, is
clear; but was this alone, it may be asked, the motive of their production, or did he himself regard them seriously, and in some way
receive from them aesthetic pleasure? To this it may be answered
that the view, not only of these devices but of all musical means,
taken by Josquin, and indeed by Okeghem also, probably resem-
bled the view of any material which is entertained by the work-
man who is to deal with it, and who is before all things desirous of
full knowledge with respect to its capacities. In creating these
difficulties for themselves, and in overcoming them, the pleasure
of the masters lay not only in the exercise of the utmost ingenuity,
but also, and much more, in the actual development itself of their
material, which was the reward of their struggle, in the discovery
of its powers, and in obliging it to perform, quite perfectly, things
hitherto unknown. Similar phenomena may be observed in the
history of all arts during their periods of growth, when often
apparently unreasonable and unmeaning activities, irritating and
disturbing to the student, are seen as occupying for awhile a large
place in the scheme of artistic effort. Their results indeed seldom
continue, certainly not in their first shape; but always something,
more or less, which may be traced to the impulse that created
them, appears as part of the finished and perfected technique.

The element of aesthetic pleasure, then, does not properly exist in the artificial system of musical contrivance, considered in itself; yet it may always be derived in some degree from the work of Josquin in this kind, even in its most recondite phases, since the ingenuity is always combined—and more obviously than in the work of Okeghem—with beauty of effect; nay, often indeed the uninstructed hearer might suppose the composition, from its musical charm, to be most devoid of artifice when in fact it is most concerned with it. And this strain of beauty, dependent upon purely musical effect, which is natural to Josquin, is of course more apparent in those works in which he is governed by no necessity—in his motets, hymns, and psalms.

Reference has more than once been made above to the small transitional school, as it is called by Ambros, which was led by Busnois and Obrecht—contemporaries of Okeghem—and also to their aims, different from those of their contemporary, and eventually merged in those of Josquin; indeed we gave lately, at pp. 189 and 197, specimens of their work. Returning now for a moment to these, after our examination of the remarkable canonic and proportional feats of Okeghem and Josquin, we are struck by the simple and rational use of imitation in the chanson by Busnois, *Je suis venut*, where the device, though truly constructive in character, is presented not as a gigantic puzzle in which all the parts throughout are equally concerned, but rather as a form of counterpoint, designed to please the ear by the repetition of a phrase, now in one voice and now in another. The methods adopted in this little work still need simplification, no doubt, but with this improvement they are to be recognized in the superior method of Josquin, in whose motets and psalms, for instance, points of imitation of the same nature as those of Busnois are frequently taken.

The work of Obrecht is even more obviously and unmistakably important than that of Busnois. We have often remarked upon the fact that the music of Dunstable and Dufay, though beautiful, was both lacking in character of its own and unable in any degree to reflect the character of the 'words, and that a joyful subject would convey in their music the same sensations to the hearer as a mournful one. This limitation was of course a part of the nature of the early polyphonic music itself. In plainsong the modal phrases no doubt to a certain extent conveyed the impression of the special modal *ethos*, so that joyous or sorrowful feelings might be created merely by the choice of mode; but the methods of early polyphony were such as to confuse and destroy any expression of special feeling which might have been contained in the ecclesiastical *cantus*, and to reduce all modes to one. For even when the composition ended in the tenor upon the final of the mode, and the various passing closes occurred upon appropriate notes, yet the absence of harmonic propriety in the progression of the parts, which was prolonged in some degree even after the death of Dufay in 1474, prevented the establishment of a sufficient harmonic relation between the sentences and their closing notes, and thus for the hearer everything was left unsettled. Now, however, as a part of that astonishing awakening of the musical understanding which came during the last quarter of the fifteenth century, the sense of harmonic propriety is seen as already almost completely established, and the true qualities of the modes are at last apparent in their harmonic treatment. Expression, therefore, at least so far as it may convey the general sense of the words, now for the first time became possible in polyphonic music, and that Obrecht must have been largely concerned in the development of its means is evident from his motet *Parce Domine*, if we consider that this splendid production dates from before 1500 and less than twenty-five years after the death of Dufay.

That this work exercised a powerful influence upon the mind of Josquin is in itself highly probable; moreover the younger man has left at least four motets which are modelled apparently, in principle, upon the plan of Obrecht's composition, and two at least of these—*Planxit autem David*, and *Absalon fili mi*—were celebrated, and have remained famous, for the qualities of pathetic expression which they display. The first could not be presented here, for lack of space, but *Absalon fili mi* is given entire. The mode chosen for this fine study in expression is Hypomixolydian, a mode, curiously enough, which Guido declares to be unsuitable to pathos: 'et difficile et ineptum est in eodem modo fieri lamentabile carmen.' Nevertheless Josquin, by frequently forming cadences upon D, the lowest note of the mode, and by a choice of the minor intervals of the scale as much as possible for the melodies of the separate parts, gives to his harmony throughout a certain melancholy; while towards the close, by a licence difficult to defend, he goes definitely out of the scale of the mode, or rather, by the sudden introduction of two flats converts it into a twice transposed Aeolian. The effect of the whole is extremely sad, and at the words *non vivam ultra* it becomes poignant from the introduction of two experimental discords—marked in our copy—which fall under no rule, and will remind the student of certain attempts by the later Purcell. The augmented fifth in the final cadence also is remarkable, and terribly effective. Finally, in passing we may notice, in the opening point of imitation, made upon the first four notes of the authentic scale of this species, the formula afterwards chosen for the famous canon *Non nobis Domine*.

MOTET. ABSALON FILI MI.

Novum et insigne opus musicum, &c.
Noribergae, 1563,   Josquin Desprès.

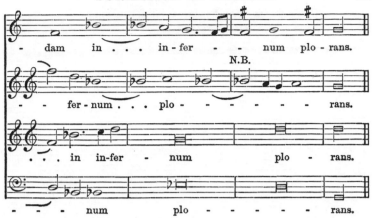

- dam in . . . in - fer - - num plo - rans.

N.B.

- - fer - num . . . plo - - - - - - rans.

. . . in in-fer - num plo - rans.

- - - num plo - - - - - rans.

In this composition we see for the first time, in a somewhat
rough and even crude form, the type of the sixteenth-century
motet. The writer had not yet perceived the true use of points,
except as regards the opening, for the purpose of declaring the
mode; it is evident that the notion of their constant employment in comparatively short passages throughout the work,
entering at the proper moment and again in turn withdrawing
from the imitation after a brief prominence, had not yet
occurred to composers; but the solid foundation of the form is
here, and in the works of subsequent authors we shall trace its
development.

Our small selection of examples would be incomplete without
a specimen of Josquin's rendering of joyous feeling; an extract
is therefore given from the Psalm *Laudate pueri*, a composition
which, from its choice of mode (the Ionian transposed), and its
general treatment, presents a remarkably modern aspect, and in
which tranquillity and joyful confidence of spirit are beautifully
exhibited. Verbal expression is seen for a moment at the word
suscitans, but it is evident that the author is unwilling upon the
whole to injure the simplicity of his representation; the music
flows on, in pure concord, undisturbed in the happiness of the
moment, and creating throughout a corresponding sentiment in
the mind of the hearer.

FROM THE PSALM.   LAUDATE PUERI.

Select Psalms, vol. ii. (Montanus) 1553.   Josquin Després.

In considering the work of Josquin, between 1470 and 1520, in the point of view of its special contribution to the technique of music, it will probably be felt that the actual degree of progress which it represents, especially as seen in the treatment of motets and psalms, is incomparably greater than that attained by any other musician in a corresponding period of time. Even if we suppose that the works in which this progress is seen as most completely established were not produced in the earlier part of his life—that is to say, not before 1500—the advance which they represent, as compared with the work of Dufay, is enormous. The technique of Dufay is still archaic in principle, for although already in the methods which that composer received from Dunstable the seeds of harmonic propriety existed, yet he did little to develop them, and their growth is scarcely apparent in his work; in the work of Josquin, on the other hand, we find this principle not only recognized, but developed to an extent which was sufficient for the purposes of music during the next fifty years after his death. It is not, however, necessary to suppose that the whole of this development is due to Josquin himself; its commencement is more probably to be ascribed to the early labours of Okeghem and Obrecht, and it may even have been begun by them during the lifetime of Dufay; but it is in the work of Josquin that the principle of harmonic propriety, which alone renders possible the construction of sentences conveying a clear and distinct musical intention, first appears as the most essential motive of musical means and methods. And it is upon this that the whole success and fame of Josquin, in our later point of view and apart from that which encouraged the recondite canonic and proportional devices, is founded; for it is to his perception of this principle above all that we may ascribe those qualities which especially delight us in his work, because more than any others they impress us with a sense of its modernity, namely, its intelligibility when regarded as pure music, and its intensity of expression in rendering the sense of words.

It is perhaps worth observing that the great awakening and activity in the art, beginning probably soon after 1450, to which this result is finally due, corresponds to similar phenomena in other creative spheres, and more particularly to the important enlargement of pictorial means and ideals which dates from the early years of the century; and that the special benefit derived from the movement of which Josquin is the accepted exponent —the potentiality in music of a closer approach to the objects of its imitation in nature—is of the same kind as that which had been already conferred upon painting, when suddenly it became possible to represent as round and isolated in space appearances which formerly could only be exhibited in two dimensions.

CHAPTER II

THE NETHERLAND SCHOOL

ALTHOUGH, as has been said, the great forward movement, seen chiefly in an advance towards intelligible musical expression founded upon harmonic propriety, which marks the close of the fifteenth century, was probably begun by Okeghem and Obrecht, the great extent of the progress which was actually accomplished by Josquin may be partly seen in a comparison of his work with that of the contemporaries who equally with himself inherited the traditions of the original reformers; and from this it will appear as probable that these composers did little, as compared with their great associate, in this special branch of the necessary work of the time. Pierre de la Rue, for instance, the master who perhaps among the contemporaries of Josquin stands next to him in talent, prefers to compete with him in general in the field of canonic and proportional contrivance, while in respect of clear and intelligible harmonic progressions, such as are constant and well sustained in the work of Josquin, his compositions do not even apparently invite comparison. The same is true as regards Gaspar, Alexander Agricola, Ghiselin, De Orto, and even of Anton Brumel, though with some modification in the case of the latter master, whose natural sense of harmonic propriety was perhaps as acute as that of Josquin himself, if not so frequently indulged. Indeed it may be said that while most of the masters just mentioned were perfectly able to construct a series of agreeable progressions, in any mode, in the form of simple chords, the old indifference to propriety is still generally apparent in their contrapuntal writing. Josquin's counterpoint, on the other hand, is rendered limpid by means of its harmonies, as we saw, for instance, in the extract given in our

last chapter from the Psalm *Laudate pueri*, and in an even more
remarkable example, considering the elaborate treatment—the
Sanctus from the Mass *L'homme armé*.

The situation perhaps most often chosen for the display of
harmonic passages in the work of Josquin's contemporaries is
at the beginning of the composition, where now in fact, and
henceforward, groups of solid and closely related chords become the accepted and usual alternative of the fugal opening.
A good example of the employment of plain harmony in this
situation, from a motet by Pierre de la Rue, may be shown in
short score:—

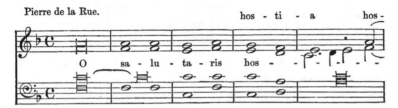

The same method is finely employed by Anton Brumel in
the great motet for men's voices, *O Domine Iesu Christe*:—

Pas - - tor . . bo - - - - - ne, &c.

The more extended examples of the immediate contemporaries of Josquin which here follow will give a fuller idea of
their methods, and will probably confirm our opinion of the
superior perception of Josquin himself in respect of the claims
of harmony as an integral portion of the scheme of intelligible
and expressive music. Were anything known as regards the
early circumstances of these composers it might no doubt be
possible to trace in their works influences and common tendencies of a more particular kind than a general descent from
Okeghem and Obrecht will suggest; but our information respecting them—and indeed this is true in almost every case during
the existence of the school—is chiefly confined to the collections
printed by Petrucci and others, in which their numerous names
and works appear. Of Pierre de la Rue, for example, we know
little beyond the fact that from 1492 to 1510 he was a member
of the Burgundian ducal chapel, that works by him were published by Petrucci in 1501, 1505, 1513, 1516, &c., and that he
was probably therefore popular. His fine Mass *De Sancto
Antonio*, which appears in several collections, might illustrate
not inappropriately our criticism of his methods; the effect of
the progressions is somewhat vague, but the fact that Hypo-
phrygian harmony was quite familiar to the writer is obvious.

Our example of Brumel is taken from an often-mentioned
Mass, *De dringhs* or *dringhis*; the name, of which no explanation is ever offered, is printed by Glareanus in Greek. Here,
as we should expect from the example already given of this

composer, the harmonic element is very distinctly perceptible, notwithstanding that the mode chosen—the transposed Lydian —is unusual, and its appropriate progressions and closes not immediately recognizable by our ears; the composition, indeed, in this point of view is extremely beautiful, the harmonies, whether simple or conveyed in figures, being quite full and rich in sound throughout. Brumel went in 1505 to Ferrara, to direct the chapel of Alfonso d'Este, and remained there till his death; it is not perhaps impossible that in the inclination of subsequent Italian composers, in Bologna, Ferrara, and Venice (before Willaert), towards the qualities which are conspicuous in his work, we may partly trace the influence of the master.

Gaspar, or Casper, van Weerbecke, to whom we may next turn our attention, occupied in the chapel of the Sforza at Milan a position similar to that of Brumel at Ferrara, but since his style is far from being so distinct and characteristic as that of Brumel, it is impossible to trace any influence which he may have exerted upon the music of north-western Italy. Our example gives a good idea of his contrapuntal writing. The opening of the *Agnus*, here shown, is perhaps interesting from its fugal passage consisting of a double point; little however comes of this device, and the rest is somewhat tedious. From the close too it is evident that Gaspar, like Brumel, is still far from perceiving the principles which govern the accompaniment of certain suspended or syncopated discords. Indeed this may be said of all the composers of this time, for all were still experimenting with this portion of their material; only quite at the end of the whole development, when perfectly satisfactory formulae had been evolved from these experiments, were composers in a position to distinguish the principles towards which they had been striving.

MASS: DE DRINGHIS.

KYRIE.

Missarum diversorum auctorum liber primus.
Venice: Petrucci, 1508.

Antonius Brumel.

MASS.

N'AS-TU PAS ?

AGNUS DEI.

Missarum diversorum auctorum liber primus.
Venice : Petrucci, 1508.

Gaspar van Weerbecke.

peccata

miserere nobis.

Ambros, in his *Geschichte der Musik*, iii. 252, includes within the group which we have just examined one other composer, of the same generation apparently as Josquin and belonging originally to the same school—Loyset Compère, an important writer, whose music is illustrated in our next following example. The general date, however, of Compère should probably be stated as somewhat earlier, since we may perhaps gather from the words of a composition in the Trent Codex 91, fol. 33,[1] that about the year 1468, at the beginning probably of his career, he belonged, together with Josquin, to the circle which had formed round the aged Dufay at Cambrai. Not many of his works are known, but those which have been examined reveal, upon the whole, strongly harmonic tendencies, and may well have played a great part in that transition from vague tonality to decided and intelligible progression, which, as we have already said, must have been one of the chief results obtained from the great awakening of music during the latter half of the fifteenth century. In the beautiful example which we give, a fragment from the motet *Bone Iesu*, the harmonic tendency is visible throughout. The chords employed are triads; the progressions are such as are proper to Mixolydian harmony, and they are everywhere used with the most perfect taste and judgement. It will no doubt be observed that the accompaniment of the cadence is unsuccessful at the place marked; but in this matter Compère is not behind his time, since the essential structure of the parts in concluding passages—except as regards

---

[1] A hymn to the Virgin, *Omnium bonorum plena*, &c., which concludes with a prayer for intercession on behalf of musicians, naming especially Dufay, and continuing, 'proque Dussart, Busnois, Caron, Georget de Brelles, Tinctoris, Okeghem, Desprès, Corbet, Heniart, Faugues, Molinet, Regis, omnibusque canentibus. Simul et me Loiset Compère orante.' Dr. Adler, in his admirable edition of the Trent MSS., assigns the codex in which this hymn appears to the year 1470, just before the death of Dufay.

the suspended fourth to the bass, respecting which there was now no doubt—was still undetermined.

To the same group also properly belongs Heinrich Isaak, a powerful and prolific composer, in learning and ingenuity but little inferior to Okeghem, and nearly the equal of Obrecht as regards expression. No very special characteristic can be said to mark his compositions, which rather partake of most of the excellences of his fellow workers in turn. Glareanus, who especially admired his work, gives many specimens, and among them draws particular attention to an enigmatical motet, of which he also prints a solution. This well exhibits the 'proportional' ingenuity of the composer; our own example, on the other hand, reveals his mastery of canonic imitation. The constancy with which the leading point appears throughout the composition in fresh relations, the opening phrase also closing the work, is most remarkable. It is said that Isaak came from Germany. Certainly he ended his life in that country, where for some years he had formed the centre of a small circle, including Hofhaimer, Holzer, Heinrich Finck, and his own pupil Senfl, the contemporary and friend of Luther. Isaak also paid two visits to Florence[1]—the first being mentioned (for so Glareanus says) by Politian, and the second by P. Aron in his well-known work on music—but it does not appear that he originated there any tradition of composition. Such influence as he was able to exert was displayed in Germany, where his followers are often said to constitute a German School.

[1] He was for some years in the service of Lorenzo the Magnificent, setting to music Lorenzo's sacred drama, *SS. Giovanni e Paolo*, and also his carnival songs. Isaak was by birth a Bohemian, and, according to Machiavelli, married in Florence. Many of the Netherland composers visited Italy. Josquin Desprès worked in Rome under Sixtus IV, and also visited Florence, as did Obrecht. [1931.]

MOTET.

BONE IESU.

(*Middle Portion.*)

Motetti della corona,
Lib. iii. Petrucci, 1519.   Loyset Compère.

In ma-nus tu-as Do - mi - ne com-

In ma-nus . . tu-as Do - mi - ne com-

In ma-nus tu - as Do - mi - ne com-

In ma-nus tu - as Do - mi - ne com-

-men - - - do . . . spi - ri - tum . . me - um;

-men - do spi - ri-tum . . me - um . . . . ; &c.

-men - do spi - ri - tum me - um . . . ; &c.

-men - do spi - ri - tum me - um . . ; &c.

MASS: 'CHARGÉ DE DEUIL.'

AGNUS DEI.

Misse Henrici Izak.
Petrucci, 1506.

Heinrich Isaak.

miserere   no - bis

nobis

Before passing on to consider the next generation of composers, mention should be made of Josquin's younger contemporaries—of the men, that is to say, to whom the methods of
the reconstructed art of music came not directly from the
original reformers but through Josquin himself. Of these some
no doubt were his actual pupils, receiving personal instruction,
while others followed his methods closely by means of the MSS.
in circulation and of the various printed collections which were
now, about the year 1510, beginning to appear; in the work of
all may be seen, in various degrees, the same governing principles, both technical and ideal, as in that of Josquin, namely,
the use of fugal imitation as an essentially constructive device,
and of intelligible harmonic progression not only as imparting
a general intention to the composition apart from words, but
also as a means of creating definite states of feeling in the mind
of the hearer. The principal composers of this group are Mouton,
Divitis (both singers in the chapel of Louis XII), Lhéritier.
Anton de Févin, Carpentras (Eleazar Genet), director of the
Sistine Chapel under Leo X, Lupus, F. de Layolle, and Andreas
de Silva—all excellent. In giving a few examples from their
works we may begin with the first Kyrie from the Mass *Sancta
Trinitas*, by Anton de Févin. This admirable writer did not

5 1162

live to fulfil entirely the promise of his earliest compositions, dying young indeed, in 1516, four or five years before Josquin himself; but though his life was short the contribution towards the formation of the new music which is contained in his remaining works is very considerable. It is also of a kind rather unusual at this period, in which the establishment of the new technique alone seemed all-important. Févin, as we see, was perhaps not so much concerned either with harmonic propriety or with fugal imitation as were some others of the group; he devotes himself rather to the study of combined sounds from the point of view of an increase of their beauty. Passages in which this aim may be thought to be apparent are to be seen even in our short example, especially at the word 'eleyson.' The author shows in general a strong predilection for the exquisite effect of overlapping cadences, which, though not absolutely new even in his time, is more beautifully introduced by him, and with greater correctness, according to the later standard, than hitherto.

The motet, *Noë noë*, by Mouton, is entirely in the style of Josquin, and might indeed very well pass for a work of that master, in the somewhat hard manner which he sometimes employs; for notwithstanding its two fine points, one of which —that at the opening—is shown in the specimen given below, there is sometimes a considerable bareness of effect in the work, owing to open fifths and octaves and the choice of wrong notes to double. In short, a greater contrast than this to the work of Févin, in all respects, could hardly be found; yet the composition presents an appearance of ease and mastery in the application of the current means, which renders it a worthy example of the central school, and of its accomplishment.

There is little, on the other hand, to remind us of Josquin in the methods of Layolle, a French Fleming who was much in Italy, where he taught music, and is said indeed to have numbered Benvenuto Cellini among his pupils. The work from which we give a fragment—a *Noël*, like that of Mouton—affords an excellent indication of one of the chief possible sources of variety and beauty in polyphonic composition, namely, the definite effect produced in the whole work by the character of the phrases adopted as subjects of imitation. Even when the aim is also largely harmonic, the flow of the individual parts, repeating and echoing the same phrase—as for instance in the author's second point in this composition, the charming 'hodie natus est nobis'—gives to the whole passage in which the point is worked a peculiar colouring, due to the constant reflection in all directions of the special melodic quality of the phrase employed. This fact is of real importance, for as a rule it is the presence or absence of this melodic quality in the individual points of the composition which principally constitutes the polyphonic work as either interesting or wearisome. Josquin himself was of course not ignorant of this means of effect; but in the work of Layolle we see it somewhat more specialized, and in a somewhat more advanced form.

Mass: Sancta Trinitas.

KYRIE.

Missae Antonii de Févin.
  Petrucci, 1515.   A. de Févin.

MOTET.

NOË NOË.

(*Opening portion*).

Motetti della Corona, Lib. 2, 1519.   J. Mouton.

Motet.

NOË, NOË, NOË, HODIE NATUS EST.

Secundus liber cum quatuor
vocibus. Motetti del fiore. *(Opening portion.)*
(Lyons, Moderne, 1532.)

F. de Layolle.

II   P

The tendencies which we have just seen displayed in the compositions of Josquin's younger contemporaries, tendencies towards the elaboration of the more beautiful and enjoyable qualities of music, are even more strongly evident in the work of the succeeding generation, where no means were now employed which could hinder the clear and spontaneous expression of the particular kind of sentiment which it was the desire of the composer to suggest. 'Proportional' devices, therefore, and intricate fugal problems, being of no use, but rather the contrary, in conveying the expression of feeling, were now, since the death of Josquin, banished from the composition, and the remainder of the technique bequeathed to the school by the master was adopted as the whole of the available means. It is to the perfection of this remainder that we now see the younger generation applying itself as its complete duty, and in the compositions of Gombert, Richafort, and Willaert, for instance, we perceive the earliest results of the effort. In the examples which we give from the works of two of these masters it is already evident that their technique is, or may soon become, amply sufficient for the attainment of all that is most desirable in music—purity of sound and beauty of expression, embellishing a perfect structure. It is true that perfection, of any kind, is not yet reached, nor even perhaps yet perceived; but the way is at last opened by which it will actually be found.

To these examples may be added a specimen of the composition of a rather younger contemporary, Jacques Clément (commonly called *non Papa*), in the whole of whose work the most noble and elevated pursuit of the new aims is remarkably exemplified. We there perceive especially the effort towards the production of a fuller and closer texture of parts in the composition than any that had hitherto been thought sufficient. The long pauses, therefore, of the old style, which often gave to a composition of five real parts the power and effect of only three or four, are abandoned in the works of Clément, and the entire strength of the means is seen as exerted throughout. And this method, which is here combined with a perfect balance of polyphonic interest in all the parts, gives rise to works which in themselves are the most triumphant vindication of the banishment of the elder forms that could be desired, and heralds of that ultimate complete success, and establishment of unalterable forms of beauty, which was now the conscious end of all effort.

Motet.

(<i>First Part.</i>)

SUPER FLUMINA.

Motetti del fiore, liber primus.
Lyons, 1532.   N. Gombert.

- da - re - mur . . tu - i, . . Sy - on . . . .

. . tu - i, Sy - on . . . .

re -cor- da - re - mur   tu - i, Sy-on . . . .

. . . . tu - i, Sy - on . . . .

MOTET.

QUEM DICUNT HOMINES.

(*Opening portion.*)

Motetti del fiore, liber primus.
Lyons, 1532.   Iohannes Richafort.

Quem   di-cunt ho-mi - nes .

Quem   di-cunt ho-mi - nes . .   es - se   fi - li - um ho -

. es - se   fi - li - um ho-mi - nis,   es - se   fi - li - um

Quem   di-cunt ho- mi-nes . .   es - se   fi - li - um ho - - -

- - mi - nis .   es - se   fi - li-um   ho- mi-nis ho - - -

Quem   di-cunt ho-mi- nes   es- se   fi-

Et ait . Ie - - - sus, ...   Be- &c.

- - - - - - - sus,   Be - a - - &c.

Ie - - - sus,   Be - a - tus es . . . Simon,&c.

Ie - - - - - - sus, ...   &c.

Motet.

VOX CLAMANTIS.

Printed by Commer
in *Collectio Operum
Musicorum Batavorum*, vol. i.   Iacobus Clemens non Papa.

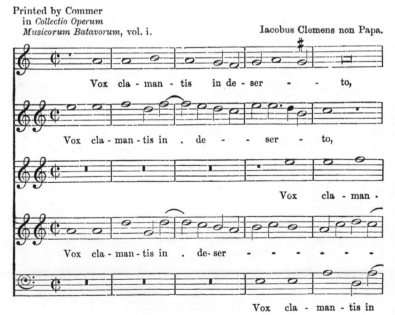

Vox cla - man - tis   in de - ser - - to,

Vox cla - man - tis in . de - - ser - to,

Vox   cla - man .

Vox cla - man - tis in . de- ser - - - - - -

Vox   cla - man - tis in

Secular Music.

We have already seen that the composition of music to secular words was from the earliest times, and in all schools, carried on side by side with that which was devoted to the divine service, and that both kinds were produced by the same men. Also, it will have been remarked, that while in those early periods in which music was still incapable of variety the treatment of both kinds was necessarily exactly similar, in proportion as the resources of the art became more extended an increasingly marked difference between them is discernible. This difference, however, was still comparatively small until the time of Dunstable, who in fact himself made an important, though perhaps not original, step in that direction; intending apparently to distinguish his setting of the chanson *Puis que*

m'amour, for instance, as secular, by the use of canonic imitation in its composition, a device which was not employed in his
sacred music. In *Cent mille escus* also, ascribed to Dufay, the
points of imitation are far more numerous than in the Masses
and motets of that master, where these embellishments are
still used with comparative reticence. But it is not until the
recognition of the triad (about 1500) as a musical factor of
importance, and the consequent discovery of modal harmony,
which before had not been in the least perceived, that the true
distinction between sacred and secular composition becomes
obvious in music. For composers had now at last a material
which they could treat in an expressive manner, and could thus
fully exhibit the difference which exists between the function
of secular music as a vehicle for the representation of moods
of feeling, and that which belongs to the music of the divine
service as the essential manifestation of a settled and constant
aspiration.

The first definite and important utilization of the new means
for secular purposes is seen in the works of a group of musicians,
all of French or Franco-Flemish origin, and almost all pupils of
Josquin, who frequented the French Court during the reigns of
Francis I and Henry II. The chief of this group was Clément
Janequin or Jennequin, a writer possessed of the most brilliant
fancy, and of extraordinary ability in converting music to all
sorts of unaccustomed uses; bringing vividly before the mind
not only the characteristic sounds of a hunt, or the street cries
of itinerant vendors, which we have already seen attempted by
the old Florentine school, but representing even subjects as
difficult and as widely different from each other as the shock of
battle and the songs of birds. From this it will be seen that
secular music was already, in some directions, at the very beginning of its free existence aiming at a point almost beyond the
bounds of the art ; fortunately, however, it does not appear either

that the fancy of Janequin was always exercised upon such matters or that his less desirable example was at all generally followed. The charming collection of thirty-one chansons, for instance, published by Attaignant in 1529, eight years after the death of Josquin—which is perhaps the most excellent monument of the school—contains nothing extravagant, and in introducing us to a new kind of music represents this in the most favourable aspect possible.

The collection contains compositions by Claudin de Sermisy, Consilium, Courtoys, Deslouges, Dulot, Gascongne, Hesdin, Jacotin, Janequin, Lombart, Sohier, and Vermont, all men of mark in their own day; most of them indeed are mentioned in the contemporary literature, and with special commendation by Ronsard and Rabelais, as also by more directly musical writers, such as Danckerts. Our example is the beginning of a chanson by Gascongne, a composition remarkable for its simplicity and beauty, so combined as to afford already a perfect model for secular treatment. The buoyant nature of the melody, the lightness of the point and its sparing use by the composer, who 'takes the best of it,' as Morley says, 'and then away to some close'—to notice only the most superficial of its characteristics—create an impression very different from that which we receive from the contemporary sacred music, with its great formal opening in deeply studied phrases, and its elaborate treatment of the various subjects, as they enter solemnly from time to time.

Chanson.

JE NY SÇAUROYS.

Paris, Pierre Attaignant, 1529.   Gascongne.

Je ny sçau - roys, je ny sçau -

Je ny sçau - roys, je ny sçau-roys chan-

Je ny sçau-roys, je ny sçau -roys, . .

Je ny sçau-roys, je ny sçau-

-roys chan - ter . . ne . . ri - - re, tous mes plai-

-ter ne ri - - - - - - - re, tous mes plai-

je ny sçau-roys chan - ter . . ne . . ri - - re,

-roys, je ny sçau-roys chan - ter . . ne ri - re,

-sirs ne sont . . que plours, tous mes plai-sirs ne sont . . que

-sirs ne sont . . . . que plours, tous mes plaisirs ne . . sont que

tous mes plai-sirs . . ne sont . que

tous mes plai-sirs ne sont que

As in the sacred music, so also in the secular kind, the alternative, with respect to the opening form, lies between a point and plain chords. In the latter, in this collection, we are struck by the remarkable correctness of the modal progressions, and in Janequin's *Ce moys de May*, for instance, this appears very strongly. Our space unfortunately will not admit of the exhibition of this

charming song, but room may be found for a few of the opening
bars, in short score:—

Twenty-three years later we find Janequin again contributing
to an interesting collection of secular pieces, composed as settings of *Les Amours de P. de Ronsard*; and here he is associated
with ecclesiastical composers of the highest rank, such as Certon,
director of the Sainte Chapelle, Crequillon, for some time, about
1544, Maestro di Capella to Charles V at Madrid, and with the
great Goudimel himself. Compared with the work of these
composers, disciples in the school of Gombert, that of Janequin,
though excellent, has now a somewhat old-fashioned air, and
does not seem to demand the exhibition of a specimen; the
secular work, however, of such masters as Certon and Goudimel

cannot be passed over, and we therefore give a short extract from each.

SONNET.

J'ESPÈRE ET CRAINS.

Les Amours de P. de Ronsard, Paris, 1552.   P. Certon.

J'ad-mi - re tout, et de rien ne me chault, Je me de -

Je

- la - ce, et puis je . . me . . re - li - e . . . &c.

me de - lace, et puis . je me re - li - e . . . &c.

&c.

SONNET. QUAND J'APPERÇOY.

Les Amours de Ronsard, 1552.   Claude Goudimel.

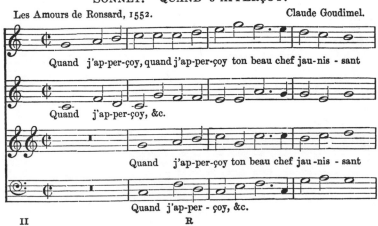

Quand j'ap-per-çoy, quand j'ap-per-çoy ton beau chef jau-nis - sant

Quand j'ap-per-çoy, &c.

Quand j'ap-per-çoy ton beau chef jau -nis - sant

Quand j'ap-per - çoy, &c.

II   R

Qui l'or fi - lé des char - i - tés ef - fa - ce, Et ton bel œil . . qui

Qui l'or fi - lé des char - i - tés ef - fa - ce, Et ton bel œil . . qui

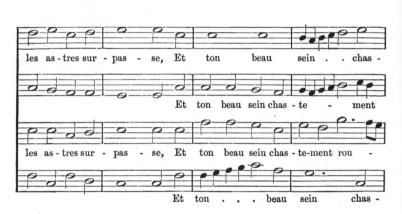

les as - tres sur - pas - se, Et ton beau sein . . chas -

Et ton beau sein chas - te - ment

les as - tres sur - pas - se, Et ton beau sein chas - te - ment rou -

Et ton . . . beau sein chas -

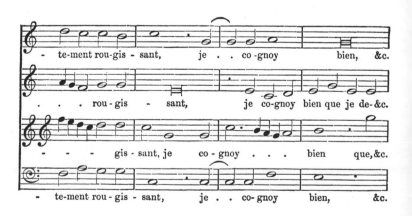

- te-ment rou - gis - sant, je . . co - gnoy bien, &c.

. . . rou - gis - sant, je co - gnoy bien que je de - &c.

- - - gis - sant, je co - gnoy . . . bien que, &c.

- te-ment rou - gis - sant, je . . co - gnoy bien, &c.

Not only at the Court of France and in the French chansons did pupils of Josquin find material for a development of the new music. A considerable number made their way also into Italy, where they received employment in every Ducal chapel, in the Sistine, and in St. Mark's at Venice. The secular music which they found in use was written to various forms of light and unsubstantial verse—*Frottole, Villanesche,* and such like, descendants probably of the *Ballate* and *Canzonette* of the fourteenth century, of which we have already seen specimens. Some of the Flemings —Layolle, for instance, Willaert, and Verdelot—attempted competition with the Italians in the production of these lighter forms; but soon the school as a whole, in composing for the chamber, turned to the old serious form of secular verse, the Madrigal, which though no longer set to music had survived, as it would seem, as poetry, and had retained also much of its original structure and characteristic expression; and with this as their subject they gradually raised, from very simple beginnings, the noble fabric in which the ideal of secular music was eventually to be perfected.

The early madrigals were chiefly the work of Willaert and the Flemish pupils who resorted to him from time to time during the first ten years after his appointment to St. Mark's in Venice—Verdelot, for instance, Archadelt, and Waelrant. Their compositions of this kind are for the most part studiously simple both in form and style of melody, the music following the metrical structure closely, yet enriching it—as appears in our example from Archadelt—with graceful points of imitation and the simpler forms of ornamental cadence.

MADRIGAL.
'SE LA DUREZZA.'

Il terzo libro dei madrigali
novissimi di Archadelt, &c.

Archadelt.

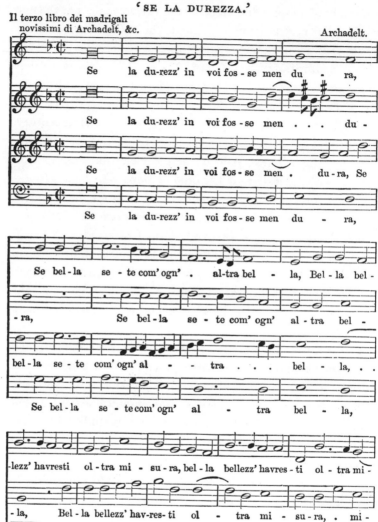

Already, while the early Flemish madrigalists were thus pursuing their somewhat cautious way, and keeping as a rule within, or at the most not far from, the outlines of their original models, the *Frottole* and *Villanesche*, an Italian, a singer in the Papal choir, Costanzo Festa, had already revealed a path of his own making for the new musical species, a path leading more directly than that adopted by the Flemings to the broadly ornate form in which the madrigal eventually arrived at perfection. In the fine *Così soave*, given as our example of Festa's work, the characteristics of the Roman method are very evident. Though not approaching the gravity of the motett in general style, the composition is certainly more indebted to that form than to the models adopted by the Flemings for its methods, being in figured counterpoint throughout with frequent points of imitation. It is true that the opening is somewhat slight in character, but the interest increases as we proceed, both points and closes becoming more and more important, yet without solemnity or greater seriousness even than befits the purely artificial sentiment of the epigrammatic verse.

MADRIGAL.
'COSÌ SOAVE.'

Venice.   Gardano, 1541.   Costanzo Festa.

Co - sì soav' è 'l fuo - - - co,

Co - sì soav' è 'l fuo - co,

Co - sì soav' è 'l fuo - co, .

Co - sì soav' è 'l fuo - -

* G in original.

The success of the madrigal, which was soon generally cultivated in North and Middle Italy, greatly stimulated the composition of the lesser and lighter kinds of secular music. In substance these remained still much the same as the *Frottole* and other forms proper to the ante-madrigalian period; but they were now enlarged in form and improved as regards musical merit. Such were the *canzoni* and *balletti* with which we are familiar in the works of later writers—Gastoldi and Ferretti, for instance. Though Morley speaks slightingly of them, they are extremely neat and workmanlike in construction, and often contain much beauty.

The condition of the Venetian madrigal in the middle of the century may be seen in two examples by Cipriano da Rore and Costanzo Porta, both pupils of Willaert. From these it will be observed that the old form of composition in plain counterpoint, which was still, it may be said, continued elsewhere by Giaches de Wert and others, has here given place to a mixed method, inclining upon the whole to the figured style adopted, from the beginning, by Costanzo Festa. In the *Chi non sa* by Cipriano there is still much simple writing, though this is intermixed with points and passages of florid counterpoint. This method, employed in so short a work, is inferior in dignity to that of the Roman, since variety is obtained in it by the use of various means, rather than by varying, as in the work of Festa, the character of one; yet in its effect it is often expressive, and its changes are not altogether unwelcome.

It is of course well known that, apart from the class of composition to which our example belongs, Cipriano wrote 'Chromatic madrigals'; it has not, however, been thought necessary either to describe these or to give examples of them, since they were purely experimental, and moreover quite unsuccessful.

The method adopted by Porta in our example is that which consists in the division of the text into the smallest portions

II   S

consistent with the preservation of the sense—too short as
a rule to admit of a point—and the embellishment of these by
means of clear and expressive contrapuntal writing, leading in
each case to some pleasing and often unexpected cadence.
This method was much in favour during the latter half of the
century, since it afforded excellent opportunities for the display
of those refinements which characterized the practice of this
period, and avoided the necessity for sustained effort. Nor is
this the only sign of the times, for it will be observed in our
fragment of Porta's *Amorose viole*, that the chromatic note is
now approached and quitted by leap, as if it formed an actual
part of the scale in which it occurs, a licence not sanctioned
by a strict observance of the rules of *musica ficta*. And this
tendency, although still absent from sacred music, continued to
increase in the madrigal, which thus became one of the principal
agents in the disintegration of the Modal system. Indeed, Orazio
Vecchi's *Pastorella gratiosella* (published in 1589), of which we
give a few bars in concluding this account, would seem to be
written frankly in the key of G minor.

MADRIGAL.

'CHI NON SA.'

Venice. Gardano, 1571.   Cipriano da Rore.

MADRIGAL.
'AMOROSE VIOLE.'

Venice.   Gardano, 1575.   Costanzo Porta.

MADRIGAL.

'PASTORELLA GRATIOSELLA.'

Venice. Gardano, 1589.   Orazio Vecchi.

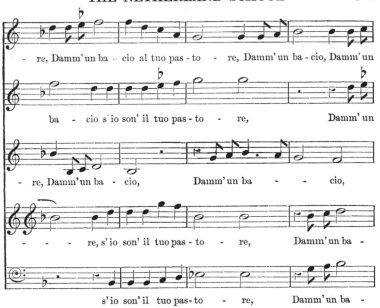

- re, Damm' un ba - cio al tuo pas - to - re, Damm' un ba - cio, Damm' un

ba - cio s' io son' il tuo pas - to - re, Damm' un

- re, Damm' un ba - cio, Damm' un ba - cio,

- - - re, s' io son' il tuo pas - to - re, Damm' un ba -

s' io son' il tuo pas - to - re, Damm' un ba -

ba - cio, un ba - cio, Damm' un ba - cio, &c.

ba - cio, un ba - cio, Damm' un ba- &c.

s' io son' il tuo pas - to - - - re, &c.

-cio, damm' un ba - cio, s' io son il tuo pas- to - re, &c.

-cio, damm' un ba - cio, s' io son' il tuo pas - to - - - re, &c.

THE OFFSHOOTS OF THE FLEMISH STOCK.

While the constant presence of Flemish composers for many years in Venice, and the influence of their teaching and example, were beneficial to the musical life of the city in many ways, in one respect especially these influences had created an advantageous situation of the highest value—in the transformation, that is to say, of the casual association of native practitioners into a true local school, whose work, not only in the secular kind but also in the music of the divine service, was brought to exhibit a special character. Its solidarity, moreover, was not affected by the death of its Netherland founder, but continued intact through many years of a long and interesting career. Even during the short period subsequent to the death of Willaert which is covered by the limits of the present work, the school numbered among its native leaders Zarlino, Andrea and Giovanni Gabrieli, and Giovanni Croce; and at a comparatively early date in its history it had enriched the art with a new form—the double choir, alternately antiphonal and united, which, immediately upon its invention, made its way throughout musical Europe.

Mention of the Venetian offshoot of the Netherland school suggests to our minds the case of France. From the frequent references to the French pupils of the Flemings which necessarily occur in any historical account of music, it might naturally be supposed that these composers should also be considered as forming a school, properly so called. But, in fact, by most historians, apparently, this distinction is denied to them; and not without reason, for though their individual works were often of great beauty and merit, they neither formed a coherent association based upon original aims, nor worked out systematically among themselves ideas derived from the Flemings, but were for ever recurring to their preceptors, with whose growth and development they associated their own. They were, however, unable to follow the Flemings in those later and higher flights which brought the art of composition to the threshold of perfection, and their methods had become out of date, and their music relatively weak, even before the appearance of Lassus or the rise of the Roman school.

With respect to Germany and Holland, it may be said that their schools had not, before the year 1600, which is our limit, declared themselves; but in Poland, and more particularly in Cracow, we find that long before that period a school already deserving the name undoubtedly existed.[1] Its beginnings are thought to have originated with Heinrich Finck, probably a German pupil of Dufay and Isaak, who was director of the Royal Chapel from about 1492, under John Albert, to about 1506, under Sigismond, for it is not certain that anything of importance was composed in Cracow before the earlier of those dates. Indeed, none of the existing music of this school is earlier than the sixteenth century; it begins with a book of hymns, composed at the request of Sigismond I, and printed in Cracow in 1522, by Sebastian Felzstyn, whose more elaborate compositions, contained partly in a Gradual of the Virgin, are to be found in MS. in the library of the Cathedral. Felzstyn was apparently also a theorist and an excellent teacher, numbering some of the best native writers of the succeeding generation among his pupils.

Cracow was far from the principal centres of musical interest and influence, and but for a fortunate circumstance the school might have dwindled from its birth, languishing in a half-starved mediocrity. This circumstance, which communicated

[1] The best thanks of the present writer are due to Count George Mycielski, Professor of Fine Art in the University of Cracow, for much kind and valuable information with respect to this school and its productions.

the needful stimulus—the desire to excel in closely united effort
—was the establishment, in 1543, of a select choir, called the
College of Roratists, consisting of a rector, nine chaplain-singers,
and a clerk, founded by Sigismond chiefly for the performance of
Masses for defunct members of the Royal house. Here at once
therefore were created conditions favourable to the growth of
an elevated style of composition; and accordingly, as it would
appear, this choir soon became the centre of musical life in
Poland, and all the principal native writers of sacred music
were to be found among its members. Its first director was one
Nicholas of Posen, of whom little is known; his successor however, Christopher Borek, was a distinguished musician, whose
ability is revealed in a Mass of some importance which is still
in existence. But the really remarkable members of the college,
the men upon whom its reputation may be said to depend, were
Martinus Leopolita, organist of the chapel, Venceslas Szamotulski, director, and Thomas Szadek, chaplain-singer. The first
of these was considered to be the most important, and was
certainly the most prolific, of the three. His principal works
are the Masses *Rorate, De Resurrectione,* and *Paschalis*; and
of these the last is probably the best, and indeed may be considered as the representative work of the school. Szamotulski
printed much; a number of motets by him were brought out
in Cracow in 1556, and two of these—*Dies est laetitiae,* and
Christe qui lux es—have been reprinted in Poland in modern
times. Two others—*In te Domine speravi,* and *Ego sum Pastor
Bonus*—appeared in the lifetime of the composer in collections
by Montanus, published in 1553 and 1583. We give examples
of Leopolita and Szamotulski, and from these it will be seen
that the style of their music is late Flemish—later, that is to
say, than that of Gombert; indeed, not only from the entire
absence of long pauses, except in the fugal opening, but also
from the general tendency to preserve the pulse-beat or minim

as the standard of movement, we might suppose the music to represent an attempt to compose in the methods of Clemens non Papa, or of Christian Holländer. It has not, however, always either the clear harmonic flow or the melodious voice parts of those masters, yet it is still estimable, and if not perfectly excellent, is nevertheless entitled to a place among the good work of its time.

'MASS: PASCHALIS.'

KYRIE.

From *Monumenta Musices Sacrae in Polonia.*
Ed. by l'Abbé Jos. Surzinski, 1887.   Martinus Leopolita.

MOTET.

EGO SUM PASTOR BONUS.

From *Monumenta Musices Sacrae in Polonia.*
Ed. by l'Abbé Jos. Surzinski, 1887.   Venceslas Szamotulski.

With regard to Spain it was once usual to disallow the claims of that country to possess a school of musicians. That it produced much music is admitted, but the originality of its productions, considering its sixteenth-century connexion with the Nether- lands, was denied. Remarkable documents, recently brought forward, have affected our judgement with respect to the posi- tion of Spanish music very considerably. The earliest polyphonic music known to exist in Spain is to be found in a twelfth- century MS. preserved in the Cathedral of Santiago de Compo- stela, the so-called 'Codex Calixti II'; but just as the majority of pilgrims to the shrine of St. James were not inhabitants of Spain, so the composers named in that MS. are not Spanish but French. A later collection of pilgrims' songs, however—the *Llibre vermell*, or 'Red Book' of Montserrat,[1] a fourteenth- century MS.—contains a number of compositions for two and three voices which can certainly be attributed to Spanish com- posers. They exhibit, in fact, so many peculiarities of form as to render it probable that they arose independently in the country in which they were written, while the determining influence seems to have come, not from France or even from Italy, but from Flanders—150 years earlier than has usually been sup- posed. By the middle of the fourteenth century Spanish musi- cians had begun to travel through France to study their art in Flanders, and to learn the new Flemish methods of composition which the young composers of the North were beginning to practise. Foreign musicians, also, had begun to arrive in Spain from Flanders, from England, and from other countries, as is shown by the entries in the municipal archives at Barcelona and elsewhere, and among the minstrels in attendance on medieval

[1] P. Suñol, *Els Cants dels romeus*, 'Analecta Montserratensia', i. 1917, 100 ff. See also O. Ursprung, ZMW., iv. 1921, 136–60, and, for other early polyphonic music in Spain, H. Anglès *Die mehrstimmige Musik in Spanien vor dem 15. Jahrhundert*, in Beethoven Centenary Congress Report, pp. 158–63. (Vienna, 1927.)

kings of Castille and Aragon are often found men described as Englishmen or Scotchmen.

It is clear, then, that the connexion between Spanish and Flemish music may have arisen long before the 'Flemish Chapel' of Charles V or the marriage of his parents, the Archduke Philip and 'Crazy Jane', in 1496—dates which have sometimes been conjectured as being those of the introduction of Flemish music into Spain. It had begun at least a century and a half earlier; while as early as 1500 and the years immediately following, Spanish musicians were able to produce a work like the *Cancionero musical*, edited by Barbieri,[1] in which the old national forms of popular song were treated in a new manner derived ultimately from the early polyphonists of Flanders.

This is a MS. in the library of the Royal Palace at Madrid (2, i, 5) containing between four and five hundred 'songs', both sacred and secular, set by sixty-four named composers, most of them native, together with many anonymous who may no doubt be presumed to have been Spanish also. Another MS. of the same period, not yet published, is the collection of *Cantinelas vulgares*, in the Columbus Library at Seville (7, i, 28), containing over a hundred compositions, both sacred and secular, of which some 20 are also found in the *Cancionero musical*. Notwithstanding the great number of works contained in this collection—works illustrating every kind of sentiment, religious, serious, and amatory, historical and chivalrous, pastoral, jocular, &c.—the composers are representative of a short period only, and all flourished probably during the last decade of the fifteenth century and the first twenty years of the century following. The music itself, as we should naturally expect, considering the period at which it was written, is in principle Flemish, and as regards the earlier works, apparently, derived

[1] *Cancionero musical de los siglos XV y XVI*, transcrito y comentado por Francisco Asenjo Barbieri. (Madrid, 1890.)

from the teaching and example of pupils of Dufay and Okeghem, among whom Alexander Agricola and Anton de Févin are known to have been for some time in Spain. Yet a consideration of the very large number of native workers, and of native workers only, represented in the *Cancionero musical*, and their firm grasp throughout of the current principles of composition, affords now apparently, in itself, sufficient reason for admitting the body of Spanish musicians of this time already among the schools.

The chief composer of this collection is Juan del Enzina (1469–1534), a poet, one of the founders of the Spanish theatre, who was employed by Don Fadrique, Duke of Alba, to write musical entertainments for performance in his palace at Toledo. Most of his music (he tells us) was written between his fourteenth and twenty-fifth year; i. e. between 1483 and 1494. He was in Rome in 1514, but there is no evidence for the statement which has sometimes been made that he was ever a singer in the papal choir. Enzina is a powerful writer, of considerable variety, who displays also great harmonic beauty within the limits of the simple forms of the *Cancionero musical*. Many of his little pieces were sung in the course of his dramatic 'Representations' and 'Eclogues', and the *Cancionero* also contains a number of musical settings of the songs in the plays of the contemporary Portuguese dramatist Gil Vicente. We give a specimen of his work, as also that of Escobar, another important contributor to the *Cancionero musical*. The following is based on the street-cry of a travelling tinker.

VILLANCICO.   CALDERO Y LLAVE.

Cancionero Musical, no 432.   Juan del Enzina

- don - na. [*più mosso.*]

- don - na.
- don - na.

- don - na. Ju - ra di per vos a - mar,

Je vo - leu vos a - do - bar. . . . . &c.

VILLANCICO.

LAS MIS PENAS, MADRE.

Cancionero Musical, no. 48. Escobar.

Las mis pe-nas, ma - dre, de a - mo-res son.
[*Fin.*]

[*three times.*]

Sa - lid, mi se - ño - - - ra,
de sol na - ran - ja - - - le,
que sois tan her - mo - - - sa. [*D.C.*]

No compositions in ecclesiastical forms by either of these musicians have as yet been discovered, although ecclesiastical works by other composers named in the *Cancionero musical* (e.g. Francisco Peñalosa) exist in MS. at Barcelona and else-where. The absence of church music by Juan del Enzina has been accounted strange, seeing that his whole life was passed in ecclesiastical surroundings, and he became successively Arch-deacon of Málaga and Prior of León. He is at his best in broadly humorous or satirical pieces, some of which indeed have necessitated ecclesiastical or editorial censure, such as the amusing Cuckoo-song (No. 406), an early example of a theme which was popular throughout the sixteenth century. Another fruitful source of musical merriment practised by Enzina and the composers of the *Cancionero musical* is to be found in the compositions based on street-cries, in which the pedlar is generally not a licensed vendor but a gallant in pursuit of his lady. The street-cry in the example, however, is that of a genuine tinker, though he is an alien, and can only speak Spanish very imperfectly. The cry is taken as the refrain, or the beginning of the refrain, and treated polyphonically, being followed by a homophonic setting of the stanza, in which the tinker declares his devotion to the lady on the balcony in words belonging to the technical processes of his trade. This form is directly derived from the poems in vulgar Arabic which were sung by Spanish Muslims from the tenth century to the conquest of Granada in 1492. Under the name of *villancico* it persisted in Christian Spain throughout the sixteenth and seventeenth centuries, while in the eighteenth century the word became practically synonymous with 'Christmas Carol'. The greater number of the pieces in the *Cancionero musical* are in *villancico* form; and secular Spanish compositions of the sixteenth century, whether they resemble *frottole* or the various types of madrigal, are known indistinguishably as *villancicos*. Two characteristic collections of these were published in 1551 and 1560 at Seville by Juan Vasquez, a composer who, with the solitary exception of an *Agenda defunctorum*, is believed to have devoted himself entirely to secular music. The words of the earlier *villancicos* in the *Cancionero musical* are not so much popular songs, as court poetry masquerading as popular songs. A vulgar refrain was often used with a sentimental stanza, for contrast; words and music were sometimes deliberately ill-assorted, for comic effect. Vasquez, on the contrary, gives the impression of being a composer who was genuinely fond of folk-song, and there is a delightful freshness about his work, both in the music and in the words. They became popular with the Spanish lutenists, whose books of tablature contain a number of transcriptions from Vasquez, arranged as solo-songs. That Vasquez's own arrangements were sometimes intended to be performed as solo-songs with instrumental accompaniment is shown also by the method of writing. The melody, in the cantus, altus, or tenor, is treated in something the same way as is 'the first singing-part' in Byrd's 'Psalmes, Sonets, and Songs' of 1588, though Vasquez is a long way from possessing Byrd's musical resources or beauty of workmanship. A somewhat similar printed collection of Spanish *villancicos*, of from two to five voices, is preserved in the University Library of Upsala, in Sweden.

Madrigals conforming to current Italian types were written by several Spanish composers, although the word 'madrigal' has, apparently, no recognized musical significance in the Spanish language. Pedro Vela published in 1561 at Barcelona a collection, *Odarum quas vulgo madrigales appellamus . . . Lib. I*, with words in Spanish and Catalan; while Juan Brudieu (a Frenchman settled in Catalonia) composed a set of stiff, rather wooden madrigals for performance in the open air, as part of the festivities for the wedding of Charles Emmanuel of Savoy with a Spanish Infanta, in 1585.[1] Other Spanish composers of madrigals, e.g. Mateo Flecha, uncle and nephew; Pedro Valenzuela (or Valenzola), Sebastian Raval, and Pedro Ruimonte (Rimonte), were men who lived abroad at foreign courts and

[1] *Els Madrigals i la Missa de Difunts d' En Brudieu.* Edited by Higini Anglès. (Barcelona, 1921.)

often preferred to set Italian words rather than Spanish. The younger Flecha, however, composed a number of *Ensaladas*, (literally 'salads'), comic parodies of madrigals in Spanish, which were printed at Prague in 1581. Ruimonte was in the service of the Spanish Governor of Antwerp, and his set of madrigals, published by Phalèse in 1614, contains, besides a number of typical chromatic madrigals of the period, with Spanish words, several interesting arrangements of popular *villancicos*, with the refrain sung by two or three voices only and the stanza set for six. A valuable MS. collection of earlier Spanish madrigals exists in the library of the Duke of Medinaceli at Madrid, excerpts from which are to be found in 'The Music of Spanish History' (Oxford, 1926); while an example of secular part-songs with words adapted for devotional purposes, on the principle of the Italian *Laudi Spirituali*, exists in the *Canciones y Villanescas Espirituales*, published in 1589 by Francisco Guerrero, a native of Seville and a prolific composer of church music.

Few compositions by any of these composers have as yet been published; either in secular or ecclesiastical forms, and we cannot therefore form a complete idea of their capabilities; but already it will probably be felt, from the short extracts alone, that the Spanish music possesses a peculiar quality of beauty, in which both passion and melancholy appear. This impression is strengthened by the examples quoted in Eslava's *Lira Sacro-Hispana*, and in Pedrell's *Hispaniae Schola Musica Sacra*. Thus the *Sancta Mater* of Francisco Peñalosa, printed by Eslava, is designed, as regards its outward form, in a somewhat dry Flemish style, containing long pauses between the voice parts, yet the composer has made this method not only tolerable but enjoyable from the beauty of his effects.

In the work of Bernardino Ribera, another of the group, we again find expression, but combined with the beauty which distinguishes the school as a whole. This is seen, for instance, in the opening of his *Magnificat* in the first tone transposed,

where the melodious and flowing character of the voice parts is
most remarkable.

MAGNIFICAT.

Lira Sacro-Hispana.
H. Eslava, Madrid, serie 16, tom. i. p. 61.   Bernardino Ribera.

Andrés Torrentes and Cristóbal Morales, two remaining
members of the group, were each in turn Maestro de Capilla at
Toledo (where the greater number of their works is preserved
in immense, illuminated choir-books), Torrentes having died
in 1544, immediately preceding Morales, who was appointed in
1545, after his return from Rome. The reputation of Morales,

the contemporary of Gombert, has naturally overshadowed that of his predecessor; yet Torrentes was an excellent composer, whose method may be seen in the opening of a *Magnificat*, in the seventh tone, which is quoted in Eslava's first volume.

The earliest known works of Morales are secular, consisting of several undistinguished madrigals to Italian and (in one instance only) Spanish words, and two fine Latin cantatas, the first of which was written for the peace conference of 1538. It is a monumental work, for six voices,[1] constructed on a well-known Flemish principle, derived, probably, from Josquin Desprès and employed all through the sixteenth century down to Orlandus Lassus. Five voices sing the text in florid counterpoint, while the sixth has the one word *Gaudeamus*, which it repeats again and again to the same six notes. Morales saw that the device might be used as an important principle of construction, and the greater number of his motets for five and six voices are planned in this way, one of the inner parts singing the same phrase and the same words over and over again, at regular intervals, until the other voices have finished. A beautiful example is the *Emendemus in melius* (five voices) printed by Eslava and Pedrell, in which the first tenor repeats a long melody to the words: *Memento, homo, quia pulvis es, et in pulverem reverteris*; while equally characteristic of the composer are the *Veni, Domine, et noli tardare* (six voices) and *Andreas Christi famulus* (five voices), illustrated in 'Music and Letters', Vol. VI, No. 1 (January, 1925). The principle depends for its success on the independent voice having a striking phrase to sing, and with Morales this is generally the case; he seems to have had a considerable feeling for the expressive possibilities of a good tune. He also applied this principle to the Mass. In the four-part 'Ave Maria', and the five-part 'De beata Virgine' (both printed in his *Missarum Liber II*; Rome, 1544), one voice sings the theme on which the Mass is based, but using its own

---

[1] R. Mitjana: *Encyclopédie de la Musique: Espagne*, p. 1978. (Paris, 1920.)

words, while the other voices proceed with the liturgical words of the Mass, as is the case in Palestrina's Mass 'Ecce Sacerdos magnus'. Morales' early five-part Mass, 'Tristezas me matan' (MS., Sistine Chapel) is even more curious, for the independent voice sings not only the tune of the Spanish popular song, but also the Spanish words to it, while the other voices continue in Latin.

Morales was the first Spanish musician to win European admiration; and, at the same time, his mind remained intensely Spanish. There were personal qualities in his style which could be recognized, together with a 'psychological basis' which, to a Spanish musician like Pedrell, seemed to confirm his nationality. He had considerable feeling for the effective spacing of the voices, and of the expressive value of purely homophonic passages when the words gave particular point to the music—as in the passage quoted later from the motet 'Ecce Virgo concipiet'. To this was added an acute realization of the expressive possibilities of the third and fourth modes, as may be seen in the example mentioned above, and in the motet ' O vos omnes ', printed by Eslava and Pedrell, and by the Faith Press. These two modes indeed have been favourites in Spain from that day to this, and are seldom absent even from popular Spanish music at the present time. Our first example of Morales, 'Puer natus est', reveals him as a somewhat dry composer when he is dealing with few voices, but possessed of admirable means, including many contrapuntal figures which later formed part of the perfected method; we see, moreover, that he was capable also of great beauties, such for instance as the lovely *Alleluia* subject which haunts all the latter half of the motet, and takes complete possession of the last twelve or thirteen bars. The true beauties of Morales, however, can only be learned from his compositions for five and six voices, the majority of which remains in MSS. or in part-books printed in the sixteenth century. As a further example, a few measures are added from the 'Lamentations' in the sixth tone, from the MS. in the Escurial.

MOTET.
'PUER NATUS EST.'

Motetta trium vocum ab pluribus authoribus
composita.   Venice, Gardano, 1543.

Morales.

MOTET.

(ECCE VIRGO CONCIPIET.)

Seville Cathedral, MS. Morales.

Ad - mi-ra-bi - lis, De - us

Ad - - mi - ra - bi - lis
Ad - mi - ra - bi - lis

Ad - mi - ra - bi - lis, De - us

for - tis, De - us for - - tis
De - us for - - - - tis
for - tis, ... De - us for - tis &c.

LAMENTATIONS.

Escurial MS. 6th tone Morales.

Hie - ru - sa - lem

Hie - ru - sa - lem

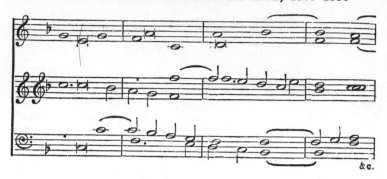

&c.

CHAPTER III

THE ENGLISH SCHOOL

THE communication of the special methods of the school of Dunstable to Dufay and his contemporaries was, as we have seen, a fortunate circumstance for the art of music, far-reaching both in its immediate effects and its final consequences; yet the Englishmen themselves were apparently quite unprepared to join in the development of these methods which immediately followed upon their adoption by the Gallo-Belgic composers, and having unconsciously set on foot the great reform in music, they took no further part in it. The consequence of this renunciation may of course easily be imagined; Tinctoris, for instance, writing twenty-five years after the death of Dunstable, when the first results of the great awakening were already beginning to take shape in the works of the 'moderns', as he calls them— Okeghem, Regis, Busnois, Caron, Faugues[1]—says that the original relations of the two schools had become reversed, and that the English must now come to their old pupils; 'for the moderns in these latter days have discovered much that is new, while their former teachers (which is a sign of the most pitiful capacity) continue composing in their old method, ever the same[2].'

That the purely English methods had but a comparatively short vogue among the Gallo-Belgians, and were soon deserted in favour of others which in fact they themselves alone had rendered possible, is quite clear from the account of the work of Okeghem and his school which has already been given, but it might also partly appear from an analysis of the collections in which the English compositions are found. In the Trent codices, for instance, this decline in favour may perhaps be traced in a comparison of the number of English works contained in them at different periods. Two of the six volumes, for example, Nos. 87 and 92, the contents of which may be said,

---

[1] 'These musicians,' says Tinctoris, 'can boast that they received their instruction from the lately deceased Dunstable, Binchois, and Dufay.' *Cousse. Script.* iv. 77.   [2] *Cousse. Script.* iv. 154.

according to Professor Adler, to date between 1420 and 1440—
a period which would include the discovery of the English music
by Dufay and his school—contain a large number of works, in
all about thirty-two or thirty-three, by our countrymen; three
volumes, Nos. 88, 89, and 90, dating between 1444 and 1465, a
period within which falls the year of Dunstable's death, contain
each only two or three; in the volume No. 91, dating between
1460 and 1480, the period during which Tinctoris was writing,
there is none. But whatever the importance of these facts may
be, there can be little doubt, from the entire absence of English
names among those of the 'moderns' in the collections about
the beginning of the following century, that before the year
1500 the foreign branch of the English school was extinct.

The censure passed by Tinctoris upon the followers of Dunstable applies also, though with less force perhaps than we
should have been inclined to suppose, to the main body of the
English composers who practised in this country. We last
considered the work of this school as it is exemplified in the
Old Hall MS., which represents the native methods of serious
composition from about 1430 to about 1450, and we may now
observe its continuation in a volume of equal importance—a
large choir-book preserved at Eton College—dating probably
from 1490 to 1504, that is to say during the latter half of the
reign of King Henry VII. In comparing the latter volume
with the former two points especially attract our attention,
namely, a considerable difference in the character of the later
music, and a relatively small advance in respect of technique.
On the one hand, we see that the composers have here almost
entirely abandoned the continuous plainsong subject in the lower
part[1], and that all the voices therefore are now entirely free; on
the other, it is plain that no effective substitute for this ancient
means of giving form to the composition has been clearly adopted;

---

[1] The Eton MS. contains chiefly motets, a form less commonly founded
upon plainsong themes. In settings of the Mass, however, both at this
date and later, a plainsong was generally present in one voice, though
not continuously.

the system includes neither of the admirable methods for this purpose which were now becoming common in the Netherlands, and we find but rarely either the passages in canon and fugue, or the clear harmonic progression of groups of chords, which Okeghem and his fellow workers were at this time already employing as the corner-stones of their compositions. The counterpoint, however, is regular, arbitrary discords are as a rule abolished, and there is an evident attempt towards smoothness of effect. But although agreeable sounds are often produced, the whole is vague, and suffers from the absence both of structure and of harmonic propriety.

The Eton MS. would seem to have been intended as a collection of motets and hymns in praise of the Virgin. Originally it consisted of nearly one hundred compositions, but the volume is imperfect, and now contains little more than half that number. The list of composers is considerable, and includes several names which appear frequently in later collections—Fayrfax, for instance, Gilbert Banaster, William Cornysch, Richard Davy, and Wilkinson the transcriber of the volume—but none of those which occur in the Old Hall MS. Our examples are the first two sentences of a *Passio Domini*, by Davy, who was organist of Magdalen College, Oxford, and the beginning of a *Salve Regina* by Cornysch, of Henry VII's establishment.

Eton MS. PASSIO DOMINI. R. Davy.

HYMN.

SALVE REGINA.

Eton MS.

Wilhelmus Cornysch.

The methods of this period are seen again in a fine volume of secular music, now in the British Museum, and marked Addl. MSS. 5465. The collection contains five songs by Robert Fayrfax, and since it is supposed to be in the handwriting of that composer himself, and moreover was in the seventeenth century found in the possession of a Fayrfax family in Yorkshire, it has come to be known as the *Fayrfax Book*. Several of the composers represented in the Eton MS. are found again here—Davy, for instance, Browne, Cornysch, Banaster, and Turges. New names also appear—Phelyppis, Newark, Sheryngham, and Tudor. In other MSS. also, in the British Museum, at Lambeth Palace, in the Bodleian, in Cambridge at the University Library and at Peterhouse and Caius Colleges, and elsewhere, we find collections of works of the more serious and important kinds—long compositions, elaborately treated—Masses, motets, and hymns to the Virgin; and here, in the lists of composers, the name of Fayrfax always appears, together with others well known and some new—Pasche, Ludford, Aston, Pygott, Hyllary, Hawte, Prowett—most of them men of ability, and all hardworking and productive. It is evident, too, that a new and reactionary school is forming, sincere in its devotion to the traditional English methods, and convinced that pure counterpoint, together with an occasional short point of imitation in the body of the movement, is sufficient to supply the necessary interest in music; and of such a school Fayrfax, whose work perfectly represents the aims of the men about him, is the natural head.

MASS: REGALI.

CREDO.

Bodl. Lib., MSS. Mus. Sch. E. 376–81.   Robert Fayrfax.

When, or in what manner exactly, the new Flemish music came to England it is impossible to say; but since there is no known record of any visits of Flemish composers to this country during the period with which we are at present concerned, it is probable that it came by way of MSS. and printed books. Petrucci, for instance, had been printing compositions by the Netherlanders since 1503, and these works might very well have been brought to the notice of the Chapel by Henry VIII [1], himself a composer, though a poor one [2]. But however this

---

[1] A small book, formerly belonging to the king, and containing compositions by Josquin and his circle, is preserved in the Pepysian collection at Magdalene College, Cambridge.

[2] A few words upon the subject of the king's compositions will be expected here, and it may be said at once that they are remarkably inferior in merit to those of his predecessor, Henry VI. The work of 'Roy Henry' was equal in ability to the best produced in his Chapel; that of Henry VIII, on the other hand, is for the most part unworthy of serious attention. The present writer, having scored the whole of the thirty-three 'Songs' by the king contained in the Brit. Mus. Add. MS. 31922, is after all unwilling to occupy valuable space with an example. They reveal no settled method; some are composed quite in the old style, with bare intervals, notes badly doubled, and constant arbitrary discord, while in others the methods remind us of those more lately in favour abroad. Probably these pieces were composed

may be, the date of the introduction of the Flemish methods into English music cannot be later than the year 1516, since in a volume dated in that year, containing two motets by Sampson, dean of the Chapel Royal, we find examples of the unmistakable imitation of foreign workmanship [1].

Flemish influence may certainly be detected in the work of John Taverner (c. 1495 – c. 1545); and in his use of canon (cf. the second example quoted) and proportional devices we may compare him to Okeghem and Josquin. He was, however, typically English in his boldness of rhythm, his habit of varying the vocal texture by sections of two- and three-part writing, and the vast scale and grandiosity of his construction, a quality which sometimes misleads him into long-windedness.

at different times and under the direction of instructors of widely different views; but though this might account for their wavering phases of style, absence of talent and of musical individuality in the composer can alone account for their extreme dullness. Two of these songs, *Pastyme with good Company*, and *Whereto should I expresse*—the best in fact in the collection, —were printed by the present writer in his edition of William Chappell's *Old English Popular Music*, 1893.

[1] The volume also contains a few anonymous motets, entirely in the current Flemish manner, and one also, in the same style, to which the name of 'Benedictus de Opicijs' is affixed. Concerning this composer, whose name is not met with in any other known collection, we have no information; but it is certainly a curious circumstance that the date of this MS. coincides, within one year, with that of the last information which we possess with respect to Benedictus Ducis of Antwerp, an important composer, of whom nothing is known after 1515. Fétis says that in that year he came to England at the invitation of Henry VIII; but in the absence of any record of this visit the supposition has generally been rejected.

MASS. GLORIA TIBI TRINITAS. MISERERE NOBIS FROM AGNUS DEI.[1]

Bodl. Lib., MSS. Mus. Sch. E. 376–81, &c.   John Taverner

[1] This and the following excerpt taken from *Tudor Church Music*, vol. 1 (Oxford University Press, 1923), with the kind permission of the Carnegie U.K. Trust.

bis.

bis.

bis.

bis.

bis.

bis.

MASS. O MICHAEL

(six voices).

FILIUM DEI.

Bodl. Lib., MSS. Mus. Sch. E. 376-81. John Taverner.

Fi - li - um De - i un - i - ge -

Fi - li - um De - - -

Fi - li - um . . . . . De - - -

The motet ◯ *Splendor* is attributed, in Ch. Ch. MSS. 979–83, to 'Taverner and Tye'; and though it is dubious how far modern criticism can disentangle the workmanship of the two composers, the fact that on this occasion they worked together is of interest in the consideration of Tye's development. Tye was born about

1500, and was first a chorister and afterwards a lay clerk in the chapel of King's College, Cambridge. Here, therefore, probably he received his musical education, and especially that complete instruction in the old style of pure counterpoint which enabled him to employ the foreign methods, when they came to his knowledge, to such excellent purpose. That Tye embraced these methods eagerly, or such of them at least as were concerned with the treatment of fugue, and that he must have made himself well acquainted with some of the more important foreign works, is evident from his compositions. The fine early Miserere, for instance, for five men's voices, which is to be found in more than one of the principal manuscript collections of the time, opens with a two-voiced canon at the distance of a semibreve, continued after the entry of a third voice with the same subject, which reminds us of Dufay and his pupils; and throughout, in fact, vague counterpoint is banished, and the whole work is constructed entirely of fugal passages. In choosing a popular English tune, ' *Westron Wynde* ', as the subject for one of his masses Tye was following the precedent of Netherland composers (cf. Dufay's *Se la face ay pale* and Josquin's *L'homme armé*). Masses upon the same theme were also composed by Taverner and Shepherd. In all that he attempts in these early works, Tye is quite the equal of his models, and in his great six-voiced Mass, *Euge bone*[1], the characteristic work of his maturity, he clearly shows that in middle age also he had not fallen behind his Netherland contemporaries, but had kept pace with their development. In some respects indeed—in the melodious freshness, for instance, of the fugal subjects in this admirable composition—he passes beyond them.

[1] For all known particulars respecting Tye's life and works see the preface to Mr. G. E. P. Arkwright's edition of this Mass. Oxford, Parker, 1893.

MASS : EUGE BONE.

AGNUS DEI.

Bodleian Library,
MS. Music School, E. 376–81.   Christopher Tye.

Respecting the early education of Tallis (*c.* 1505–85), we have
no information; but from an examination of his remaining
works it would appear that he, like Tye, was brought up in the
purely contrapuntal school, and that he also, comparatively
early in life, began to abandon the methods of that school to
follow those of the contemporary Netherland composers. In an
interesting work of his youth, as we may suppose, a *Magnificat*
for four voices, we observe the early methods still in full opera-
tion—the careful avoidance, that is to say, of any resemblance
to fugue in the opening, and the employment of one conceded
point of imitation about the middle of the movement, which we
have already seen not only in Tye's early music, but also in
the work of Cornysch; moreover we may note the strange experimental construction of the final close, so characteristic of the
old school, a construction in which the essential members of the
cadence do not appear. But the consideration which not least
perhaps induces us to assign this work of Tallis to the period

of youth and inexperience arises from its lack of beauty; the vocal phrases are devoid of interest, and the harmonic effect is often disappointing. The same demerits are to be observed in the four-part Mass (B.M. Add. MSS. 17502–5), and this also is probably an early work. The influence of such composers as Brumel may perhaps be traced in the use of blocks of chords, and of the small points ornamenting the close. The conduct of the voices displays many experimental discords, not all of which can be considered satisfactory.

A much greater mastery of technique is to be observed in the motet *Audivi media nocte*. It is true that the division of the work into short sections each ending with an important close, which was one of the fundamental old English notions of forms, renders the work in its general aspect different from anything to be found abroad; but upon examination it will be seen that each of these sections is now full of canonic imitation, and in fact consists of little else, while their closes are at last perfectly regular and intelligible. The voices, too, are delivered from the necessity of those progressions to awkward and often unexpected intervals to which they were so often obliged by the old English method, in its aim towards beautiful sound by means of pure counterpoint only; they now proceed therefore smoothly, in conjunct movement chiefly, as in the foreign contemporary compositions. The whole work is full of power and beauty, and must be taken to represent a period not far from that in which the master's technique arrived at its perfection. Among the very few signs of backwardness still to be observed in this fine work, the construction of the final cadence with the descending portion in the lowest place may be mentioned; this method was still often employed abroad for the passing closes in the body of the work, but since about 1485 it had been, as we saw, banished from the end of the composition, to make way for the more powerfully conclusive form in which the lowest voice either rises by a fourth to the final or descends by a fifth to its octave.

MOTET.

AUDIVI MEDIA NOCTE.

Brit. Mus. Add. MSS. 17802–5.   Thomas Tallis.

But it is in the *Cantiones*[1], the two sets of Lamentations, and some of the shorter motets that Tallis's finest work is to be found. These exhibit a serene contrapuntal mastery, and a suavity of phrasing which is peculiarly Tallis's own. It is a far cry from the awkwardness of the four-part Mass and Magnificat, or the prolixity of those motets such as *Gaude Gloriosa*, which may almost certainly be dated as belonging to the period when he held a post at the Abbey of Waltham Holy Cross: that is to say, before 1540, when the Abbey was dissolved. Indeed, the compression of the *Cantiones* is especially noteworthy; through them, Tallis may be honoured as the first of the English School to have realized 'the grace of not too much'[2].

[1] *Cantiones quae ab argumento sacrae vocantur, quinque et sex partibus autoribus Thoma Tallisio & Gulielmo Birdo Anglis serenissimae Reginae Maiestati a private Sacello generosis & Organistis. Excudebat Thomas Vautrollerius typographus Londinensis . . . 1575.*

[2] No account of Thomas Tallis can be complete without mention of his celebrated motet in forty real parts, *Spem in alium nunquam habui.* The voices are disposed in eight choirs. During the greater part of the motet, which is of considerable length, these choirs are grouped antiphonally; but in the three climaxes of the composition all the forty parts are employed: in the last climax, for seventeen measures consecutively.

Laudate Dominum.[1]

(part of)

Christ Church MSS. 979–83.
Tenbury MSS. 341–4.

Thomas Tallis.

Quo - ni - am con - fir - ma - ta est su - per po - pu - li.

Quo - ni - am con - fir - ma - ta

Quo · ni - am con - fir - ma - ta est

e - um o - mnes po - pu - li.

o - mnes po - pu - li.

nos mi - se - ri - cor - di - a e - - - -

est su - per nos mi - se - ri - cor - di - a e -

su - per - nos mi - se - ri - cor - di - a e - - ius,

Quo - ni - am

[1] Taken from *Tudor Church Music*, vol. vi, with the kind permission of the Carnegie U.K. Trust.

II   B b

It would seem probable that both Tye and Tallis were called to Henry's Chapel about the same time, Tye coming from King's College, Cambridge, about 1537, and Tallis from Waltham Abbey. It is supposed, not without good reason, that Tye, who became a fervent Protestant, resigned his post upon the accession of Queen Mary, and it is known that in the second year of Elizabeth's reign he took orders and became a country clergyman, dying eleven years later; Tallis, on the other hand, continued in the Royal Chapel under Edward, Mary, and Elizabeth, ending his life in fact in the service of the last-named sovereign.

The great event, musically speaking, of this period in the history of the English school, was the reformation of public worship. Seldom, probably, has a political occurrence exerted so considerable an influence upon the course of any art, as that which obliged the English composers of the middle of the sixteenth century to abandon the natural development of their material, and deliberately to devise new methods; for as a rule political events, even the most violent—wars, subversions of government, and so on—though they may convulse society, leave both the springs of art and the actual forces which shape it unaffected. But here, by the alteration of the bases of public worship, the conditions also of sacred music were entirely changed; it was now not only constrained to apply itself to new forms, but was also required to give expression to a new kind of sentiment, corresponding to the outward change from the original language of Christian devotion to the vernacular; and not only were the composers subjected to this necessity of inventing new methods, but they had also to realize the fact that of all that they had hitherto done, nothing was any longer of any use. The complete disappearance from collections, about this time, of many accustomed names, reveals the fact that this blow had seriously affected the school, and indeed nothing but the wonderful inherent vitality of the English music could have supported it under so great a shock; it responded, however, in some degree to the demands which were made upon it, and in Tye's *Acts of the Apostles*, and in the Dorian Service of Tallis, we may perceive the nature of the first attempts to produce some sort of suitable composition [1].

Tye's setting of his own metrical versification of a portion of the *Acts of the Apostles* is for the most part in plain counterpoint; but the sternness of the method generally dissolves towards the close of each composition in running notes and short points, the parts coming together at the last in a beautiful florid cadence.   None of the numbers, indeed, is quite plain, while some though plain in appearance are really elaborate—one especially, which contains a double canon; and all, whatever the particular character of their treatment may be, are united in the exhibition of a peculiar kind of metrical melody, in a style both popular and jubilant, yet so chastened by the contrapuntal influences as to escape the suggestion either of indecorum or of vulgarity.   Tye composed much for the reformed service, and seems, of all the composers of this period of enforced transition, the one most at ease in adapting himself to the new conditions.   Many of his small offertory anthems are almost perfect examples of the Anglican ideal of good musicianship directed by good sense—one might almost say, by good breeding.   The following specimen shows with what tact he could comply with the official demands for simplicity and directness of word-setting

---

[1] The following printed books belong to this period and represent the endeavour to provide a style of church music, in the English tongue, and conforming to the new demands. Merbecke: *The Booke of Common praier Noted*, 1550; John Day: *Certaine Notes set forth in foure and three parts to be sung at the morning Communion, and evening praier*, 1560. A MSS. collection (Bodl. MSS., Mus. Sch. e. 420-2) contains settings of the canticles from the primers of 1535, 1539, and 1545. It also contains adaptations of two of Taverner's Masses to English words. It is noticeable that some of the music in this early collection is slightly more florid than the music in John Day's book. It was not until rather later and under the Genevan influence that the plain style was strictly enforced.

while yet preserving an independent musical interest of finished part-writing and melodic propriety. To combine simplicity with distinction is at no time a common achievement; but in order to appreciate Tye's work in this kind at its full value, it must be remembered that he came at a period when the impulse of musical development had been towards magnificence and complexity, and that in his post-Reformation music he was handicapped by many of the difficulties of the pioneer.

OFFERTORY.

GIVE ALMES.

Brit. Mus. Add. MSS. 30480–4.   Christopher Tye.

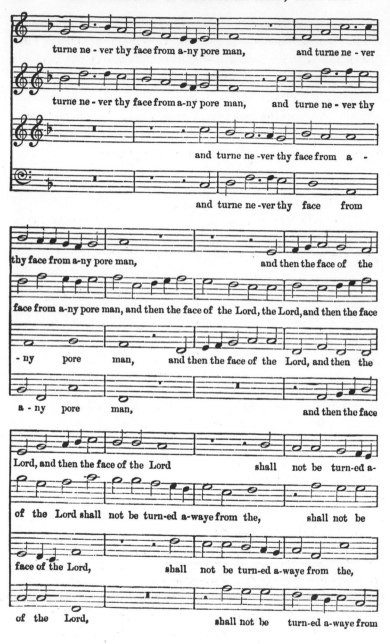

turne ne - ver thy face from a-ny pore man,   and turne ne - ver

turne ne - ver thy face from a-ny pore man,   and turne ne - ver thy

and turne ne -ver thy face from   a -

and turne ne -ver thy   face   from

thy face from a-ny pore man,   and then the face of   the

face from a-ny pore man, and then the face of the Lord, the Lord, and then the face

- ny   pore   man,   and then the face of the   Lord, and then   the

a - ny   pore   man,   and then the face

Lord, and then the face of the Lord   shall   not be turn-ed a-

of the Lord shall not be turn-ed a-waye from the,   shall not be

face of the Lord,   shall   not be turn-ed a-waye from the,

of   the   Lord,   shall not be   turn-ed a-waye from

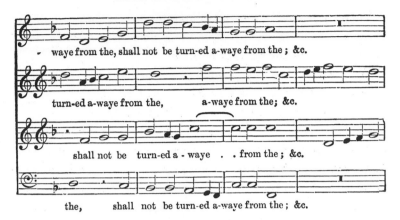

waye from the, shall not be turn-ed a-waye from the ; &c.

turn-ed a-waye from the,   a-waye from the; &c.

shall not be turn-ed a - waye . . from the ; &c.

the,   shall not be turn-ed a-waye from the ; &c.

The essential feature of the Dorian Service of Tallis is the use of plain counterpoint, in unbroken notes and without points of imitation. The model was probably given as early as the year 1544, in the Litany harmonized according to the directions of Cranmer; for these directions especially enjoin an absolutely plain treatment, note under note, and one syllable to each note[1]. This method was probably suggested in order to meet one of the principal objections urged by the reformers, Catholic and Protestant alike, against the actual condition of ecclesiastical music; an objection based chiefly upon the practical extinction of the sacred text in the passages in running notes, and in the overlapping repetitions of phrases, inevitable in florid composition.

Besides the Dorian Service Tallis composed two other English Services, both incompletely preserved, a setting of the plain-song of the Litany, Preces, and Responses, some psalm-tunes, and some anthems, four of which were printed in John Day's *Certaine Notes*. Of these, one, *I call and cry*, is an adaptation of *O Sacrum Convivium*, possibly made by the composer himself.

[1] It is worth pointing out that Cranmer's injunctions contain no restrictions upon rhythmical invention. Such a veto would not have occurred to any sixteenth-century censor of church music.

It would seem that after a short investigation of the possibilities
of music under the new conditions he decided to abstain from
further effort in the cause of reformation.

Be this as it may, one notable modification in the style of his
subsequent compositions may probably be traced to his period
of compliance with the demands of Cranmer: the *Cantiones* are
largely syllabic in the treatment of the words, in some instances,
almost entirely so. Moreover, this collection contains items, such
as the hymn-settings, *O Nata Lux de Lumine*, and *Procul Recedant
Somnia*, which in their note against note construction would be
perfectly fitted for the English rite, had they not set a Latin
text. It is as though Tallis, finding that something valuable
could be learned from the English restrictions, had decided to
try them out in Latin, although the use of that tongue would
disqualify any composition from performance in the national
church. This cannot be attributed to religious convictions, for
Tallis had held his post at the Chapel Royal with impartial
persistence under the varying dispensations of Henry, Edward,
Mary, and Elizabeth; moreover the same preference for the old
tongue was displayed by other composers born after the Reformation, and holding posts in the English Church. The reason can
better be sought in a conjunction of two facts: one, that the
body of sacred music known to and studied by the English
musicians was predominantly Latin; the other, that Latin had
in itself a hold on men's minds as being a more creditable
language for any intellectual pursuit than the mother-tongue.

The same faithfulness to Latin texts characterizes Robert
Whyte (d. 1574), who was Tye's son-in-law, and succeeded him
as Master of the Choristers of Ely Cathedral in 1561–2. He
subsequently held an appointment at Chester Cathedral, and
at the time of his death was Master of the Choristers at West-
minster Abbey. This career makes it the more remarkable that
he should have left so little music for the English rite. In his

Latin work two styles may be clearly perceived. In his Magnificat he employs the floridity and lavishness of the earlier tradition, and this may be assumed to be an early work. In his great motets (of which thirteen survive) and in his Lamentations he employs a more close-knit style and exhibits, especially in the Lamentations, a marked attention to harmonic richness and poignancy. Whyte was undoubtedly one of the finest English composers of the sixteenth century, and his command of technical resources was thorough and extensive.

O vos omnes[1]

from Lamentations for five voices

Bodl. MS., Mus. Sch. e. 1–5
Ch. Ch. MSS. 979–83, 384–8, &c.   Robert Whyte.

[1] Taken from *Tudor Church Music*, vol. v, with the kind permission of the Carnegie U.K. Trust.

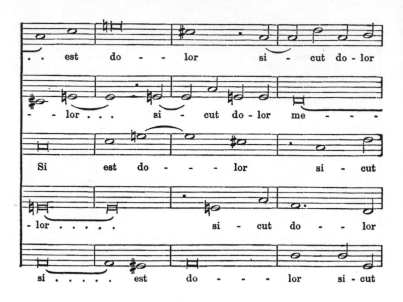

CHAPTER IV

THE PERFECTION OF THE METHOD

By the middle of the sixteenth century a point in musical history
is reached at which the distinctive characteristics of the art of
various nationalities become less clearly marked. Free inter-
play between England, the Low Countries, Avignon, and Rome
is of course a marked feature of the earlier centuries; but the
spread of printing, coupled with the attainment of relative perfection in the art of diatonic choral composition, shows the
masters of Flanders, France, Spain, Italy, and, to a large extent,
England arriving at a common goal. This is not to deny that
national characteristics survive; but each nation, while expressing its own thoughts, uses henceforward a common tongue. And
first we may notice the completion of the Netherland tradition.

LASSUS

Typical of this almost cosmopolitan musical culture stands out
the figure of Orlandus Lassus, climax and crown of the Flemish
schools. Born in the town of Mons about 1530, his boyhood and
youth were spent in Sicily, Milan, and Naples: as a young man
he lived in Rome till 1554, and then went to Antwerp for two
years, visiting France and England *en route.* About the age of
26, however, he settled at the ducal chapel at Munich, and in
Bavaria he remained until his death in 1594, this period of
38 years being interrupted by various important journeys to
Italy, France, and Flanders. His earliest existing publication
is a book of madrigals, dating from the Antwerp period, written
in the advanced style of Cipriano da Rore, and published in
Venice, in which he appears as the follower of Willaert, Verdelot,
Archadelt, Waelrant, and other Flemish madrigal writers of the
first rank. Indeed, so great apparently was his delight in secular

music that from 1555, when his first book appeared, until 1562, when he brought out a collection of twenty-five *Sacrae Cantiones quinque vocum* at Nuremburg, every work that he published was either purely secular or of a mixed character; from this time forward, however, having been appointed Kapellmeister to Duke Albert of Bavaria, he composed chiefly sacred music for the Munich choir.

The praise which has been bestowed upon the ecclesiastical compositions of Lassus is doubtless due, at least in part, to the impressiveness of effect which they display, and to the composer's excellent use of the harmonic material bequeathed to him by his predecessors. For although the melodic constituents of polyphony were emphasized and cultivated to a certain extent, and insisted upon at some periods more than others by the Flemish writers, yet the harmonic aspect of the vocal conjunctions was upon the whole that which is most apparent in the work of the school, and chiefly suggested in the special efforts in which its members were on the whole most successful. This tendency to explore vertical possibilities as well as horizontal (seen contemporaneously in the Englishman Taverner) produces in Lassus a facility and a success in expression which, though not sufficiently developed in form to merit the title of dramatic, corresponds almost exactly to the ideas conveyed by the phrase of the French doctors of Plainsong—*l'accent pathétique*.

If Lassus, therefore, in his mature and most characteristic works falls behind other masters in melodic beauty of outline and freedom from *cliché*, if his voice parts seem not to spring complete from the imagination of the composer and to flow thence in parallel streams, but rather to have been put together with a view to creating an harmonic effect, he is not, for this reason, the less representative of the school as a whole, or the less worthy of admiration for the grandeur and pathos of works in which this particular deficiency also appears.

Lassus, like all the great exponents of a closing art, supported by a vast body of production and called upon by circumstances to complete it, was a most prolific composer. Modern lexicography brings his total of compositions to the almost incredible number of 1,250 and upwards, and though the majority of these are short pieces, such as Motets and Madrigals, there are more than fifty Masses under his name. Employed, as he was, by a reigning prince whose love of music was intense and whose admiration for the master himself was unbounded, the succession of his works could hardly have been otherwise than continuous; and in fact this stimulus, which in some form or other is seldom wanting in the lives of the greater artists, brought forth in the case of Lassus a volume of composition larger than that which can be ascribed to any other musician. Probably his greatest work is the famous setting of the Seven Penitential Psalms, composed in 1565—two years later than the traditional date of the reformed Masses of Palestrina—and remarkable for its expressive qualities. In this fine work Lassus displays not only the science of the school, but his own personal feeling also, and in a degree perhaps greater than in any other of his works. It is with reluctance, therefore, that we pass from this composition without an illustration, but its particular merit could not be exhibited in a short extract. We may, however, give part of a Magnificat as a fair example of his workmanship, and from this it will probably be seen that though inferior in some respects (in melodic beauty, for instance) to some of his immediate predecessors—to Gombert and Clément, for example—he nevertheless heads the school and sums it up by virtue of his presentation of the general Flemish methods in a form more nearly perfect than hitherto, and that he also brings it to a point which, considering its nature and its inherited character, is evidently its extreme limit.

MAGNIFICAT

Tone iii

Three other short extracts will show specimens of Lassus' style in dealing with (*a*) vertical use of block chords, (*b*) fugal entry, (*c*) 'accent pathétique'.

(*a*) Block Chords
Missa Quinti Toni

Downside Masses
No. 6. 1905.   Orlandus Lassus.

(b) Fugal Entry

VELOCITER EXAUDI ME

Penitential Psalms
No. vii.

Orlandus Lassus.

- tas fa - ci - em tu - am . a me, &c.

fa - ci - em tu - am a me, &c.

fa - ci - em tu - am a me, et si - mi - &c.

- ver - tas fa - ci - em tu - am a me, et &c.

- - ci - em tu - am a me, et si - &c.

(c) Accent Pathétique
ADORAMUS TE

Collection Palestrina.
Chanteurs de St. Gervais,
Paris. n.d.

Orlandus Lassus.

Qui - a per san - - - ctam

Qui - a per san - ctam cru - cem

Qui - a per san - ctam cru -

cru - cem tu - - - am re - -

tu - - am re - - de - mi -

-cem tu - - - - am re - de - mi -

- de - mi - sti mun - - - - dum : &c.

- - sti mun - - - - - dum : &c.

- - sti mun - - dum : Do - &c.

Byrd and the English Madrigalists

We have seen that the natural development of the original
English ecclesiastical school of composition was forcibly arrested
at the Reformation, and the school itself broken up, and it has
also appeared probable that the work of the second or Protestant
school of sacred music, which might have redeemed the loss of
the first, was so effectually obstructed by the Genevan ministers
that, notwithstanding the splendid example of Tye, and the
sincere attempts of many minor composers, such as Packe,
Redford, Causton, and Heath, together with the less whole-
hearted co-operation of Tallis, it failed—like the corresponding
school in Germany—to arrive at its logical conclusion. English
music, nevertheless, continued to develop, and outwitted an
historical accident; though as a result of that historical accident
we must look for its greatest achievements, for the most part,
elsewhere than in the bosom of the Church.

Though Tallis and Whyte continued to compose to Latin
words, their faithfulness did not extend to the Latin rite. After
the Reformation a great change may be noticed in the choice of
texts set; the former natural choice of the Mass, with liturgical,
Marian, or patronal Motets is succeeded by a tendency to select
texts from the Psalms (in the Latin rite sung to plainsong) or
from Latin hymns and collects. The Lamentations (from the

service of Tenebrae) were also a frequent choice, and at a rather later date passages from Latin books of devotion were made some use of. Since the Latin tongue was practically banished from public worship,[1] none of these compositions would be eligible for performance in church; but the language would not be a reason against private performance, and the choice of a sacred, as oppose to a liturgical, text would be in favour of it. These compositions must undoubtedly have been sung somewhere, for no composers, however highly principled or however wrong-headed, would have continued for years to produce works which had no possible chance of performance in the land of their origin; and despite the great length and extreme technical demands of many of these compositions we must conclude that the demand for them came from contemporary patrons who enjoyed them as chamber music. The printing of such collections as the Byrd-Tallis *Cantiones* and the Byrd *Gradualia* and *Cantiones Sacrae* is evidence of this; and the quantity of works in this kind by many composers which exist in the MS. part-books commissioned for private ownership is further evidence.

This phenomena, which we may call the Secularization of the Motet, is a most important aspect of the history of English music at this period. It provided an outlet to the energies of composers to whom the old fields were forbidden and the new uncongenial, an outlet in which tradition and innovation were inspiringly mingled. Till the coming of the madrigal, English composers found no form so apt to their purpose as the secularized motet; and even when the madrigal was at its most flourishing and most fashionable, William Byrd, the head and culmination of the English school, ennobled by his adherence to it the form which had stood his forerunners in such good stead.

[1] By the Act of Uniformity of 1549, and by Royal Letters Patent of 1560, permission was given that in college chapels of the two Universities services might be in Greek, Latin, or Hebrew.

Byrd was born in 1543. There is a tradition that he was a pupil of Tallis's. Be this as it may, their musical connexion is undoubted, for Byrd shared with Tallis the appointment to the Chapel Royal (he was previously organist at Lincoln Cathedral) and in 1575 the two musicians combined to publish a volume of Latin sacred music, the *Cantiones quae ad argumento sacrae vocantur* (*vide sup.*). Amongst his contemporaries Byrd was acknowledged to be pre-eminent. His versatility, the extent of his output, and the consistent dignity and high aim of his style, assured him of the veneration in which he was held amongst his fellow-artists, and so well-founded was his reputation that it endured through the after-period when the glories of the school which he summed up were slighted and forgotten. Contemporary estimates inevitably (and rightly) give peculiar consideration to technical mastery; even if Byrd had been a technician only, Morley would still have been justified in his sentence of 'never without reverence to be named among the musicians'; but while Byrd's skill seems to-day as fresh and convincing as ever, the residual impression of a hearing of his music is not of skill, but of character; after the lapse of centuries he still speaks to us in his music with a personal accent. At this remove of time it is perhaps beyond the powers of analysis to detect the particular element which enables the work of one man, among so much music whose chief attraction for us is in exemplifying the work of a period, to hold us by being the work of a person; but in this connexion it is a fact worth stressing that Byrd's music, whilst summing up the achievements of his period, shows a certain definite inattentiveness to the niceties and conformities of contemporary standards. He absorbed the Italian lessons of smoothness and singability, but there is nothing Italianate in the candour and directness of his melodic curve, and in the light of Italian refinement the robustness of his texture may even have seemed a little inelegant. In his use of the diatonic clashes which in a ruder form characterized the earlier style of Tallis, but which the elder man subsequently abandoned, he may well have seemed to critics of his own time old-fashioned and unprogressive; his chromatic freedoms have laid him open to a charge of decadence from later scholars.[1]

Byrd was an adherent of the old faith, and in his three Masses and the *Gradualia* his choice of text was probably dictated as much by devotional as by musical reasons. He composed much, however, for the English rite, and in his Great Service, a portion of which we give as our first example from his writings, he produced a work wherein the rhythmic vitality and impressive proportions which signalize the great six-part masses of Taverner are combined with the finish and resource of a later technique.

[1] 'Byrd's vocal music . . . is independent in style, containing, especially in its later phases, many innovations; and of these perhaps the most remarkable are the simultaneous employment of the flat and sharp seventh of the scale, and the introduction of two chromatic notes at once, as for instance D♯ together with F♯ before a close upon E. It is a curious fact that of these two innovations, frequently to be found in the works of Byrd, the former * is to be defended, if at all, upon purely melodic and modal grounds, while the second is based entirely upon harmony, and in the case of our suggested example destroys the ecclesiastical mode, and creates a scale of E minor. The confusion which is revealed in these two departures from established principles indicates that the end of the Polyphonic period is approaching.' *Oxford History of Music*, vol. ii, First Edition.

---

* Byrd was not the inventor of this licence, but he uses it more fully, perhaps, than any other composer. Its use cadentially became so common that Morley observes: 'If you will but once walke to Poules Church, you shall heare it three or foure times at the least, in one seruice, if not in one verse.' (*Plain and Easy Introduction*.) It would seem that Byrd himself was aware that some details of his style might cause misunderstandings, for in the preface to the *Psalms, Sonnets, and Songs* (1588), he writes: 'In the expressing of these songs, if ther happen to be any jarre or dissonāce, blame not the Printer, who (I doe assure thee) through his great paines and diligence doth heere deliver to thee a perfect and true Coppie.' (1931.)

GREAT SERVICE [1]

Close of Nunc Dimittis

William Byrd.

[1] Taken from *Tudor Church Music*, vols. ii and vii, by permission of the Carnegie U.K. Trust.

QUOTIESCUNQUE MANDUCABITIS

Gradualia. Lib. I, 1605.   William Byrd.

&c.

ni - at,   do - nec ve   -   ni - at :   i - ta - que

&c.

ve - ni - at,   do - nec   ve - ni - at :   i -

&c.

- nec ve - ni - at, ve   -   -   ni - at : i - ta - que   qui -

&c.

do - nec ve - ni - at :   i   -   ta -

Though falling beyond the period assigned to this work a word must be said of the later composers of English church music. John Barnard's collection, *The First Book of Selected Church Music* (1641) contains, besides services and anthems by Byrd, Tallis, and Tye, works by later composers such as Morley, Farrant, and Orlando Gibbons. Two features of the English church music which emerged at the end of the century from the Genevan influence may be noticed in the Barnard collection: the antiphonal convention, whereby alternate sections of the music were allotted to the *decani* and *cantoris* choirs; and the rise of the Verse-Anthem, containing passages for solo voice, accompanied by the organ part, or, occasionally, stringed instruments. The verse-anthem is generally considered a token of the disruption of the polyphonic tradition. This form is, nevertheless, of a comparatively early date. Byrd wrote several verse-anthems (two examples with instrumental accompaniment are included in his *Songs of Sundry Natures* (1589)); and that the practice of this form was perfectly consistent with a command of the resources of the traditional manner is shown by the work of Orlando Gibbons (1583–1625), and Thomas Tomkins (*c.* 1573–1656) whose *Musica Deo Sacra* was published posthumously in 1668. The late date of this publication is significant as suggesting that the polyphonic style did not go out of repute quite so early, or quite so completely, as is supposed by some writers. It is, however, possible that other than purely musical considerations were concerned in its preservation. Both at Durham and at Peterhouse, Cambridge, there are important collections of seventeenth-century transcripts of the church music of the preceding century. These collections have many peculiarities in common, and are certainly connected; it is probable that their compilation was promoted by Dr. John Cosin; and Cosin was a Laudian.

Yet it cannot be denied that despite the contributions of Byrd and Gibbons, many admirable compositions by lesser composers, and a high level of seriousness and dignity, official church music never recovered from the effect of the Reformation, and must be placed below both the secularized motet which is the true heir to pre-Reformation church music and the madrigal. Byrd himself may be taken as an example of this. With the exception of the *Great Service*, his music for the English church is inferior to his compositions to Latin texts; it is less inventive, less at liberty, and markedly less expressive and moving. It might be claimed that this is but the expression of his religious views, and that he could not with perfect spontaneity and conviction sing the Lord's song in a strange church. But this view can with difficulty be supported in the face of the fact that Byrd did write many English sacred compositions which display the characteristic ease and naturalness of his Latin motets, having far more in common with them than with his church services; and that he published these in his madrigal volumes, a fact which would presumably debar them from church performance. What is true of Byrd in this respect is even more true of the lesser composers of this epoch; and it is

undeniable that in order to find English composers at their best
in setting their mother-tongue, we must look to the madrigal.

We can have no doubt that from the earliest times secular
composition had flourished in this country, and that it was often
undertaken by the greatest composers, who willingly adopted
their learned methods to its lighter necessities. This was especially
evident, for instance, in the works of Cornysch, who, although
himself one of the chiefs of the old elaborately contrapuntal
school of ecclesiastical music, produced also a large number of
plain compositions, chiefly in three parts, note under note, as
settings of secular and frequently humorous words. This form,
with the addition of a fourth voice part, and of simple points
of imitation at the beginning of the song, constituted the pattern
of secular music until about 1580. This simple style had a
remarkable revival and apotheosis in the polyphonic versions
of the Air form (see later under *Song*) as practised at the end of
the century; and something of the manner persisted throughout
the madrigal period in the lighter forms, such as the Ballet.[1]
But the essentials of the earlier style of secular composition—
directness, little repetition of the words, and a preponderance
of block movement—are properly those of the part-song, and
thus absolutely opposed to the essentials of the madrigal.
Perhaps the clearest way of expressing this distinction is to say
that in the secular compositions of the first half of the century,
and their derivatives, we are always conscious of the stanza,
whereas in the madrigal the structure is a purely musical one.

The English madrigal school is generally dated as beginning
in 1588 with the publication, on the one hand, of the native
product, Byrd's *Psalmes, Sonets, and Songs*, and, on the other,
of the first volume of Yonge's *Musica Transalpina*, a compilation of foreign examples. As dates go, this is good enough; but

[1] The settings of the metrical psalms which form the first section of
Byrd's 1588 Set are examples of the simple manner as it appeared in the
hands of an accomplished technician.

it must not be overlooked that Thomas Whythorne's *Songs of Three, Four and Five Voices* were published in 1571. These may be said to stand half-way between the early part-song and the madrigal. Whythorne's reputation has suffered at the hands of post-Burneyan historians, who have relied upon Burney's opinion that his music was 'truly barbarous'. It would be equally short-sighted to fly to the opposite extreme, and consider him to be the first English madrigalist *pur sang*; but it may be held that Whythorne was as much of a madrigalist as circumstances would allow him to be. The madrigal form must almost certainly have been known to him, for at the time of his publication foreign examples had already reached this country. A set of part-books in the Fellows' Library at Winchester College, containing examples of the work of Willaert, Lassus, Archadelt, and others, is dated as early as 1564, and the quantity of foreign madrigals in MS. collections shows that there was a decided cult of the transalpine madrigal. Nicholas Yonge may be considered the founder of the first madrigal society in this country. His friends met daily, he tells us in his dedication of *Musica Transalpina*, at his house to practise, and he supplied them with music-books from Italy. Nor need we suppose that they sang only foreign madrigals. Several of the items in Byrd's first Set exist in MS. part-books (Christ Church Mus. MSS. 984–8) which bear the date 1581.

But the most conclusive proof that a well-established feeling for the madrigal existed in this country previous to 1588 is supplied by the dates of the madrigal publications in the years that followed. Byrd's 1588 Set includes a promise of 'some other things of more depth and skill to follow these'; and in 1589 appeared his second Set, *Songs of Sundry Natures*. In 1590 came another collection of Italian madrigals, in this instance 'Englished', compiled by Thomas Watson.[1] 1593 saw

[1] Including two madrigals by Byrd. Two others are included in *Musica Transalpina*.

the publication of Morley's *Canzonets to Three Voices*, 1594 of
a volume of John Mundy and Morley's *Madrigals to Four Voices*.
In 1595 Morley published his *Ballets*,[1] and a little book of two-
voice Canzonets. In 1597 came his fourth volume (belied by the
modesty of its title: *Canzonets or Little Short Airs to Five and
Six Voices*, for it contains some of the most highly wrought and
impressive examples of his mastery of the form), the *Madrigals*
of Kirbye, and the first madrigal volume of Weelkes. The
following year saw another Weelkes volume and the first Set
of *Madrigals* by Wilbye. In 1599 appeared the Sets of Farmer
and Bennet, in 1600 the two great Weelkes Sets, the *Madrigals*
of five and six voices respectively, and in 1601 the *Triumphs of
Oriana*.[2]

Were we to judge on grounds of fertility alone these twelve
years of madrigal production [3] must be acknowledged as a
remarkable achievement. But the quantity of the output sinks
into comparative unimportance when we come to consider the
quality. It would seem that the madrigal form was especially

[1] The Ballet was a light madrigal form whose compact dancing rhythms
were probably retained from its original form of a true *chanson à danser*.
It is distinguished from the madrigal proper by the Fa-la-ing passages
between the clauses. But compare the example *Hence, Care* (p. 229), where
Weelkes has adapted the ballet convention to a madrigal in the grave
manner, using the fa-la passages to procure a definite emotional effect.

[2] Historical and antiquarian sentiment has caused undue importance to
be attached to this Set of congratulatory madrigals addressed to Queen
Elizabeth. The individuality of the contributing composers is swamped in
the uniformity of mood demanded by the character of such a collection.
Moreover, a number of the composers represented are second-rate. The
Triumphs tend to have a slightly Royal Academy Banquet air when compared with the more personal work of the period.

[3] The madrigal endured for some time into the new century, the last
madrigalian publication being Hilton's *Airs or Fa-las for Three Voices*
(1627). With the exception of Gibbons no madrigalist of the first water
emerges in this period; but Byrd and Wilbye both published further volumes,
and the Bateson Sets of 1604 and 1618, together with the Ward Set of
1612, must be given honourable mention in any account of the English
madrigal.

welcomed as affording an outlet for the imagination and poetical feeling which was brimming the literature of the period; for the English madrigals are pre-eminently distinguished by their expressiveness, and the wide field of emotion which they cover. Their dexterity and technical accomplishment may be paralleled in the Italian school, but in depth of feeling and range of sympathy the English surpass their models; indeed, such composers as Byrd, Morley, Weelkes, and Wilbye, poured so much imagination and invention into the existing form that the English madrigal may almost be considered a thing standing by itself. It is significant that the feeling for mass and splendid proportions which characterizes our national architecture and literature, and had assisted to build up such works as the extended Masses of the Fayrfax and Taverner period, exhibited itself in our treatment of the madrigal also. Another noteworthy feature is the number of serious and passionate madrigals. With but one exception, the chief English madrigalists, Byrd, Wilbye, Weelkes, Gibbons, are at their happiest in expressing the more permanent emotions. The exception is Morley. Morley composed several beautiful madrigals in the grave manner, but his peculiar excellence is in the swiftness and gaiety of his handling of light subjects, and in the possession of a quality which might almost be described as wit. He seems to have had a particularly genial eye for character (it is seldom realized that his *Plain and Easy Introduction to Practical Music*, 1597, is an extremely deft and alert record of musical psychology, as well as an admirably conducted account of musical theory); and the specimen of his work in this volume has been chosen to illustrate this aspect of his genius.

MADRIGAL FOR FIVE VOICES

The first set of English madrigals to
3, 4, 5 and 6 voices. Newly composed by
John Wilbye. London: T. Este, 1598.   John Wilbye.

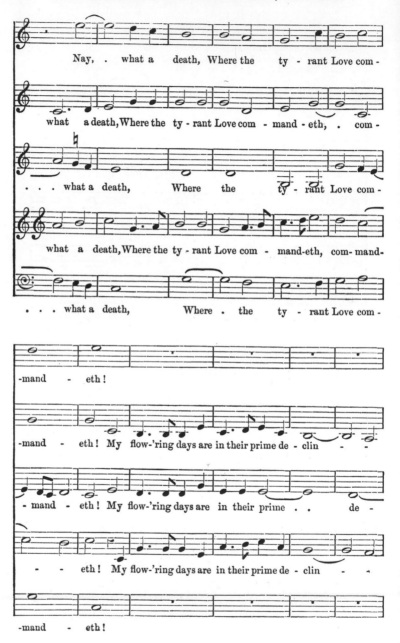

HO WHO COMES HERE

Madrigals to
Four Voices, 1594.

Thomas Morley.

O Care, Thou Wilt Despatch Me

From 'Madrigals of
5 and 6 parts', 1600.

Thomas Weelkes.

PALESTRINA

In contrast to the cosmopolitan character of Lassus's early career, Giovanni Pierluigi da Palestrina (1525–94) is a lifelong Roman. His very name, taken from his birthplace, bears a territorial significance, and his appointments were all in the Eternal City—choirmaster of the Cathedral of Palestrina, 1544–51, of the Cappella Giulia, 1551–5, singer in the Papal Chapel for a brief six months, *maestro di cappella* at St. John Lateran, 1555–8, at the Liberian Basilica, 1561–7, at St. Peter's from 1571 until his death.

The work which Palestrina accomplished in the perfecting of polyphonic composition was chiefly, in its general relation to the technique of composition, a work of taste and judgement and insight, consisting in the formation of a completely satisfying and altogether beautiful method from given materials; for it is probable that all the best figures of contrapuntal melody, and most of their combinations, were already to be found in existing works, scattered among less beautiful and less expressive forma, awaiting selection to form an authoritative style. And for this duty Palestrina was well prepared, not only by his own genius but also by his education in the school into which he was born; for the ideals of the Roman school, though of course Flemish in origin, had been softened and beautified through the influence of the Italians and Spaniards of the Papal choir, and its music had been brought to exhibit the smooth and flowing quality which is characteristic, for instance, of the work of its well-known member and leader, Constanzo Festa. Archadelt, Morales, probably Willaert and possibly Goudimel directly influenced the young composer.

But the view of Palestrina extended beyond the bounds of his native school. That he was also well informed with respect to the work of the Flemish composers, from Okeghem and Obrecht onwards, is clear, not only from his first published volume, which is full of scholastic devices, canonic and proportional, but also from his comparatively frequent adoption, from the later men, of points of imitation, which, however, he worked out in a manner different from the original.

Melody.

The governing principle, technically speaking, of Palestrina's melody is of course that of conjunct movement: but this is varied with consummate art by the constantly changing values of the notes, and also by occasional disjunct intervals; these latter are permitted upon the condition of not continuing in the direction of the leap, but immediately returning by gradual motion towards the point of departure. This rule may also, of course, be deduced from the methods of Palestrina's predecessors since 1450, but there is in his application of it a certain final elegance of proportion, representing the ideal in such matters, which had been aimed at generally hitherto, but was now for the first time attained.

Of all the qualities that go to the making of a good melody, contour is perhaps the most important. There are three main types of contour; the 'ecstatic', which works up to its climax; the 'contemplative', which states its point early and then descends ruminatively to its final; and the 'proportionate', a discreet and artistic compromise, where ascent and descent are balanced harmoniously against one another. Palestrina conforms on the whole to the second of these types, though there are, as we should expect in one whose dominant character is a right sense of proportion, many instances of the third, e.g. the following, from an Ave Verum for five voices:

From a Roman MS. of 1875 in the Library
of the Plainsong and Mediaeval Music Society.

Cu - jus   la - tus   per - fo - ra - tum

Modality.

But not only does Palestrina adopt in his contrapuntal melody the most beautiful forms available from conjunct movement; he also insists upon a modal treatment of the separate voice-parts, a treatment, that is to say, which clearly displays the peculiar characteristics of the mode of the subject in its authentic and plagal forms. And over modal and chromatic questions he is a conservative; for the master, limitations which irk lesser men and make them strain to break the bonds, are but so many incentives to greater flights of technique. 'His attitude towards his predecessors in art was critically revisional.' [1]

Knud Jeppesen, *The Style of Palestrina and the Dissonance* (English translation), 1927, p. 26.

The gain to music from the variety obtained by the clear definition of modal tonality is very considerable, since the same character is perceived in the harmonic progressions proper to each mode, when based upon the true scale, as in the plainsong melodies themselves. It would be interesting to trace these characteristics through either or both of Palestrina's complete series of *Magnificats*, in which, owing to the arrangement of each number of the series under each mode in turn, they are susceptible of masterly treatment; but the limits of our space render this quite impossible, and we must be content with a specimen from one only of these admirable compositions, the *Deposuit* from a *Magnificat* in the seventh mode. In this work the characteristic note of the mode, F♮, its minor seventh, is so used as not only to keep the peculiarities of the Mixolydian scale constantly before us, but also to render more exquisite the sweetness of the F♯ in the cadences upon the final. Another lovely specimen of modal character in all the parts is the *Plange quasi virgo*, sung during Holy Week for a respond after the lesson from the Lamentations. This is in the third and fourth modes, and its strictness is marvellous if we consider the freedom and beauty of the harmony; the first phrase, for instance, upon which, occurring in all the parts, the whole of the opening is built, consists of three notes, of which the first and last are the final of the mode, and the remaining one its characteristic minor second.

MAGNIFICAT. Tone vii

DEPOSUIT POTENTES

Proske—*Musica Divina*, annus 1, tom. 3.
Ratisbon, 1861.   Palestrina.

RESPONSORIUM

PLANGE QUASI VIRGO

(Opening portion)

From Paolucci.   Palestrina.

From the IMPROPERIA

From Paolucci.   LITANY of the B. V. M.   Palestrina.

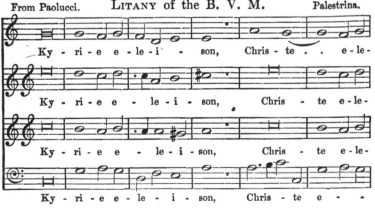

We have insisted upon the consideration of Palestrina's melodic methods, because it is by way of melody that the whole of his meaning and intentions are conveyed. His settlement of the laws of modal harmony, of the accompaniment of discords, of the ornamental forms of cadence, and of the absolutely best courses to adopt in approaching finality—for upon all these matters, for the complete explanation of which a separate volume would be necessary, it may justly be claimed for him that he said the last word in his own day and in his own state of things—is presented in the form of concurrent melodies, each of which pursues an untrammelled course, so apparently spontaneous that it is difficult to realize that any common end or purpose is proposed in them, or that they are pursuing any object beyond the exhibition of their own separate beauty; meanwhile, however, their mutual agreement has been carefully planned, and its development guided with the most scrupulous exactness in all the windings of the florid counterpoint, and through the long-drawn-out notes of the holding pedal. Even in the solemn chants of the *Improperia* and Litanies, which are constructed to all appearance mainly upon harmonic principles, the melodic character, though in abeyance during the recitation, appears in all the passages in which there is movement.

Missa Papae Marcelli.

In considering the work of the composers of this time, the Mass is rightly to be regarded by us, as it was by them, as the highest point of their artistic effort. Out of the ninety-four Masses written by Palestrina two are especially well known, at least by their titles; the *Missa Papae Marcelli* and the *Missa Aeterna Christi Munera.* Round the former service still hang the shreds of a lively controversy; for a picturesque story was long current on the authority of Baini to the effect that the fate of church music, which the Council of Trent in 1562 had felt to be far too elaborate, was decided by the composition and trial performance of three Masses specially written for the occasion, including the *Missa Papae Marcelli.* This story is now generally discredited, and the Rev. J. R. Milne, writing in the 1927 edition of Grove's Dictionary, goes so far as to say that 'there is no real foundation for the imaginative story of Baini. . . . His whole story must be dismissed into the realm of fable.' But the outlook for polyphonic music in the church service was certainly serious in 1563, and the efforts of well-meaning men like Ruffo at Milan and Cranmer's obedient Merbecke, Heath, Stone, Tallis, &c., in England, might have landed us in a dreary wilderness of homophonic block chords. From such a fate church music was saved by the inherent greatness of its great men; and the masterpiece of the *Papae Marcelli* may well be taken as a symbol of a great deliverence for Italy. Both these two Masses do indeed produce in the rendering an idea of clarity of diction, of faultless harmony between text and music, of a victory over the dangers of complexity inseparable from the polyphonic system; dangers, that is, viewed from the side of the text and of its ecclesiastical guardians; and hearing Palestrina in contrast to many of the lesser great men of his time, we instinctively feel that he is indeed *facile princeps* in this connexion.

KYRIE ELEISON.

From the Mass *Aeterna Christi Munera.*   Palestrina.

The recent elaborate investigations of Dr. Jeppesen (*op. cit.*, p. 37) into the technique of Palestrina reveal that the boasted 'simplicity' of the *Papae Marcelli* is no empty tradition, but a fact susceptible of mathematical demonstration. But before 1562 the master had, though perhaps not perfectly in any Mass, adopted the simplicity of technique which is so characteristic of his finest works; for the Lamentations and the eight-part *Improperia* in which his later methods are strongly fore-shadowed, were earlier in date than the *Papae Marcelli*, which clearly therefore cannot have been the means of turning the attention of the composer to the advantages of simplicity. Nay rather, regarding on the one hand the advanced condition of music generally at this time, and the consequent variety and complexity of its methods, and on the other the simplicity which notwithstanding the possession of immense resources controls the technique of the great Roman, and brings within the compass of a brief utterance the creations of a profound and comprehensive imagination, may we not say that the consistently increasing appearance of this quality in the work of Palestrina is the consequence and the sign of his artistic mission as the consummator of all things musical; and that it corresponds, in the form in which it is seen in his compositions, to the sudden and final mastery appearing in some individual in the close of all arts, when he, by unconscious selection and without apparent effort or attention to detail, renders at a stroke the essential beauty and perfection towards which the art itself has tended since its first beginning?

When we pass from the work of Palestrina to that of his followers and contemporaries, we are still able to agree with the general impression of the last generation, that he stood head and shoulders above every one else: only in the case of Victoria is it now necessary to modify any such dictum. With this one exception their work may be said to reveal, quite as clearly as anything written by himself, the power and genius of the master; for notwithstanding every advantage of association and instruction, not one of them was quite like him, or ever able to attain to the special character of his interwoven melodies. Victoria, the Spaniard, perhaps most nearly resembles him in technique, though he is more passionate and more obviously tender in expression than Palestrina. Soriano lacks both the more elaborate forms of technique on the one hand, and on the other the strong devotional feeling of the master; his use, however, of the simpler forms displays fine taste, and perfect propriety, if not great intensity, of sentiment. G. M. Nanino also, though decorous, reveals but little of the kind of feeling proper to sacred music in his compositions for the church, displaying rather an elaborate knowledge of technique; in his madrigals, however, the technique is simple and the sentiment remarkably appropriate. Nanino was somewhat advanced in tendency, and his madrigals by a curious chance—for it can scarcely be more—foreshadow in character some of those of the middle, and even of the latter half of the seventeenth century.

Pedrell, the editor of the complete works of Victoria published by Breitkopf and Härtel, pointed out that the Spanish composer while in Rome was influenced by G. M. Nanino and Luca Marenzio, both of them famous for madrigals rather than for church music. All the music of Nanino published before Victoria left Rome for Madrid in 1579 was secular music; and Marenzio, whose first set of madrigals was published the year after, concentrated his attention on secular music, and is usually regarded as the greatest of all composers of madrigals. It is improbable that Victoria was a pupil of Nanino; both men were about the same age, and Victoria's first book of Motets appeared in 1572, the year before Nanino opened his school of music. Nanino began by training his pupils in the severe contrapuntal style, and warning them against florid writing; but he ultimately adopted the newer style of composition, like Victoria, and his Psalms for eight voices (1614) are full of rapid, syllabic rhythm, unexpected modulations, and dramatic effects.

The music of Victoria has been described (in a saying quoted by Baini) as being 'generated from Moorish blood'. There is a simpler explanation. A Castilian by birth, a Roman by education, Victoria is a representative—one of the last and one of the greatest—of the Flemish-Roman school of polyphonic church music. The mystic realism of his music owes much to the discoveries of the madrigalists; he set Latin words to music as easily as if they had been his native tongue, while the fervour of his expression (which, after all, is mainly a question of technique), was due to his consummate mastery of all the musical resources of his time, and to the example of composers like Marenzio and Nanino, who achieved their highest flights not in the Mass but in the madrigal. Victoria's expressiveness sometimes oversteps the bounds of propriety and degenerates into an almost gushing sentimentality—as, for instance, in the motet 'Vere Languores' (at the words *Ipse tulit*, or *dulces clavos*). Yet this kind of expression, and the morbid sensuousness of 'Jesu dulcis memoria',[1] are less congenial to him than the noble and dignified contemplation of 'O magnum mysterium', the swirling rhythms and flowing contrapuntal texture of 'Duo Seraphim clamabant', or the rapturous splendour of the six-part 'Nigra sum, sed formosa' from the *Song of Songs*.

Compared with Palestrina, Victoria is a composer who looks forward rather than backward; there are moments, indeed, when he looks forward to no less a master than J. S. Bach. Even for his own time, his work is full of novel and interesting methods. Many of his Masses are built not on liturgical melodies or popular tunes, but upon fragments of his own motets. The

---

[1] This motet, however, is found in no *editio princeps*, and its attribution to Victoria must be considered doubtful.

different movements of the Mass are not necessarily built upon the same theme, but on different themes, all of which, however, are derived from the motet from which the Mass takes its name. Mr. R. O. Morris, in his admirable study, *Contrapuntal Technique in the Sixteenth Century*, gives various examples of Victoria's methods—his fondness, for example, of following up a full close by a plagal cadence by way of reinforcement; while Padre Martini, who praised Victoria for his happy invention and melodic gift, admired his intellectual honesty in not pretending to write for more 'real parts' than he actually employed. Victoria was a man of his time; he seems to have been fully aware of the developments which were going on in contemporary music. Though his last work, the splendid *Officium Defunctorum* for six voices (1603), is in the older manner, the collection of Masses, Magnificats, Motets, and Psalms, published at Madrid in 1600 (when the composer was nearly sixty) is written for large numbers of voices in several choirs and provided with an organ accompaniment.[1] In the earlier 'Ave Regina' quoted by Padre Martini in his *Esemplare*, vol. i, p. 134, the eight voices are divided into two choirs which sing alternately. Yet from the beginning they overlap, the second choir entering on the heels of the first before the phrase is finished; and the distance between them becomes smaller and smaller, until at the end all eight voices are singing together in a brilliant close at the words *Lux est orta*. In the Mass from which our example is taken, rapid, syllabic passages, and broad homophonic effects in which all the voices are employed, alternate with quiet polyphonic sections for few voices, conceived in the older manner; while the organ usually accompanies the first choir and often merely doubles the voice-parts. The voices—eight, nine, or twelve—are arranged in groups, after the manner invented by

---

[1] The organ part is missing from the set of part-books in the British Museum, but there are copies of it at Munich, Florence, and Modena.

Willaert, and practised with such success by the Venetian composers, and in the seventeenth century by Juan Bautista Comes
at Valencia and Orazio Benevoli at Rome.

MOTET

NIGRA SUM, SED FORMOSA

(*De Beata Virgine*)

Opera omnia (ed. Pedrell.)   T. L. de Victoria.

II   K k

NIGRA SUM, SED FORMOSA (*conclusion*)

T. L. de Victoria.

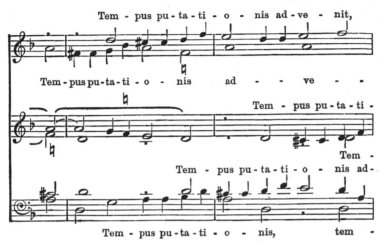

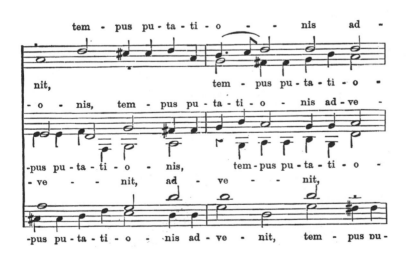

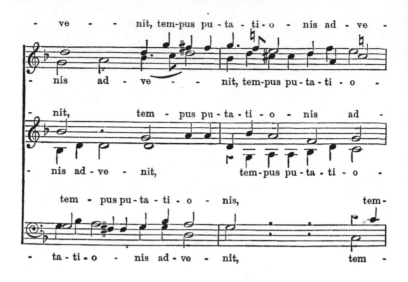

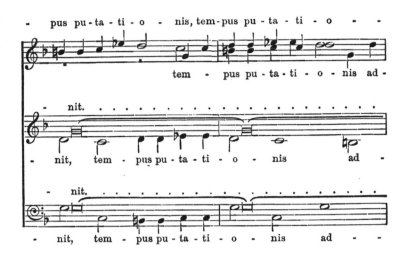

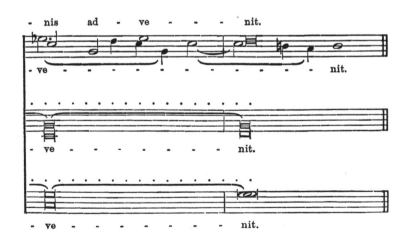

MISSA

PRO VICTORIÂ

Opera omnia, ed. Pedrell.   T. L. de Victoria.

CHAPTER V

SONG

INTRODUCTORY

IT is hardly necessary to demonstrate the existence of secular song from the very earliest times. Singing, especially in concert with others, is such an admirable and obvious outlet for human energy that even if no records of primitive song survived one might reasonably assume that vocal music had had a prominent place both among our savage ancestors and in those civilizations which appear at the dawn of history. Much of this vocal music was inevitably associated with the popular cults, and in fact a distinction between sacred and secular in primitive times has little meaning. It is rather in civilized society that one looks to find cult and secular music co-existing as different manifestations of the same artistic impulse. In Athens the music for the drama is as much sacred music as modern settings of the *Te Deum*, and it is this music about which we know most. But from a number of isolated references it is clear that apart from this music, which must have been very elaborate and intricate, there were songs which everybody knew and sang, and whose titles would be recognized when they were mentioned. Thus in the *Acharnians* of Aristophanes the Boeotian trader says to the pipers who accompany him:

> ὑμὲς δ' ὅσοι Θείβαθεν αὐληταὶ πάρα,
> τοῖς ὀστίνοις φυσῆτε τὸν πρωκτὸν κυνός.

'Pipers of Thebes, come play "The dog's rump".' [1] The Pin-

---

[1] There have been other interpretations of these lines, but this seems the most probable. Cf. in the same play, line 13:

> ἡνίκ' ἐπὶ μόσχῳ ποτὲ
> Δεξίθεος εἰσῆλθ' ᾀσόμενος Βοιώτιον.

and *Thesmophoriazusae*, 1175:

> σὺ δ', ὦ Τερηδόν, ἐπαναφύσα Περσικόν.

See also Athenaeus, 693 f and foll.

daric hymn and the choric song were far from being the only types of musical composition. Much of this secular music was doubtless of the kind which we now describe as 'folk-song', a term which has received a variety of interpretations and still defies adequate definition. It has in fact no real meaning other than that of song which is known and sung by the folk, and the latest popular dance-tune is as much 'folk-song' as a seventeenth-century air preserved in a distorted form by the failing memory of some toothless rustic. There seems to have been a considerable vogue for the music-hall type of song under the Roman Empire, and guests who were invited to sing at receptions frequently performed these excerpts, undeterred by the lack of vocal technique.[1] But this chapter is concerned neither with the popular song as transmitted from one generation to another, nor with the history of singing as a social accomplishment. 'Song', in the sense in which it will here be interpreted, means vocal composition as a conscious artistic creation which has been preserved for us by intelligible records, and though it will be necessary to glance briefly from time to time at examples of 'folk-music', it is the history of the solo song and part-song as musical forms which will principally engage our attention.

The most significant event in the early centuries of our era was the spread of Christianity and with it the development of the ecclesiastical chant. Nor did the Church confine itself to the maintenance of the sacred offices. It took the drama under its wing, and by assimilating various pagan elements produced those liturgical spectacles to which the subsequent invention of the opera may ultimately be traced. It did not so much crush secular art as embrace it. Through the welcome which the

---

[1] 'Ipse etiam taeterrima voce de Laserpiciario mimo canticum extorsit': Petronius, *Satyricon*, 73. Cf. also 'Coepit Menecratis cantica lacerare sicut illi dicebant, qui linguam eius intellegebant': ibid., and the old man who was (he says) a fine singer in his young days—'apposita ad os manu nescio quid taetrum exsibilabat, quod postea Graecum esse affirmabat'.

Church afforded to all that might beautify and adorn the celebration of Christian rites much has been preserved which otherwise might have perished irretrievably. Thus the Church adopted the scansion of popular poetry by rhythm and tonic accent instead of by quantity as in classical Latin, and produced a large number of hymns which are the ecclesiastical counterpart of secular song. As early as the tenth century secular tunes were used for hymns, and some prose melodies which have survived, such as *Orientis partibus* and *O Filii*, which can be traced back to early sources, are indistinguishable from the style of secular songs.

Comparatively few of these songs have survived with music, and the neumatic notation, despite the efforts of transcribers, hardly allows us to form a trustworthy opinion of their merits. Apart from more serious songs, such as the well-known *Planctus Karoli* and the *Modus Ottinc* reproduced by Coussemaker, there are pieces of a lighter type like those in the Cambridge song-book,[1] which appears to consist of the repertory of a travelling singer.

CHANSONS DE GESTE

The Latin popular songs of the eleventh century are interesting enough, even though their melodies defy satisfactory transcription. Far more interesting, however, as being less nearly related to the Church, are the songs or poems in the vernacular. In their simplest form, the epic, they occur all over Europe, in the songs of the Welsh bards, in the Norse *kviŏas*, in the Finnish *runos*, and in the Spanish *romancero*. But they reach their height as a literary form in the *chansons de geste*, recitations of the heroic deeds of Roland, Oliver, Charlemagne, and other notable figures of the glorious days of Gallic chivalry. Of the music of these epics practically nothing remains. There is, however, a very clear and concise definition in the treatise of

[1] Edited with facsimiles by K. Breul (Cambridge University Press, 1915).

Johannes de Grocheo,[1] which enables us with the help of one or two fragments to get some idea of how these long poems were performed. Johannes de Grocheo writes as follows:

Cantum vero gestualem dicimus, in quo gesta heroum et antiquorum patrum opera recitantur, sicuti vitae et martyria sanctorum et adversitates quas antiqui viri pro fide et veritate passi sunt, sicut vita beati Stephani protomartyris et historia regis Karoli. Cantus autem iste debet antiquis et civibus laborantibus et mediocribus ministrari, donec requiescunt ab opere consueto, ut auditis miseriis et calamitatibus aliorum suas facilius sustineant et quilibet opus suum alacrius aggrediatur. Et ideo iste cantus valet ad conservationem totius civitatis. . . .

Versus autem in cantu gestuali qui ex pluribus versiculis efficitur et[4] in eadem consonantia dictaminis cadunt. In aliquo tamen cantu clauditur per versum ab aliis consonantia discordantem, sicut in gesta quae dicitur de Girardo de Viana.[5] Numerus autem versuum in cantu gestuali non est determinatus, sed secun-

By a *chanson de geste* we mean a poem in which are recited the deeds of heroes and of the early fathers, such as the lives and martyrdoms of the saints[2] and the adversities which men of old suffered for faith and truth, e.g. the life of St. Stephen, first martyr, and the story of Charlemagne. The *chanson de geste* should be sung to the aged[3], to citizens that labour and to those of humble birth, while they rest from their accustomed toil, that by hearing the miseries and misfortunes of others they may more easily bear their own, and that one and all may set to their work with more alacrity. Thus the *chanson de geste* helps towards the preservation of the whole state. . . .

The lines in the *chanson de geste* (which is made up of several short lines) close with the same rhyme. In some *chansons*, however, the poem ends with a line by itself having a different rhyme, as in the *Chanson de Girart de Viane*. The number of lines in a *chanson de geste* is not fixed, but can be extended according to the

[1] Printed by Wolf in *S.I.M.*, i, pp. 69–130. Cf. vol. i, p. 237.

[2] Two such religious epics survive, a 'Passion' and a life of St. Léger, noted in neumes. See Beck in *Comptes rendus de l' Académie des Inscriptions*, &c., 1911, p. 41.

[3] Contrast the recommendation on the *cantus versualis*: 'Cantus autem iste debet iuvenibus exhiberi, ne in otio totaliter sint reperti.'

[4] 'et' is otiose. Wolf supplies 'in eodem sono' after 'efficitur'. This hardly improves the sense.

[5] 'Viana' is Rechnitz's emendation, adopted by Beck, *op. cit.*, p. 40.

dum copiam materiae et volun- tatem compositoris ampliatur.	amount of subject-matter avail- able and the inclination of the
Idem etiam cantus debet in omnibus versibus reiterari.	author. The same tune should be repeated for all the lines.

The important points to notice in this extract are: (*a*) the *chanson de geste* was sung; (*b*) the same tune is used throughout; (*c*) an extra line with a different rhyme (and hence a different tune) is sometimes admitted. The example which best con- forms to this definition, though it is not actually itself a *chanson de geste* is the *chante-fable* 'C'est d'Aucassin et Nicolete'.[1] The music is composed of three elements, *A B C*. The couplet *A B* is repeated as many times as is necessary, until the musical section is closed by *C*, 'versus ab aliis consonantia discordans'. In the *chante-fable* sung portions alternate with spoken text, but otherwise the parallel with the *chanson de geste* as described by Johannes de Grocheo is exact. The following is the opening section of 'Aucassin et Nicolete'. All the other sections follow the same plan.

Ex. 1.[2]
(A)

(1) Qui	vau - roit	bons	vers	o - ir
(3) De	deux biax	en - fans	pe - tis,
(5) Des	grans pai - nes	qu'il	sou - fri
(7) Por	s'a - mie	o	le	cler vis?
(9) Et	cor - tois	et	bien	a - sis.
(11) Tant	do - lans	ni	en - soit	tre - pris
(13) Se il	l'o - it	ne	soit	ga - ris

[1] Paris, Bibl. Nat. fr. 2168 (13th cent.). Facsimile published by Bourdillon (Clarendon Press, 1896).

[2] Line 8 is hypersyllabic. There are other examples in this poem. Some editors omit the second 'est'. In some of the sections the tune is slightly modified to accommodate a feminine ending. The notation of the original is non-mensural (see p. 265).

(B)
[l. 8.]

(2) Del	de - port	du	viel	an - tif,
(4) Ni - cho - lete	&	Au - cas - sins,
(6) Et	des	prou - e - ces	qu'il	fist
(8) Dox est li	cans,	biax	est	li	dis
(10) Nus	hom	n'est	si	es - ba - his,
(12) De	grant	mal	a - ma - la - dis,
(14) Et	de	ioi - e	res - bau - dis.

(C)   [rall.]

Tant   par   est   dou - ce . .

It is interesting to notice that *B* occurs in an anonymous *lai*—
the 'Lai des Amants', noted a fourth higher. This naturally
suggests a connexion between the *chanson de geste* and the *lai*,
and there is in fact evidence of connexion in some of the more
primitive *lais*. Thus in Ernoul le Vieux's 'Lai de l'Ancien et
du Nouveau Testament' there are 265 lines and twenty-three
laisses or sections, but only nine musical themes, a type of
economy which recalls the *chanson de geste*, sung throughout
to the same melody. This repetition of the same theme is not,
however, a characteristic of the *descort* (the Provençal counterpart of the *lai*), whence perhaps its name (? *descort = discordans*).
As we shall see, the *lai*, though musically related to the epic by
this system of repetition, belongs none the less, like the sequence,
to the realm of lyric poetry. It has in fact a double ancestry [1].

Two fragments of tunes for *chansons de geste* remain. One was
used by Adam de la Hale for his 'Jeu de Robin et de Marion',
but actually belongs to a poem on Audigier, from which Adam
borrowed one of the lines. The tune is as follows:

[1] Beck, *op. cit.* For further notes on the *lai* see p. 284.

Ex. 2.[1]

Au - di - gier, dist Raim - ber - ge,   bou - se vous di.

Here, again, it must be admitted that the poem from which this is taken is not in reality a *chanson de geste* but an indecent parody of an epic poem. Being, however, a parody, it follows very closely the style of the *chanson de geste*, and our example can be claimed as representative of the music. The only other surviving fragment is a tune for Thomas de Bailleul's 'Bataille d'Annezin'[2]. It is indeed not surprising that these melodies have not been preserved. They were so short that they laid no tax on the memory, and a performer who had once sung a *chanson de geste* would never be in danger of forgetting the music. What does seem surprising to modern ideas is that people should have been satisfied with so many repetitions of the same melody, until we reflect that chanting (whether Anglican or plainsong) is open to similar objections. A curious nineteenth-century echo of this practice is mentioned by Castil-Blaze in his *Théâtres Lyriques* (p. 25). He there relates that at Monteux (near Carpentras, Vaucluse) on the 14th of May, 1808, a mystery play representing the adoration of the Magi was represented. Five hundred actors took part, and the piece, which consisted of several thousand couplets, was sung throughout to the same 17-bar tune and lasted nine hours.

We need hardly lament the non-survival of the music of the *chansons de geste*. It seems probable enough, if we may judge from the examples quoted above, that this music lacked distinction and had hardly room enough to secure that expansion

---

[1] Printed thus by Gennrich in *Der musikalische Vortrag der altfranzösischen Chansons de Geste*, p. 13, after Aix MS. 166, with a slight emendation.

[2] Printed by Gennrich, *op. cit.* The music of some of the Spanish *romanceros* was printed by Salinas in the sixteenth century, but traditional versions of so late a date are unlikely to be completely trustworthy.

which is necessary for a work of permanent interest. In style
the music belongs to the same class as the popular song of the
same time. From the point of view of the historian of music the
glory of this period is not in the epic but in the lyric, which in
spite of the many difficulties which attend its interpretation
remains one of the most significant phenomena in the history of
musical activity.

TROUBADOURS AND TROUVÈRES

In a word the art of the troubadours and trouvères may be
said to introduce a new feature into the history of song—
sophistication. Not that the composition of solo song in any
sense originated with them. All folk-songs have an author, and
given the necessary data it would be possible to trace any
popular melody back to its individual source. But there is that
in the music of the troubadours which is lacking in popular song.
The public for which such songs are composed is content with
the simplest ingredients. Many early songs of this type are mere
scraps of melody, charming enough in their way, but unsatisfying to the cultured listener who demands something that will
appeal, not necessarily to his intellect, but at least to his finer
emotions. The following, taken from Adam de la Hale's 'Jeu de
Robin et de Marion', the tunes of which are selected from
popular sources, is a fair specimen of the early popular songs in
the vernacular:

Ex. 3.[1]

[*Fast.*]

Ah! Ro - bi - chon,   leu - re, leu - re va,   Viens

[1] Music from Coussemaker's edition of the works of Adam de la Hale,
words from Langlois's edition of the 'Jeu de Robin et de Marion'. The
notation of the original is mensural.

près de moi, leu - re, leu - re va, Al - lons jou-

- er du leu - re, leu - re va, Du leu - re, leu - re va.

As will be seen from some of the examples which follow, the work of the troubadours and trouvères often shows traces of having been influenced by popular song, and some of the more simple and artless of their melodies have a certain affinity with the style of Ex. 3 [1]. But their music has always the air of having been composed, whereas a popular song conveys the impression of having come into existence of its own accord. They were not composers in the strict sense (Adam de la Hale and Moniot were exceptions) in that they did not produce polyphonic works. They may best be described as poet-musicians, distinguished amateurs who cultivated both the arts at the same time. It is not always certain, however, that the author of a song composed the music. Different melodies survive in many cases for the same words, and the author may not have composed any of them (cf. p. 268). Some of these alternative melodies may be by *jongleurs*, travelling singers who were responsible for the performance of the songs. At least one of these, Colin Muset, wrote the words and music of songs himself, and there must have been others who were composers as well as performers. We know from miniatures and from references in the poems that it was usual to accompany the songs on the *vielle* [2] and other instru-

---

[1] e.g. the delightful spring-song of Thibault de Champagne—'En mai la rousée' (Paris, Arsenal 5198, p. 318), printed by Beck in *Riemann-Festschrift*, p. 171.

[2] Cf.:　　　　　'Li auquant chantent pastourelles,
　　　　　　　　　Li autre dient en vielles'
　　　　　　　　　Chançons royaus et estampies,
　　　　　　　　　Dances, notes et baleries,

ments, but no examples of these accompaniments appear to have survived. They were most probably improvised by the *jongleur* and must have been very primitive and simple in character (cf. p. 289).

The music of the troubadours, covering roughly a period of two centuries (from the end of the eleventh to the end of the thirteenth), has only in comparatively recent years been the subject of detailed study. Examples from their works were printed by Burney and subsequent writers, but the method of transcription employed was vague, illogical and unsatisfactory. This is scarcely to be wondered at, as the notation of the original manuscripts (with a few exceptions) gives no indication of the time-values of the notes. The most satisfactory solution of the problem is that set out in detail by Beck in *Die Melodien der Troubadours* (Strassburg, 1908) and *Les Chansonniers des Troubadours et des Trouvères* (Paris and Philadelphia, 1927) and developed by Aubry in a number of publications. It assumes that the rhythm of the music is latent in the rhythm of the words, and that the music must be transcribed in whichever rhythmic mode the metre of the poem proves to be the most suitable. In practice only the first three rhythmic modes are employed—the trochaic, the iambic, and the dactylic[1].

There are several arguments in favour of this interpretation

> En leüt, en psalterion,
> Chascun selonc s'entencion,
> Lais d'amours, descors et balades
> Pour esbatre ces gens malades.'
> > (Jean Maillart (1316), quoted by Droz and Thibault,
> > *Poètes et musiciens du XV*ᵉ* siècle*, p. 5.)

Also: 'Et adhuc inter omnia instrumenta chordosa visa a nobis viella videtur praevalere. Quemadmodum enim anima intellectiva alias formas virtuales in se virtualiter includit et tetragonum trigonum et maior numerus minorem, ita viella in se virtualiter alia continet instrumenta.' Johannes de Grocheo (printed in *S.I.M.*, i, p. 96).

[1] For the rhythmic modes see vol. i, p. 64. Beck's original view is here followed.

of troubadour melodies. Where these melodies are noted according to the rules of mensural notation (e.g. in Paris, Bibl. Nat. fr. 846, or in thirteenth-century motets) they are found to agree with transcriptions of the non-mensural notation made in accordance with this theory of the latent rhythm of the music. Further, in Bibl. Nat. fr. 844 and 12615 are found both songs and motets written in this quadrangular notation without any indication of the rhythm[1]. It is self-evident that polyphonic music must be measured, and indeed these same motets occur in other manuscripts in mensural notation. If then these motets, being measured, are written in a notation which gives no clue to the rhythm, it is highly probable that songs which occur in the same manuscript, in the same handwriting, and in the same system of notation, should also be measured. Lastly, there is the evidence of the *estampies chantées*. The *estampie* was a dance and therefore measured. The *estampie chantée* must also have been measured, else why was it so called? We have indeed actual evidence that songs were written to dance tunes. The biographer of the troubadour Rambaut de Vaqueiras, who flourished about 1195, tells us that the poet, when urged by Béatrice de Montferrat to compose a new song, wrote an *estampida* on an air which had been played by the *jongleurs*[2].

These are *a posteriori* arguments. But it may also be held to be *a priori* probable that these songs should be sung to a measured rhythm, seeing that the words have such a definite and constant rhythmic beat, and that that rhythm should take the shape of those forms of triple time which were current in the music of the time. The theory of the application of the rhythmic

[1] Cf. also vol. i, pp. 203–11.

[2] 'Aquesta 'stampida fo facha a las notas de la 'stampida quel joglar asion en las violas': quoted by Aubry, *Trouvères et troubadours*, p. 56. The text is there printed and also in Adler's *Handbuch*, p. 159. The difference between the two versions is only the result of the inevitable uncertainty which accompanies the transcription of these melodies.

modes has not, however, been allowed to go unchallenged[1]. It is contended that while monodies in which ligatures occur but rarely may be successfully interpreted in this way, those in which the ligatures are both numerous and extended cannot so be interpreted without resulting in absurdities which bear no resemblance to medieval music as we know it. Thirteenth-century versions in mensural notation are, it is claimed, modifications of the original melodies, made in order to bring them into conformity with later practice. It is therefore suggested that those songs which include elaborate ligatures should be understood to be in free rhythm, while those in which there is one note to each syllable practically throughout should be transcribed in one of the rhythmic modes.

There is a certain justification for these objections. It is not indeed possible to transcribe a troubadour or trouvère melody with absolute certainty, still less to arrive at a standard critical text where there are several versions[2]. It is also true that the use of plainsong melodies in polyphonic compositions might be used to show that they too should be interpreted in strict rhythm. At the same time it is clearly desirable that we should have one consistent system of interpretation for all the troubadour and trouvère songs. However dangerous generalization may be, there is a certain obvious similarity of style about all the solo songs of these two centuries, and there is strong reason for supposing that their authors were inspired by similar ideals and employed similar methods. It is not necessary to explain why a system of notation so patently obscure should have been used. The manuscripts were intended not for the public but for the

[1] See Gastoué in the *Musical Quarterly*, April 1917, p. 180. Of constructive theories other than that of Beck, those of Riemann (in *Musikalisches Wochenblatt*, xxviii, *passim*) and Ribera (see p. 298) may be mentioned.

[2] Thus 'Ausi com l'unicorne sui' by the King of Navarre is found noted in no less than eight manuscripts. For a specimen collation of several versions of a melody see Bédier and Aubry, *Les chansons de Croisade*, pp. xxv foll.

particular musician who sang the songs or the particular noble-
man who heard them. Both would be familiar with the rhythm
and would need no visible reminder.

The difficulties of transcription confront us more forcibly in
the case of the older troubadours and trouvères. The existing
manuscripts [1] are all of the thirteenth and fourteenth centuries,
when the stave was in regular use, but the earliest troubadour
songs were probably written in neumes, so that the versions
which have come down to us are themselves transcriptions of a
previous system of notation. This accounts for the large number
of variants which survive, and explains the fact that there are
often several melodies for the same words[2]. In most of the
examples where extended ligatures occur the melodies can be
rendered intelligible by a certain modification of the rhythmic
system or by making a *rallentando* at the end of a phrase, where
such ligatures most frequently are to be found. The possible
modifications are of two kinds: (1) The rhythmic mode may be
changed in the course of the song[3].   (2) Contraction or ex-

[1] The principal MSS. are: Paris, Bibl. Nat. fr. 844, 845, 846, 847, 1591,
12615, 20050, 22543, 24406, n.a.fr. 1050; Paris, Arsenal 5198; Arras,
657; Rome, Vatican, Christ. 1490; Milan, Ambros. R 71 sup.; Sienna,
H.X. 36; London, Brit. Mus., Egerton 274. The last is a good example
of a *jongleur's* book. Of the foregoing the following have been published
in facsimile: Paris, Bibl. Nat. fr. 846, by Beck (Paris and Philadelphia, 1927);
Paris, Bibl. Nat. fr. 20050, by Meyer and Raynaud (Paris, 1892); Paris,
Arsenal 5198, by Aubry and Jeanroy (Paris, 1910); Arras, 657, by Jeanroy
(Paris, 1925). Aubry's facsimiles of the 'Roman de Fauvel' (Paris, 1907),
and the Bamberg MS.—*Cent Motets du XIII* siècle* (Paris, 1908)—should
also be consulted.

[2] See, for example, three melodies to a *jeu-parti* of Adam de la Hale—
'Adam, vaurriés vous manoir?'—printed together by Ludwig in Adler's
Handbuch, p. 167.

[3] This is disputed by Aubry, but there are examples in pieces written in
mensural notation, and in some cases the change is sufficiently clearly
indicated even by non-mensural notation; cf. Ex. 7. A thorough exposi-
tion of the rules governing expansion and contraction is given in Aubry's
Cent Motets du XIII siècle*, vol. iii, chap. 3.

pansion may be employed. The latter are necessary if there are
too many or too few syllables in a particular line or lines. For
example, in the romance 'Bele Yolanz':

> Bele Yolanz en ses chambres seoit,
> D'un boen samiz une robe cosoit;
> A son ami tramettre la voloit.
> En sospirant ceste chançon chantoit:
> 'Dex! tant est douz li nons d'amors,
> Ja n'en cuidai sentir dolors.'

The rhythm of the first four lines is clearly dactylic:

$$\acute{}\,\cup\,\cup\ |\ \acute{}\,\cup\,\cup\ |\ \acute{}\,\cup\,\cup\ |\ \acute{}$$

The music is therefore in the third rhythmic mode:

In the last two lines, which would normally consist of seven
syllables and so be in Mode III, *ordo secundus,*

an extra syllable has been introduced, for which room has to be
found in the hard and fast rhythmic scheme. This is done by
assigning two syllables instead of one to the first element of the
second dactyl[1], so that the line runs:

The complete melody transcribed becomes:

Ex. 4.[2]

Bele Y - o - lanz en ses cham - bres se - oit,

---

[1] This is the easier as it was always felt that there was a connexion
between the second and third modes through the second and third elements
of the latter.

[2] Paris, Bibl. Nat. fr. 20050, fo. 64ᵛ.

D'un boen sa - miz u - ne ro - be co - soit;

À   son a - mi tra-met - tre la vo - loit.

En   sos - pi - rant ces - te chan - çon chan - toit:

'Dex!   tant est douz li nons d'a - mors, . .

Ja   n'en cui - dai sen - tir do - lors.'

In expansion the converse process takes place. The following, a *rondeau* interpolated in the 'Roman de Fauvel'[1], is a good example, as the original is in mensural notation. As in a great many *rondeaux*, the rhythm is that of the first mode—trochaic. The first line, however, instead of

[1] Paris, Bibl. Nat. fr. 146, fo. 10; fourteenth century. It will be sufficient to give here the original notation of the first two lines:

Ex. 5.

All the songs from the 'Roman de Fauvel' are printed by Gennrich, *Rondeaux, Virelais und Balladen*, i, pp. 290–306.

becomes

so as to allow room for the ligatures:

Ex. 6.

The application of this principle to songs written in non-mensural notation is naturally hazardous at times, but the principle is none the less sound and established by positive evidence. Nor does it alter the fact that if the main lines of this theory of interpretation are correct, the troubadours and trouvères were compelled to keep within the bounds of what at the present day seems a very limited rhythmic scheme. Slight variations would be permitted within the boundaries of that scheme, but any radical infraction of the principle of the rhythmic modes would be impossible.[1]

---

[1] Examples written in mensural notation show that the same tune was sometimes performed in the first or second mode according to the words sung to it. The interpretation of the third mode as $\frac{6}{8}$ is followed in this chapter. Some authorities prefer $\frac{2}{4}$ in certain cases.

In melodies belonging to the first mode *anacrusis* frequently occurs, either in the simple form of a preliminary up-beat:

or contracted into the first foot:

or expanded into a complete foot by itself:

The explanation sometimes given of the second mode that it is in reality the first mode with *anacrusis* entirely ignores the presence of the tonic accent, which is so helpful in determining the mode in which a song is written. Within the limits of this chapter it is impossible to explain in more detail the principles of transcription and the considerations which guide transcribers in their choice of mode and notation. The following example (the first verse or section of a *lai* attributed to Colin Muset) illustrates quite simply the relation between the original notation of a song and its modern transcription. The change of mode in the last line is suggested by the ligatures and, though not essential, renders the flow of the rhythm smoother:

Ex. 7.[1]

En ces - te   no - te   di - rai   D'une a - mo - re -

[1] Paris, Arsenal 5198, p. 334.

- te   que j'ai,   Et   pour li   m'en - voi - se - rai

Et   bauz et   joi - anz   se - rai :   L'en   doit bien   pour

li chan - ter   Et   ren - voi - sier   et   jou - er

Et   son cors te - nir   plus gai   En   de ro - bes

a - ces - mer   Et   cha-piau   de   flors   por - ter

Au - si   coume el   mois   de   mai.

It is usual to divide the troubadours and trouvères into three periods, the first from the end of the eleventh to the middle of the twelfth century, the second from the middle of the twelfth to the middle of the thirteenth century, and the third from the middle to the end of the thirteenth century. Of the earliest troubadours of whom we have record—Guillaume of Aquitaine and Marcabru—very little has survived. The music to one of Guillaume's songs [1] and four of Marcabru's [2] is all that remains. Among the other early troubadours few were more celebrated than Bernard de Ventadour,[3] who rose to fame from a humble origin and died in 1195. The following is an example of his serious and sometimes melancholy style:

[1] 'Pos de chantar m'es pres talenz.' The music is only known through its having been used in a Provençal mystery of St. Agnes; facsimile in Monaci, *Il mistero provenzale di S. Agnese* (Rome, 1880); reconstruction of the song in Gennrich, *Der musikalische Vortrag, &c.*, p. 36.

[2] All four have been published by Aubry.

[3] See the edition of his works by Appel, with facsimiles of the music (Halle, 1915).

Ex. 8.[1]

Can par la flor jus-tal vert fuelh E vei lo tems clar
Et aug lo chans d'au-zels pel bruelh Quem a-dos-sal cor

e se - re Mais l'au-zel chan - ton a lau -
em re - ve,

- zor, Ieu plus ai de joi en mon cor . . .

Dei ben chan - tar, car tug li miei jor - nal

Son joi e chan que no pens de ren als. . . .

Of the trouvères of the first period perhaps the most famous is
Gace Brulé, who was at one time thought to have been a contemporary of the King of Navarre, but has since been shown to
have lived in the twelfth century. His style is often elaborate
and abounds in ornamentation. The following song affords a
good example of his decorative methods:

Ex. 9.[2]

Cil qui d'a-mors me con - seil - le Que je

m'en doi - e par - tir Ne sent pas que

[1] Paris, Bibl. Nat. fr. 22543, fo. 56[v] (Appel, plate xxi). Another song,
'Lancan vei la folha', is printed by Ludwig in Adler's *Handbuch*, p. 159.
[2] Paris, Bibl. Nat. fr. 20050, fo. 55. Another version is in Paris,
Arsenal 5198, p. 55.

me res - veil - le . . Ne quel sont mei grie sos -

- pir. Pe - tit a sens et voi - di - e,

Cil qui m'en vuet chas - toi - er . . N'en ainz

n'a - ma en sa . . vi - e . . Cil fait bien ni -

- ce fo - li - e, . . . Qui s'en - tre - met del mes -

- tier Dont il ne se . seit . ai - dier.

* The G is doubtful.

The connexion between the troubadours and the trouvères, the former the poets of the south of France, the latter of the north, has been a subject for conjecture. The honour of having introduced Provençal poetry and music to the north is often assigned to Eleanor of Aquitaine, granddaughter of Guillaume and patroness of Bernard de Ventadour. It cannot, however, be shown that a solitary instance of this kind determined the origin of the trouvères. Indeed, some affirm that the trouvères learnt their art not through communication with the south of France but through the Crusades. In any case many features are common to the songs of the troubadours and trouvères, not least the celebration of the *amour courtois,* a poetic conceit which lifts illicit love on to a purely aesthetic plane, where the poet can indulge his fancy without too close an attention to reality.

Of later trouvères Gautier de Coinci (*d.* 1236) is remembered for his religious pieces, and Thibault de Champagne, afterwards King of Navarre (1201–53), and Adam de la Hale (*c.* 1230–85) for their secular songs, among a host of other poet-musicians.[1] Thibault's engaging style is well represented by the well-known 'L'autrier par la matinée', or by the almost bald simplicity of the following:

Ex. 10.[2]

Cous-tume est bien quant on tient un pri - sion
Car nu - le riens ne fet tant cuer fe - lon

Qu'on ne le veut o - ïr ne es-cou - ter,
Con grant po - voir qui mal en veut u - ser.

Pour ce, da - me, de moi m'es-tuet dou - ter,

Car je n'i os par-ler de ra-en - çon

N'estre os-ta - giez sen be - le gui-se non;

[1] Over 600 are known and several hundred melodies have been preserved. For the troubadours and their works see Beck, *Die Melodien der Troubadours*; for the trouvères see Raynaud, *Bibliographie des chansonniers français* (Paris, 1884). H. J. Chaytor's *The Troubadours* (Cambridge, 1912) gives a useful short account of the troubadours and their influence.

[2] Paris, Arsenal 5198, p. 48.

A - vec tout ce ne puis je es-cha-per. . . .

The attribution of these melodies to the authors of their words is, as we have seen, often conjectural, and it is practically impossible to say which of two or more alternative melodies was written by the author. The following is a setting of a poem by the Chatelain de Coucy, but the tune cannot with certainty be assigned to him, because another manuscript has an entirely different melody to the same text:

Ex. 11.[1]

Mer - ci cla - mant de mon fol . . er - re -
Car tra - ï m'a et mort a . . es - ci -

ment, Fe - rai la fin de mes
ent Mes ja - los cuers que g'en

chan - çons o - ïr, Si m'a mal
doi tant ha - ïr.

fet par le dit d'au - tre gent

Tout sont par - ti de moi joi - os ta -

- lent, Et quant joi - e me faut,

[1] Ibid., p. 104. Different melody (incomplete) in Arras 657, fo. 155^v.

bien   est re - sons . .   Qu'a - pres ma

joi - e   fe - nis - sent   mes chan - çons. . . .

Adam de la Hale (otherwise known as Adam le Bossu) deserves a few words to himself, as he is well known as a composer.[1]
If his solo songs are not so important for the history of music as
his polyphonic works, they have none the less a certain charm
of their own. His *jeux-partis* (a form in which the poet conducts
a debate with himself or another) are less interesting. They
display little variety and are often monotonous. The tunes for
the songs in his ' Jeu de Robin et de Marion ' (see pp. 261 and 263),
which even Coussemaker attributed to him (though he noticed
the difference in style), have long since been recognized as
popular melodies to which Adam wrote his own words. This
was a fashion of borrowing which has always been popular in
France from the earliest times right up to the present day.

The usual classification of the various types of troubadour and
trouvère song is of less importance in a history of music, as the
variety of type in the music is not so marked[2]. This does not
mean that all troubadour songs are similar. On the contrary,
it was a rule that no song should be like another. But the most
minute divergence was considered a sufficient proof of originality,
and apart from the *lai* or *descort* and the *rondeau*, which will be
considered presently, a large majority of the songs have roughly
the same musical form. This form may be expressed by the
terms *strophe, antistrophe*, and *episode*, or by the formula *A a x*,
where *x* may be of indefinite length and take almost any form.
Sometimes *x* is itself subdivided into *B b*, so that the repetition

---

[1] See vol. i, pp. 174–7.
[2] See Introductory vol., pp. 220–1.

of the first half (*A a*) is balanced by the repetition of the second. A further variation is the prolongation of the tune after *B b*, so that the complete melody is in the form *A a B b y*, where *B b y* stands for *x*. There are of course many exceptions to these general rules. For example, *A* will sometimes stand alone without the repetition *a*. Again, *x* is often little more than a short *coda* phrase added at the end. There is this also to be noted about the first section, that *a* is frequently not a mere repetition of *A*, i.e. the final note will differ, *A* being *ouvert* while *a* is *clos* (cf. Ex. 9). Occasionally the final note of the complete melody is *ouvert*, in which case it is probably intended as a transition note to the next verse and the singer will automatically alter it to the final *clos* (or as we might say the 'tonic') at the end of the last verse.[1]

The tonality of the songs varies, nor is it always clear how far the rules of *musica ficta* apply. It is generally advisable to prevent the *diabolus in musica* when both B and F occur in the same descending phrase. Where necessary the B is to be flattened throughout the song, and in some pieces it is so marked in the original (see Ex. 11). But as in the polyphonic music of the period it is often omitted. The *B quadratum* (or sharp), which also serves to correct a previously flattened note, is rarer.[2] The modes most commonly found are the 1st (D–D, also transposed A–A), the 5th (F–F, also transposed C–C), and the 7th (G–G). The melodies, however, occasionally exceed the normal range of an octave. In the following lively piece the compass of the tune is an 11th:

Ex. 12.[3]

Gai - te de   la   tor, Gar - dez   en - tor Les murs, se

---

[1] The use of *ouvert* and *clos* endings forms another point of contact with dance tunes, in which they are the rule.

[2] Accidentals are fairly frequent in Paris, Bibl. Nat. fr. 846.

[3] Paris, Bibl. Nat. fr. 20050, fo. 83.

Deus vos voi - e, Cor sont a se - jor Dame

et sei - gnor, Et lar - ron vont en proi - e.

Hu et hu et hu et hu! Je l'ai ve - ü La

jus soz la . . cou - droi - e. Hu et hu et

hu et hu! A bien pres l'o - ci - roi - e.

We have seen (p. 266) that the *estampie chantée* was a song
written to a dance tune or composed on dance rhythms. Two
other types of song are also strongly influenced by dance
rhythms—the *ballade* and the *rondeau*. The *ballade*, though at
this period it has no definite form, is commonly arranged so
that the chorus sings the refrain while the verse is left to a solo
voice. A good example is 'A l'entrade del tens clar', which may
be divided between soloist and chorus thus:

Ex. 13.[1]

A l'en-tra - de del tens clar, E - y - a,
E pir ja - lous ir - ri - tar, E - y - a,

[1] Ibid., fo. 82ᵛ. Tiersot, Aubry, and Riemann all emend the latter part
of this song.

Pir joi - e re - co - men-çar,
Vol la re - gi - ne mo -   E - y - a.

strar, K'ele est si a - mo - rou - se.   A - la -

vi', A - la - vi - e, Ja - lous, las -

- saz . . nos, las - saz . . nos bal - lar . .

en - tre nos, . . en - tre nos.

The *balerie* is akin to the *ballade* and still more closely allied
to the dance. In this form the stanzas are often divided among
several persons, and the singing may even be accompanied by
a mimed representation of the miniature drama. In Ex. 12
(though no indication is given in the manuscript), it is supposed
by Jeanroy and Bédier that a dialogue is taking place between
a lover's accomplice and a watchman in the tower.[1] The
rotrouenge is also similar to the *ballade* in that each verse is accompanied by a refrain,[2] which may be long or short and may
occur either at the end or in the middle of the stanza. Marcabru's
'Dirai vos senes doptansa' (printed in Adler's *Handbuch*, p. 158)

[1] Complete text in Aubry, *Trouvères et troubadours*, p. 89.
[2] It is possible that the refrain is of Muslim origin and came to the
troubadours from Spain. In Spanish Muslim poetry, however, and in the
'Cantigas' of Alfonso el Sabio (see p. 296) the refrain comes at the beginning.

is a characteristic example. Here the refrain consists only of
one word—'Escoutatz'—after the third line, the form being
A B a C D E, where *C* is the refrain. This example is in Provençal, but most *rotrouenges* come from the north of France,
where the form is said to have originated. The varieties of type
are innumerable, nor is there any fixed style. Many songs
which are classed as *chansons de toile* or *romances* come under the
category *rotrouenge*.[1]

In the *rondeau* the form is stereotyped and is almost invariably
A B a A a' b A B, where *A a a'* and *B b* stand for different lines
in the same metre and with the same rhyme set to the same
music. An example has already been quoted from a fourteenth-
century manuscript—'Porchier miex estre ameroie' (see Ex. 6).
The form also occurs in Latin songs of the thirteenth century,
many of which are in the Florence Antiphoner.[2] It is at once
the simplest and the most rigid of the literary and musical conventions of the period. The rhythm is generally trochaic, and
the sentiment of the poet, of necessity, free from complication.
The popularity of the *rondeau* is attested by the presence of
their elements in motets of the same period. Thus in the
Bamberg MS. (fo. 9ᵛ) a motet ends as follows:

Ex. 14.

[1] See Gennrich, *Die altfranzösischen Rotrouenge*, which includes several
examples.
[2] Aubry in *Riemann-Festschrift*, p. 216.

The words, 'En ma dame ai mis mon cuer et mon panser' (in the
upper part) are the first two lines—i.e. the elements *A* and *B*
of a *rondeau* of which the words (without music) are in Paris,
Bibl. Nat. fr. 12786, fo. 80. As only two musical elements are
employed in the *rondeau*, the tune as preserved in the Bamberg
MS. is sufficient to reconstruct the complete song:

The *lai* (or *descort* in Provençal) differs from all the types of
song which we have hitherto been considering. It consists of a
poem in several verses (or sections) each of which has a different
metrical scheme, and consequently a different musical setting. In
some of the earlier *lais* two or even more sections are in the same

---

[1] This melody has a further interest, as it is found in Brit. Mus. Egerton
274, fo. 49ᵛ, with the words of a Latin hymn, 'Veni, sancte spiritus',
also in *rondeau* form. (Text in Dreves, *Analectica Hymnica*, vol. xxi.)
This is one of many examples of the facile exchange of sacred and secular.
In the motets themselves there are often Latin words in one manuscript,
French in another. Another refrain in the Bamberg MS. (fo. 45ᵛ)—'Li
regart de ses vairs ieus'—is also the foundation of a *rondeau*. See Aubry,
Cent Motets, iii. p. 96; Gennrich, *Rondeaux, Virelais und Balladen*, ii,
pp. 96–7.

metre and have the same music (see p. 261), but the general
tendency in the more sophisticated examples is to avoid repetition
and to seek infinite variety. Ex. 7 is the first verse of a *lai* (the
music to the other verses has not been preserved). In style it
is fairly typical of the generally unaffected simplicity of this sort
of composition. It has already been remarked (p. 261) that the
lai can claim kinship with epic, as well as with lyric, poetry.
It also forms a secular parallel to the Church sequence. There
is, it is true, a difference. The sequence is composed of a series
of parallel pairs of verses preceded and succeeded by a verse
which is structurally independent.[1] But the initial stanzas of
two trouvères *lais* [2] are written on the melody of 'Ave gloriosa
virginum regina' (Brit. Mus. Egerton 274, fo. 3 and elsewhere),
and this use of a sequence melody is sufficient to suggest, if not
to establish, a close connexion between the sequence and the *lai*.
The connecting link may be the French translations of sequences

---

[1] 'Est autem sequentia ex pluribus versiculis compositus sicut *Laetabundus* vel *Benedicta es celorum*. . . . Sed sequentia cantatur ad modum ductiae,
ut ea ducat et laetificet, ut laete recipiant verba novi testamenti puta
sacrum evangelium, quod statim postea decantatur.' Johannes de Grocheo
(*S.I.M.*, i, p. 126).

Cf.: 'Ductia vero est cantilena levis et velox in ascensu et descensu, quae
in choris a iuvenibus et puellis decantatur, sicut gallice *Chi encor querez
amoretes*. Haec enim ducit corda puellarum et iuvenum et a vanitate re-
movet et contra passionem, quae dicitur amor, valere dicitur.' (Ibid., p. 93.)

Contrast: 'Est autem ductia sonus illiteratus (sc. "without words") cum
decenti percussione mensuratus.' (Ibid., p. 97.)

Though the last two extracts do not appear to be complementary, it is
clear at any rate that there was a definite connexion between the sequence
and secular song and that secular songs were performed in regular
rhythm.

[2] (a) 'Lonc tens m'ai tëu et oncor me teroie' (*Lai des Hermins*); Paris,
Bibl. Nat. fr. 845, fo. 185 (in Jeanroy, Brandin, and Aubry, *Lais et descorts*,
p. 147). (b) 'L'autrier chevauchoie pensant par un matin' (*Lai de la
Pastourelle*); Bibl. Nat. fr. 845, fo. 186 (in *Lais et descorts*, p. 139). Dis-
cussion in Beck, *Die Melodien der Troubadours*, pp. 76–9, and *La Musique
des Troubadours*, pp. 39–43.

which are not uncommon at this period.[1] On the other side the *lai* is related to the *chanson de geste* and to the popular songs of the time, to which many of the anonymous *lais* show some resemblance. The words of the *lai* may be either sacred or secular. Whatever their subject, all are notable for a looseness and incoherence which are the natural result of using a form which has no circumscribed limits and little continuity of structure.

The art of the troubadours was aristocratic. It was nurtured and flourished in the homes of the nobility,[2] and its only point of contact with the people was the employment of *jongleurs* of humble birth to perform the songs. It was inevitable that some traces of popular influence should appear in many of the melodies. But the songs which are most typical of the outlook and aims of the troubadours are those in which there is a conscious originality, even where originality results in an effect of strain and a loss of naturalness. How far these songs became known to the world at large it is impossible to say. Some must have been sung far and wide if we may believe the evidence of several manuscript versions of the same song. Again, the Crusaders' songs were probably familiar. Twenty-eight are printed with

[1] e.g. 'Hui enfantez' (Bibl. Nat. fr. 2163, fo. 224; facs. in Aubry, *Les plus anciens monuments, &c.*, Plate VI), a translation of the *Laetabundus*. Parodies of proses were also popular, e.g. 'Falvelle qui iam moreris' in the 'Roman de Fauvel' (Bibl. Nat. fr. 146, fo. 29ᵛ; mensural notation) is a parody of 'Homo qui semper moreris' (Florence, Bibl. Laur. Plut. xxix, 1, fo. 428ᵛ).

[2] 'Cantus coronatus ⟨ab⟩ aliquibus simpliciter conductus dictus est. Qui propter eius bonitatem in dictamine et cantu a magistris studentibus circa sonos coronatur, sicut gallice *Ausi com l'unicorne* vel *Quant li roussignol*. Qui etiam a regibus et nobilibus solet componi et etiam coram regibus et principibus terrae decantari, ut eorum animos ad audaciam et fortitudinem, magnanimitatem et liberalitatem commoveat,* quae omnia faciunt ad bonum regimen. Est enim cantus iste de delectabili materia et ardua sicut de amicitia et karitate et ex omnibus longis et perfectis efficitur.' (Johannes de Grocheo, *S.I.M.*, i, p. 91.) The interpretation of the last six words is disputed.

* Wolf reads 'quia'.

music in Bédier and Aubry, *Les chansons de Croisade*. Uncouth
and graceless though many of them are, they have a certain
rough simplicity which suits their subject and calls to mind, as
no historical record can, the high aims and the deep disappoint-
ments of chivalrous warfare. The following is one of the most
striking and perhaps the best known of these songs:

Ex. 16.[1]

Par - ti de mal e[t] a· bien a tur - né
K'a sun be-suing nus ad Deus a - pe - lé,

Voil ma chan-çun a la gent fere o - ïr,
Si ne li deit nul pros - do - me fail - lir,

Kar en la cruiz dei-gnat pur nus mu - rir:

Mult li doit bien es-tre gue - re - do - né

Kar par sa mort su-mes tuz ra - cha - té.

EARLY MINNESINGER

The troubadours and trouvères had no successors in France,
though their influence lasted on in a shadowy way into the
fourteenth century. But they exercised a strong influence on
contemporary art in other countries. In England, though there
was a close connexion with the trouvères, there does not seem
to have been any national school of song-writers on the same
lines. A few English songs of the thirteenth century have been

[1] London, Brit. Mus. Harl. 1717, fo. 251ᵛ; facsimiles in Wooldridge,
Early English Harmony, Plate 8, and Aubry, *Les plus anciens monuments*,
&c., Plate IV.

preserved, but they are fragmentary and unimportant.   In Germany and the Iberian peninsular, on the other hand, we have evidence of artistic movements similar to those of the French and Provençal *chansonniers* and owing their origin in a large measure to their influence.

The name of the Minnesinger—'singers of love'—indicates sufficiently the chief subject of their poems.   Like the troubadours, they were concerned with the tender passion.   But their attitude was different.   The *amour courtois* of the troubadours consisted in devotion to a single person, not infrequently the wife of another.   The German *Minne* (differing also from the modern *Liebe*) was more comprehensive and its ideal that of a devotion essentially chivalrous.   This ideal, which has in it something of the characteristic sentimentality of the German race, did not survive.   Rational persons discovered it to be a little ridiculous, and there were not wanting poets who had sat at the feet of the Provençal troubadours [1] and who were only too ready to turn their backs on chivalry and come down to particulars. But the earliest Minnesinger did uphold this ideal, and in spite of rebellion it had an obvious influence on the whole current of German poetry until quite modern times.

The year 1184 is a useful peg on which to hang the beginnings of German chivalry.   At Whitsuntide of that year a magnificent festival was held at Mainz by Frederick Barbarossa, to which not only his countrymen but persons of noble rank from all parts of Europe were invited.   This festival was celebrated with all the pomp and majesty which we associate with the upper classes in medieval times, and did much to facilitate intercourse with other countries.   In this way it is probable that German

---

[1] Wolfram von Eschenbach, a contemporary of Walther von der Vogelweide, says: 'Von Profanz in tütsche Land die rechte Mere uns sind gesannt.' Of the troubadours of the twelfth century Folquet de Marseille (d. 1231) and Pierre Vidal (d. *c.* 1215) had the most influence on the Minnesinger.

poets came into closer contact with the troubadours. Heinrich von Veldeke was a pioneer of the Minnesang, though others before him had already foreshadowed the style. But the most famous of all was Walther von der Vogelweide (*c.* 1170–1230), who was acknowledged as a master by his contemporaries. Though a noble, he spent at least ten years in wandering to and fro as a *fahrender Sänger* (= French *jongleur*), receiving hospitality and singing in return the songs which he had composed. He is the type of the best period of the Minnesinger, the singers of pure chivalrous love, and the words put into his mouth by Wagner well express the Minnesinger ideal:

> Willst du Erquickung aus dem Bronnen haben,
> Musst du dein Herz, nicht deinen Gaumen laben.

The art of the Minnesinger, therefore, though it originated in Provence, soon became something thoroughly and essentially German. Like the troubadours, they did not confine themselves to love-songs, but composed also religious and political pieces. But their love-songs are among the most attractive and characteristic of their compositions. In performance the songs were accompanied by the viol or some other instrument (cf. pp. 264 and 329), but as with the troubadours and trouvères this accompaniment was not written down but improvised at the time. The form of the *Lied* resembles that of the trouvère lyric, which, it will be remembered, was generally *A a x*, *A a* being a repeating section while *x* was a sort of episode or coda whose length and composition depended on the fancy of the writer. In the *Lied* the sections *A* and *a* (the same melody with different words) were known as the *Stollen*, and the section *x* was called the *Abgesang*, which often concluded with part of the melody of the *Stollen* (cf. Ex. 18).

Another point of comparison with the troubadours and trou-

vères is the notation of the manuscripts.[1] This, whether quadrangular or Gothic, generally gives no clue to the rhythm of the
music. Fortunately the modal interpretation, which has already
been shown to be suitable for the melodies of the trouvères and
troubadours (see p. 265), is also applicable to the melodies of the
early Minnesinger.   Sometimes there are certain difficulties
which confront the transcriber, as in the following thirteenth-
century spring song, where the *melisma* runs riot and the interpretation is bound to be a little free:

Ex. 17.[2]

[1] The most important Minnesinger MSS. with music are: Munich,
Staatsbibl. germ. 4997 (the 'Colmar' MS.); a MS. in the University Library,
Jena (the 'Jena' MS., a superb facsimile was published by K. K. Müller in
1896); Berlin, Kgl. Bibl. germ. 2ᵛᵒ, 779 ('Nithart's Song Book', formerly
belonging to von Hagen and reproduced by him in *Minnesinger*, iv, 845–52);
Vienna, Nationalbibl. 2701 (reproduced in *Denk. der Tonkunst in Öst.*, xx,
pt. 2) and 2856 (published by Mayer and Rietsch, *Die Mondsee-Wiener
Liederhandschrift*). For later Minnesinger, to whom the above remarks do
not necessarily apply, see pp. 327–31. Some of the songs in Vienna,
Nationalbibl. 2856 (which is late fourteenth or early fifteenth century), are
in mensural notation and clearly in duple time.

[2] Berlin, Kgl. Bibl. germ. 4°, 981; facsimiles in Wolf, *Handbuch der Notationskunde*, facing p. 176, and *Musikalische Schrifttafeln*, no. 21.

was   ghe - - - - - stalt. .

But in most of the early Minnesinger melodies the modal interpretation is quite successful, if occasionally less rigid. The rules
of German verse were fully as complicated as those of the French
and Provençal lyric, but many minor variations were permissible.
Thus the section *a* sometimes has an initial up-beat which is
wanting in the section *A*, and the licence of changing the mode
in the course of a song is not infrequently advisable. Later
Minnesinger melodies which are written in mensural notation
are often in duple time (cf. p. 290, note 1), and for this reason
many modern scholars prefer to transcribe the earlier melodies
also in duple time. Most of them fall as easily into duple time
as triple, and indeed there are examples of later Minnesinger
tunes noted in duple time in one manuscript and in triple time
in another. But the close connexion between the Minnesinger
and the troubadours is a strong argument for interpreting their
melodies in the same way, especially as reliable examples of
duple time are extremely rare in the thirteenth century.

The following song by Walther von der Vogelweide falls
naturally into the second rhythmic mode, with *anacrusis* where
necessary:

Ex. 18. 1
[Stollen.]

Nu al - erst leb' ich mir . . wer - de, Sint myn

¹ From a fragment discovered in the State Archives, Münster; facsimile
in *S.I.M.*, xii, facing p. 500. A tempting emendation is E for F in bars
7 and 15, but the MS. reading is quite clear both here and in the last bar
but one. An alternative interpretation of the *anacrusis* is to write

| ♪ ♪ ♪ | and | ♪ ♪ ♪ | .
Das he · re   Mir ist ge -

sun - dich   ouge er . .   sicht   Das   he - re   lant und

ouch die   er - de,   Dem man   vil   der   e - ren

[Abgesang.]

gicht.   Mir   ist   ge - schen als   ich   je   bat:

Ich   byn   ko - men   an   die   stat   Da   got

me - n[i]s - li - chen   trat.

This has all the normal characteristics of the *Lied*: the repeating section, followed by the coda, which itself concludes with the same four bars as the *Stollen*. Indeed the form offered quite a number of possibilities to any one with a feeling for balance and design. Here the very best use is made of these possibilities, and the result is an attractive and graceful composition. But there are a large number of songs which are based on the same scheme but which are of far clumsier workmanship. The *Abgesang* is often of almost interminable length, and sprawls out in a graceless fashion, now repeating scraps of tune from the *Stollen*, now introducing new matter, as in a piece by the Minnesinger known as the Tannhäuser, preserved in the Jena MS.[1] The Tannhäuser was a follower of Nithart (or Neidhart) von Reuenthal (1180–1250), whose work, though contemporary with Walther von der Vogelweide, marks the beginning of the decline

[1] ' Ey ist hirte eyn wunnychlicher tac ' (fo. 42ᵛ).

---

of the Minnesinger's art from its idealistic beginnings. Nithart's songs are simpler (and often coarser) in style and have more in common with folk-song than the works of his predecessors and contemporaries.

Apart from the *Lied* two other forms were in use—the *Spruch* and the *Leich*. The words of the *Spruch* were didactic, religious or political; it normally consisted of one long extended verse, but there are also examples of several verses sung to the same tune. The *Leich* is the German counterpart of the *lai* and *descort* and like them is composed of a number of independent sections loosely strung together. What has been said about the *lai* (see p. 285) applies in the main to the *Leich*. Some authorities repudiate the connexion with the sequence, which seems to them superficial, and regard the *Leich* as a dance-form. But its precise origin is not of any great importance. We have seen that the principle of stringing together structurally independent pieces in this way was not uncommon at this time, and all that can be said with certainty is that sequence, dance, and *Leich* are all linked up by a general similarity of method and perhaps by a common ancestry. Certainly the following example (the first section of a *Leich* by Frauenlob) suggests an analogy with dance tunes, even though it is not entirely safe to press that analogy:

Ex. 19. [1]

Diss ist unser frauwen leich oder der guldin flügel zu latin Cantica canticorum.

Ey ich sach in dem tro - ne Ein jung - fraw
Sie wol - te sin en - bun - den Susz gie die

[1] Colmar MS. (Munich, Staatsbibl. germ. 4997, Gothic notation), fo. 19; facsimile in Runge, *Die Sangweisen der Colmarer Handschrift*, facing p. 2. The last line would run a little more smoothly if written in the second mode (cf. Ex. 7), but the notation of the MS., though non-mensural, suggests that it is preferable not to change the mode.

die was swan - ger, Sie trug ein wun - der - cro -
al - ler - bes - te; Zwolff stei - ne zu der stun -

ne In my - ner au - gen an - ger.
den Kosz in der kro - nen ves - te.

This is the type of the *Leich*-verse—a single repeated section, or, in other words, a *Lied* without *Abgesang*. The complete *Leich* from which this is taken has twenty-two such verses or sections.

Frauenlob (1250–1318), whose real name was Heinrich von Meissen, is the last of the early Minnesinger. A few years before his death he founded a guild of singers at Mainz, a precedent which was quickly followed by others, until by the fifteenth century every town of any importance had its guild. The time when music and the arts were the preserve of monarchs and nobles had passed, and honest burghers now cultivated the Muse. A few survivors of the old tradition are still to be found at the end of the fourteenth century, e.g. Hugo von Montfort and Oswald von Wolkenstein (see p. 327), but they are aristocratic oases in a middle-class desert. For practical purposes the knightly art may be said to have ended, as in France, with the dawn of the fourteenth century. There is a short transition period and then the Meistersinger (see p. 335) occupy the stage, their art rising to its height at the end of the fifteenth century and declining by gradual stages until it expired towards the middle of the nineteenth century.

EARLY SPANISH SONG

From Germany we turn to Spain and Portugal. The earliest secular songs which we possess are the *Siete canciones de amor*

of Martin Codax [1] which belong to the early part of the thirteenth
century. Six of these seven songs, which are in the Galician
dialect, have the music noted on a five-line stave, but in most of
them the mutilated condition of the MS. makes it impossible
to reproduce an accurate version. The following (No. 5 in the
MS.) is a fair sample of the style and is legible throughout in
the original:

Ex. 20.

Quan - tas sa - be - des a - mar a - mi - go

Trei - des co - mi - go a lo mar de vi - go

E ban - nar nos e - mos nas on - das.

It is impossible to build theories on so scanty a fragment, but
it seems likely that the melodies are closely related to popular
songs of the time, especially the Galician *alalás*. Nos. 1 and 5
in the MS. are melodically almost identical. The notation gives
no indication of the time-values of the notes, and it has generally
been assumed that the songs are in free rhythm. The above
example, however, transcribed according to the same principles
as the songs of the troubadours, is logical and intelligible, though
it is probable enough that the time was not strictly observed.

Also to Galicia belong the *Cántigas de Santa Maria*, collected
by Alfonso X of Castille (1221–84), brother-in-law of Edward I
of England. Though in many ways an unsatisfactory sovereign,

---

[1] The name is thus written in the MS. (see the facsimile published by
P. Vindel). Codax may only have been the owner of the MS. He was
probably a Portuguese or Galician *joglar*.

Alfonso (surnamed *el Sabio*—'the Wise') seems to have had a royal appreciation of art and literature. The last of the troubadours, Guirault Riquier, is known to have sojourned at his court, and there is every evidence that the Spanish troubadours were influenced in some measure by those of Provence. The *Cántigas*, which consist of carols and hymns to the Virgin, may be regarded as the Spanish counterpart of the *Miracles* of Gautier de Coinci, though the styles of the two are very different. The notation of the MSS.[1] belongs to that intermediate period when the rigid interpretation of ligatures had not become general. Most of the melodies are written in the first or second modes, but the third is also found, written ⌐ ▪ ⌐ instead of the usual ⌐ ▪ ▪ (see Ex. 22).

In the form of the *Cántigas* the *estribillo* (or refrain) is noteworthy. This always comes before and after each *estrofa* (or verse), whereas in French songs it is generally in the middle or at the end. This is in fact the ordinary arrangement of the Spanish *villancico* and of the Arab *zajal*, from which the form of the *Cántigas* probably derives. In the simplest type of *Cántiga* the same melody does duty both for the *estribillo* and for the *estrofa*. Where the *estrofa* is longer than the *estribillo* the music is generally in the form *A B a A*, *A* being the *estribillo* and *B a* the *estrofa*. This form may be paralleled by that of several Latin *rondeaux* in the Florence Medici Antiphoner,[2]

---

[1] There are three that contain the music: Madrid, Bibl. Nat. 10069 (c. 1270, formerly at Toledo); Escurial j. b. 2; Escurial T. j. 1. The last two date from the end of the thirteenth century and the notation may be compared with that of Paris, Bibl. Nat. fr. 846. A curious feature of the Toledo MS. is the use of ▪ ♦ instead of the more customary ⌐ ▪, though the ordinary ligatures, &c., are employed.

[2] Aubry, *Iter Hispanicum*, p. 46. The words of his example are:

A   Hec est dies quam fecit Dominus,
B { Felix dies et grata,
    { Hec est dies optata,
a   Dies nostri doloris terminus,
A   Hec est dies quam fecit Dominus.

though in Aubry's example the conditions are fulfilled by single
lines, not by stanzas, and the resemblance may only be fortui-
tous. Ex. 21, a carol, illustrates the ordinary form of the
Cántigas:

Ex. 21. [1]

The style of this is not markedly Spanish, and apart from the
form and language it might easily pass unobserved in a collection
of French troubadour songs. The only detail which might be
selected as characteristic is the use of the *plica ascendens* (in this
example on the 'fa-' of 'façamos'), which, though not peculiar
to Spanish song, is of far more frequent occurrence in the *Cántigas*

[1] Madrid, Bibl. Nat. 10069, fo. 146; facsimile in Ribera, *La Música de
las Cántigas*, pt. ii, p. 96.

than in French songs of the same period. Used at the end of a melody (as in Ex. 22) it is definitely a Spanish idiom:

Ex. 22. [1]

(a) Se - nnor en to - ller coi - tas et do - o - res.

(b) se - nner das se - nno - res. [FINE.]

The tendency to seek for origins, a tendency which no con- scientious historian can altogether avoid, has led to some sur- prising theories in the case of the *Cántigas*, none more remark- able than that first propounded by Ribera with a wealth of explanatory detail in *La Música de las Cántigas* (Madrid, 1922) and developed in two volumes of transcriptions of troubadour and trouvère melodies published in 1923 and 1924. He would have us believe that the music of the *Cántigas*, like the folk- songs of Andalucia, is derived from Moorish origins. This is, in fact, nothing more than a revival on a grand scale of the Moorish, Arab, and Mozarabic superstitions which are continually re- peated about Spanish music. However racy and effective the *Cántigas* may be when transcribed as *habaneras* and the like, such transcriptions ignore the notation of the MSS. And the application of the same system to the works of the troubadours, trouvères, and Minnesinger is fantastic to a degree. Every one would readily admit that Spanish art, literature, and music were influenced by the Moors and Arabs. But that is hardly the same

---

[1] Madrid, Bibl. Nat. 10069, fo. 20ᵛ; facsimile in Ribera, *op. cit.*, pt. ii, p. 10. Another version from Escurial j. b. 2, fo. 17ᵛ (facsimile in *Bulletin Hispanique*, Bordeaux, 1911, plate viii), is printed by Trend, *The Music of Spanish History*, p. 206. (a) is the end of the *estrofa*, (b) of the *estribillo*. The exact transcription of the *plica* is always a little doubtful, especially as regards the position of the second note.

thing as pretending that these influences reigned supreme not only in Spain, but throughout Europe.[1]

If we are to look for influences in the *Cántigas*, we must look everywhere. French, Spanish, Moorish song all had their effect on the composers of the time. It is impossible to live in a complex civilization without being affected by a variety of extraneous influences, and it is as false to derive the melodies of the *Cántigas* from Spanish popular songs as it is to stress too closely their affinity with the works of the troubadours. Ex. 23 is in style not unlike the lighter type of French song. But the characteristic *plica ascendens* and the repeated notes betray Spanish influence:

Ex. 23.[2]

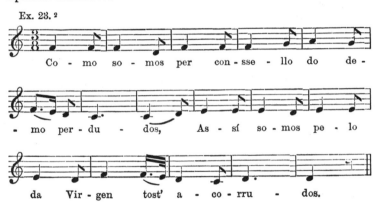

Co - mo so - mos per con - sse - llo do de - mo per - du - dos, As - sí so - mos pe - lo da Vir - gen tost' a - co - rru - dos.

---

[1] The examples from the *Cántigas* given in this chapter are transcribed according to the same plan as those of the troubadours, with the additional help afforded by the notation. If that notation is followed, there are irregularities in the rhythmical scheme which one would not expect from a close adherence to the rhythmic modes (e.g. Ex. 21). But these irregularities are not of any great importance. It is, at any rate, more prudent to follow the notation of the MS., in as far as it indicates the lengths of the notes, than to ignore it in favour of theoretical principles. In some of the songs this method of interpretation seems to conflict with the just accentuation of the words. It has been suggested that in these cases an existing melody has been carelessly fitted to independent words. This is highly improbable.

[2] Escurial T. j. 1, fo. 168^v; facsimile in *Bull. Hisp.*, plate xvi.

Again, in Ex. 24 the *ouvert* ending of the opening phrase, with the *clos* reserved for the final statement, is after the French model:

Ex. 24. [1]

[1] Escurial j.b. 2; facs. in *Bull. Hisp.*, plate x and López Chavarri, *Música Popular Española*, plate iii.

Que en Fran - des a - ques - ta Vir - gen fez,
Por hũ - a do - na que foi hũ - a vez,

A sa ei - gre - ia, d'es - ta que se - ia
No pa - ra - y - so, ú Deus dar qui - so

por nós, et ve - ia mol - a sa faz
go - yo et ri - so a quen lle praz.

D.S.

Moorish influence no doubt made itself felt in the manner of
performance. The beautiful miniatures of Escurial T. j. 1 (reproduced by Ribera) [1] show besides string instruments a very large
number of wind and percussion instruments, many of which are
of Arab origin, and as the bagpipe figures it is possible that some
of the *Cántigas* were sung to a drone bass.

The tonality of the *Cántigas* is more often purely modal than
that of the troubadour and trouvère songs, which often lean
towards modern tonality. The first mode is particularly common, either in its usual form D–D, or transposed G–G with B flat
in the signature. Ex. 22 is in the first mode transposed—in
Escurial j. b. 2 it is untransposed with final D. [2] The first mode
thus transposed is easily interchangeable with the seventh (G–G).
In the following example the refrain and the corresponding
section of the *estrofa* are without B flat, which is added for the
first (independent) part of the *estrofa*. The mode may be considered as the same throughout, with B flat added for the middle

---

[1] Also in Kinsky, *Geschichte der Musik in Bildern* (1929), p. 46, and Grove
(3rd ed.), iv, plate lx.
[2] The *plica* should no doubt be ignored the last time the refrain is sung.

section, or it may be assumed to change from the seventh to the first transposed. Probably no one would have troubled to give a definition. As with the troubadour melodies, the distinctions between the modes were tending to disappear.

Ex. 25. [1]

[1] Escurial T. j. 1; facsimile in *Bull. Hisp.*, plate xvii. Aubry, *Iter Hispanicum*, p. 56 (followed by Trend, *op. cit.*), ignores the flat.

Like the French troubadours, the Spanish school had no real successors. The traditions established by Alfonso were maintained by his grandson Diniz, king of Portugal, but there was little future for monody at a time when the wonders of polyphony had revealed to musicians the undreamt-of and unbounded possibilities of their art. Solo song was carried on in Germany by the later Minnesinger, but elsewhere (apart from popular melody) it tended to disappear in favour of accompanied song, a branch of polyphony (see p. 305). Before we consider the rise and development of this form it will be necessary to refer briefly to a phenomenon in Italy, which though of no outstanding musical importance at the time had a far-reaching effect on Italian music of the sixteenth and seventeenth centuries.

LAUDI SPIRITUALI

In 1260 there arose in Umbria a religious mania of a most fanatical kind. Terrified at the awful results of the bloody wars between Frederick II and the Papacy and anxious to propitiate, as they thought, a wrathful and avenging deity, the people turned to flagellation as a penance for their sins. Young and old, rich and poor, united together in procession and wandered through the country,[1] inflicting on each other the ghastly torments which they considered necessary, and singing as they went. In the south of Italy the movement was checked, but in the north it had more success. Crossing the Alps, it spread over France, Austria, and Germany, and even reached as far as Poland. The mania which had inspired these processions naturally died down in time, but the singing which had been a feature of the penance persisted and was kept up by lay brotherhoods known as *Disciplinati di Gesu Cristo*. Neither brotherhoods nor the singing of Italian hymns were new inventions (they can in fact be traced back to the eleventh century), but it was the

[1] A vivid account is given by a contemporary, quoted by Dent, *Proc. of the Mus. Assoc.*, xliii, p. 65.

outbreak of flagellation and the subsequent reaction which were largely responsible for the widespread popularity of *Laudi spirituali*, as these hymns were called, at the end of the thirteenth century.

The rhythm of the *Laudi spirituali* [1] has more in common with plainsong than with the measured music of the Middle Ages. They are best left unbarred in modern transcriptions, though most of them can be sung quite easily in a straightforward duple time, e.g. the following:

Ex. 26. [2]

Al - ta tri - ni - ta be - a - ta Da noi sia sem - pre

a - do - ra - ta, Tri - ni - ta . . glo - ri - o - sa,

U - ni - ta ma ra - vil - lio - sa, Tu se man - na

sa - vo - ro - sa, A tutt' or de - si - de - ra - ta.

Many examples are constructed on a similar plan to that of the Spanish *Cántigas* and the French *chansons balladées* (see p. 307), with the *ripresa* (or refrain) coming at the beginning and end and a middle section composed of two *piedi* and a *volta* (correspond-

---

[1] Three MSS. contain the music, the 'Cortona MS.' and Florence, Bibl. Naz. II. i. 122 and 212. There are parallels to the *Laudi* in the German *Geiszlerlieder* and the fourteenth-century Catalan songs in the *Llibre vermell* of Montserrat (facsimiles in *Analecta Montserratensia*, i; see also chap. ii, p. 142).

[2] Florence, Bibl. Naz. II. i. 122; facsimile in Gandolfi, *Illustrazioni di alcuni cimeli, &c.*, nos. v and v *bis*.

ing to the *Stollen* and *Abgesang* of the Minnesinger songs). The
style of the *Laudi* leans toward popular song, even though some
are overladen with decoration in the Florentine manner. In
the sixteenth century this popular tendency makes them indistinguishable from the *villanelle* of the time (see p. 123). Their
importance for the history of music rests on the use to which
they were put. The introduction of antiphonal singing and
dialogue led to the performance of *Divozioni*—miniature dramas
on religious themes. The *Divozione* developed into the *Sacra
Rappresentazione* which flourished at the end of the fifteenth
century, and to the *Sacra Rappresentazione* we owe not only the
Oratorio but also not a few of the elements of Opera as well.

Fourteenth Century—France and Italy

It has already been remarked (p. 303) that the fourteenth
century sees the virtual disappearance of pure monody. Henceforth our chapter forsakes its independent course and merges
into the main stream of musical history. Song becomes polyphonic and as such takes its place among the art-forms discussed
in the earlier part of this volume. We are here concerned not
with the development of the polyphonic style but with the
changes which came about in the conception of melody and the
function of instrumental accompaniment. No change is ever
abrupt, nor must it be supposed that monody came to a sudden
end. The change is in fact more apparent to the historian than
it was in reality. It is in the standardization of accompaniment
that the change really lies, in the substitution of a carefully
composed instrumental background for the improvisations of
the *jongleurs*. This development is naturally a gradual process,
and in the early part of the fourteenth century there are still to
be found a quantity of examples of solo song without written
accompaniment.[1] Many of these are preserved in the 'Roman

---

[1] For German solo songs of the fourteenth–fifteenth centuries see pp. 327
and foll.

de Fauvel' (Paris, Bibl. Nat. fr. 146), from which an example of a *rondeau* has already been quoted (Ex. 6). The same MS. also includes the works of Jean de Lescurel—*chansons* and *rondeaux* for unaccompanied solo voice, with the exception of the first, which is in three parts.[1] These, like the songs in the 'Roman de Fauvel', are written in mensural notation, so that from this point, as far as French song is concerned, we escape the ambiguities and difficulties of the troubadour melodies. The following is a specimen of Lescurel's songs:—

Ex. 27. [2]

A - mour, vou - lés vous a - cor - der
Que je mui - re pour bien a - mer?

Vo vou - loir m'es - teut a - gré - er, Mou -

- rir . . ne puis plus dou - ce - ment. Vrai - ɔ -

- ment, A - mours, fa - ciez vous - tre . . ta - lent.

---

[1] It is not impossible that all these pieces were originally for three voices, but that only one part has been preserved. For the other songs by Lescurel in this MS. see Gennrich, *Rondeaux, Virelais und Balladen*, i.

[2] Paris, Bibl. Nat. fr. 146, fo. 57; facsimile in Aubry, *Les plus anciens monuments, &c.*, plate xx. In bar 11 the first two notes (A G) are written ♩ in the MS., an obvious error for ♩ .

This exhibits no striking differences from the later trouvère songs. The use of the first rhythmic mode throughout and the repetition of the first line are both characteristic of the earlier melodies. There is, however, a subtlety in the melodic construction, which is less noticeable in the works of the trouvères. Thus the music of 'agréer' is a repetition of the music of 'vouloir' with just that necessary adjustment which gives finality to the phrase. To make room for the C on '-er' the notes D C B are pushed back so that the crotchet D in the 'vouloir' group has this time to be omitted. The shape of the phrase is still further carried on in the next line ('Mourir ne puis'). The same device is found in the *Cántigas*, e.g. in the *estrofa* of 'O que pola Virgen leixa' (Ex. 25), and indeed occurs in a simple form in some of the trouvère melodies, but less consciously than here.

With Guillaume de Machault (*c.* 1300–77), who like Adam de la Hale was more celebrated as a purely polyphonic composer, solo song cuts itself off definitely from the trouvères. Machault has been called the last of the trouvères, but the description is quite false. Neither his position in life nor his work qualify him for that title. Between him and the trouvères stands the *Ars Nova* of Philippe de Vitry (see vol. i, chap. vii), which liberated music from many of the crippling conventions which it had hitherto endured. The old rhythmic formulas disappear and a new freedom is born into solo song. The possibility of varying the rhythm in the course of the song offers a priceless opportunity to a man of genius. Machault's work necessarily betrays a slight awkwardness in dealing with the new method, and in some of his songs he is loth to abandon the old conventions. The following *chanson balladée*, a good example of his manner, is written throughout (except in bars 14 and 15) in the second rhythmic mode. The form is identical with that of the thirteenth-century Spanish songs. The latter half of the verse is sung to the same melody as the refrain, which is itself repeated at the end:

Ex. 28.[1]

Hé! da-me de vail-lan - ce, Vos-tre dou-

- ce sam - blan - ce M'a pris sans def-fi - an - ce Mais

au pen-re sans lan - ce M'a na-vré du - re - ment. FINE.

Car vos-tre dous ri - ant vair oueil Et
Et vos-tre gra-ci - eus a - cueil Plein

vos - tre sim - ple chiè - re
de plai - sant ma - niè - re

Ont fait par leur puis - san - ce Que

m'a-mour, m'es-pe - ren - ce, Ma joi - e,

ma plai - sen - ce Et tou - te ma fi - -

- an - ce Maint en vous seu - le - ment. D.S.

¹ Paris, Bibl. Nat. fr. 1584, fo. 482; facsimile in Aubry, *Les plus anciens monuments, &c.*, plate xxi.

In the next example, the first verse of a *lai* from 'Le Remède de Fortune', the rhythms change freely throughout. The tonality approaches the modern G minor:—

Ex. 29. [1]

The complete *lai* has twelve verses and is faithfully modelled on the *lai* type as we know it in the works of the trouvères. Each verse has a different metrical scheme and consequently a different melody, with this exception, that the twelfth verse has the same scheme and the same tune (noted in the MS. a fifth higher) as the first. The other solo pieces in 'Le Remède de Fortune' (the music of which has been published by Ludwig in the second

[1] Paris, Bibl. Nat. fr. 1584, fo. 52, and fr. 9221, fo. 23; facsimiles in Hoepffner's edition of Machault, vol. ii, supplement, p. 25.

volume of Hoepffner's edition) are a *complainte*, a *chanson roial*, and a *chanson balladée* similar in style to Ex. 28.

The importance for the history of song of Machault's works for two or more voices is that the secondary part or parts are in many cases undoubtedly written for instruments. See for example the two-part 'De tout sui si confortée' and the three-part 'De toutes flours' (quoted in vol. i, pp. 247 and 250), not by any means solitary examples. We have in these works the beginnings of instrumental accompaniment as an integral part of an art-form. The technique is hardly yet distinguishable from that of vocal composition, and many of these accompanying parts could be, and doubtless were on occasion, sung. Where words are supplied, the instruments probably accompanied the voices in unison throughout. We do occasionally get glimpses of an instrumental style, as in the following 'Déploration sur la mort de Guillaume de Machault', which dates from the end of the fourteenth century. The words are by Deschamps and the music by F. Andrieu, who, it is supposed, was a pupil of Machault, from the general similarity of style. The words are written only under the upper part, and the bass has every sign of having been deliberately composed for a string instrument:—

Ex. 30. [1]

O   flour . . . . des . . flours .

[1] The original is in the Chantilly MS. 1047, fo. 52 (see vol. i, p. 254). The above is based on the text printed in Droz and Thibault, *Poètes et musiciens du XVᵉ siècle*, p. 17.

A piece of evidence which is still more conclusive (cf. p. 329)
is afforded by one of the French three-part songs in Escurial V.
iii. 24 (fo. 49^v), where the contratenor is marked 'trompette', a
term which is capable of more than one interpretation but which
at any rate suggest that the part was executed on an instrument
of some kind. The song opens thus:—

Ex. 31.[1]

J'ay-me bien ce-lui

CONTRA-
TENOR
TROMPETTE.

TENOR.

qui s'en va.   En pri-ant

[Instr.]

[Instr.]

Dieu   que le con-dui - e

&c.

In the upper part will be noticed an example of an instrumental
interlude, a commonplace in the works of Dufay and his con-

[1] After the copy of the original printed in Aubry, *Iter Hispanicum*, p. 28.
The composer is Pierre Fontaine, a member of the Papal choir (see also
p. 41). The date of the song is early fifteenth century.

temporaries.[1] The instrument employed most probably played throughout the composition, in unison with the voice where there are words in the MS., and alone where the words stop. This practice was still common in the sixteenth century. Its application in fifteenth-century compositions would be easier if the underlaying of the words in the MSS. was always perfect. Unfortunately, in the many cases where the words are copied aimlessly without any regard for their position under the notes to which they are to be sung, it is impossible to be quite certain where the instrumental interludes, if any, begin. What would have been clear to a contemporary familiar with the conventions has become for us a source of much ambiguity.

There are, however, many simple accompanied songs where the voice part is free from excessive elaboration. For all its comparative simplicity there is a certain distinction in the following anonymous song, with its nice handling of rhythmic patterns and the alternation (common enough but always attractive) of 3/4 and 6/8. The last bar but two of the contratenor has the same suggestion of an instrumental style which we noticed in Ex. 30:—

Ex. 32.[2]

---

[1] See also chap. i, p. 41.

[2] Escurial V. iii. 24, fo. 1ᵛ (early fifteenth century); facsimile in Wolf, *Handbuch der Notationskunde,* facing p. 362.

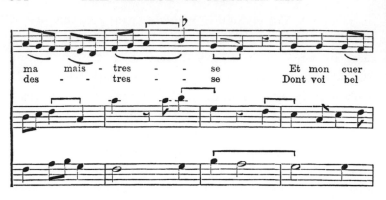

ma   mais - tres - - se   Et mon cuer
des - - tres - - se   Dont voi bel

de - vers   vous . . . .   s'en . . . .   va,
a - cuel   le . . . . .   pri - -

va.   Ain - si que pre - mier   a - ri -

-va   A   l'a - mours   de   vo   ri - ans

yeux   Que   sans . . . ble - chier . . .

moult   me   gre . . . .   Et   me   fist . .

vos - tre   si m'ait   dieux.

This example is not, of course, to be taken as necessarily typical of the French style of the early fifteenth century. At the same time it is noticeable that there is at this time a tendency to write in a simpler fashion and to abandon the long *melismata* which were popular in the fourteenth century. Many of the compositions of Dufay, Binchois, and others are very like the modern part-song—simple pieces harmonized in three or four parts and comparatively innocent of contrapuntal device. The style is polyphonic, but elaboration is avoided as far as possible. The following little piece by Grossim is composed of the simplest elements:—

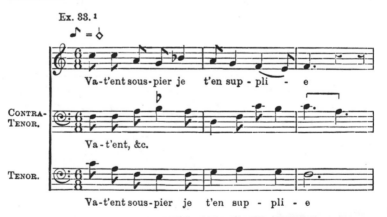

Ex. 33.[1]

Va-t'ent sous-pier je t'en sup - pli - e

CONTRA-TENOR.

Va - t'ent, &c.

TENOR.

Va-t'ent sous-pier je t'en sup - pli - e

[1] Oxford, Bodleian, Canonici misc. 213, fo. 27; facsimile in Stainer, *Dufay and his Contemporaries*, plate iii.

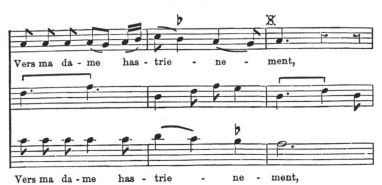

Vers ma da - me has - trie - ne - ment,

Vers ma da - me has - trie - ne - ment,

Et de par moy tres doul - che - ment

Et de par moy tres doul - che - ment

Fay li sa - voir ma ma - la - di - e.

Fay li sa - voir ma ma - la - di - e.

Bar 9 (with the preceding up-beat) is clearly an instrumental interlude, while the last three bars, which cannot conveniently be so divided, are intended to be sung. The tune, as in many of the compositions of this period, is in the tenor and may be a popular song. The use of popular melody is nothing but a continuation of the practice of introducing well-known airs in motets and *rondeaux* in the thirteenth and fourteenth centuries. In the fifteenth century the tenor remains unaltered, and the slight embroidery that is permitted takes effect in the upper parts.

If we are to see to what lengths the desire for embellishment can lead, we must look back to the works of the Italian composers of the fourteenth century.[1] Here is musical expression and imitation in its most abandoned form. Long before the Italian madrigalists were copying nature the Florentine school were indulging their fancy in those very *melismata* and *roulades* whose absence we have been noticing in the later French songs. The bare mention of a bird calls forth the most extravagant elaboration, and the resources of vocal technique are tried to the utmost. Other natural phenomena, together with various expressions of the soul's desire, are translated with an equal regard for faithful and vivid representation. One example is sufficient to illustrate these extravagances, a two-part song by Jacopo da Bologna:

Ex. 84.[2]

[1] See vol. i, pp. 256–68.

[2] Florence, Bibl. Laur. Cim. 87 (fourteenth century); facsimile in Wolf, *Musikalische Schrifttafeln*, nos. 77 and 78. Complete text, with other examples of the same school, in the same author's *Geschichte der Mensural-Notation*, ii, p. 65.

The extended runs and the decoration of phrases are not altogether unexpected in an Italian composition. Vocal expression
always seems to have come naturally to the Italians, and this
same tendency to extravagance is still noticeable at a much later
date in the operas of the eighteenth and nineteenth centuries.
By that time it had left its native confines and conquered the
greater part of Europe, but in the fourteenth century it was still
more or less a purely national disease. Dissatisfaction with
these vocal gambols has led some German historians [1] to suggest
either that the florid passages were intended to be executed on

[1] (a) Riemann in *S.I.M.*, vii, p. 529, and *Handbuch der Musikgeschichte*,
i. 2, p. 316. (b) Schering, *Studien zur Musikgeschichte der Frührenaissance.*

instruments, the simple phrases only being assigned to the voice, or that these compositions are highly decorated organ arrangements of originally simple and unembroidered vocal melodies. Riemann, who is responsible for the first opinion, would rewrite Ex. 34 as bracketed.

This interpretation is tempting enough, but it is open to question how far it is justifiable. The underlaying of the words in the MSS. in which these pieces are found is generally particularly clear and definite, and even where the pieces conclude with *ritornelli*, as many of them do, words are generally supplied. It is also to be remarked that the long runs frequently occur on vowels which are specially suitable for vocal display, such as 'a' or 'o'. The only place in these songs where it is safe to rearrange the words and to allot the music to instruments is at the commencement. The copyist naturally places the first syllable at the very beginning for the sake of his miniature, but in some cases another hand has rewritten the syllable further on, as in the British Museum version of Geradello's 'Tosto che l'alba' (see Ex. 36). Apart from this it is extremely unwise to rearrange these compositions. The florid instrumental style probably developed from the vocal style, just as early string accompaniments appear to be modelled on vocal parts. These runs and triplets for the voice need not dismay us. Their origin may be sought in those 'endless Alleluias' which were the delight of the Church in the eighth and ninth centuries, and from which the prose and sequence were hatched. Florid ornamentation for the voice, so far from being something new or requiring explanation, was in fact almost as ancient as Western European music itself.

Evidence is not wanting, however, of a more sober and restrained style of composition. This may best be seen in some of the works of Francesco Landini (*c.* 1325–97), who was unmistakably influenced by the French school and probably by

Machault in particular. Though Landini also composed pieces in the manner which we have just been discussing, there is nothing of that glittering superficiality in his best works, of which the following ballad is a sample. The extended passage at the end may have been intended to be sung, or possibly the voice should stop on the first beat of bar 20. Here the tenor does not appear to be an originally independent melody. Both contratenor and tenor are without words and are instrumental accompanying parts after the French model:

[1] After Wolf, *Gesch. der Mensural-Notation*, ii, p. 92. Only the first part is here given.

Al　lun - go　so - no　pe - ne-trò nel

co - - - - - - - re . . . . .

Le - gò　me　prese　et　ter - ra　sem -

- -pre　a - mo - - - - - - - -

Among other forms popular at this time was the *caccia* (? = English *catch*), which was written as a canon for two voices over an independent instrumental bass. The theme of these pieces was generally, but not always, the chase, from which they took their name. In one of the more elaborate of these *caccie*—the 'Cacciando per gustar' of Zacharias, who, like Fontaine, was a singer in the Papal choir—a third voice reinforces the instrumental bass from time to time, while the two upper voices continue their canon to the end of the movement.[1] The subject-matter on which this musical fabric is reared is inconsequent enough. A hunter, roaming far and wide in search of treasure, comes upon a wonderful bush, covered with masses of golden flowers in bloom. He is just about to enjoy their fragrance when he is rudely interrupted by market cries of all kinds—'Lobsters, fresh fish, rag and bones, old iron!' The remainder of the song is occupied by the reiteration of these cries and a vivid representation of the bargaining and haggling over prices which

[1] Printed by Wolf in *S.I.M.*, iii, p. 618. The opening is quoted in vol. i, p. 268.

accompanies the sale of the wares. The whole composition is extraordinarily alive, and the settings of the market cries provide an earlier parallel for Janequin's 'Voulez ouyr les cris de Paris' and the similar English settings of Gibbons and Dering.

'Cacciando per gustar' is an exceptional example, and the ordinary *caccia* is less dramatic and to modern taste a little insipid, once the interest aroused by the canon has worn off. Ex. 36 is the beginning of a *caccia* by another Florentine composer—Geradello:

Ex. 36.¹

¹ London, Brit. Mus. Add. MS. 29987, fo. 26.   Wolf in *S.I.M.*, iii, p. 626, prints practically the same text from the Florence and Paris MSS. Another *caccia* in the Brit. Mus. MS. (fo. 41ᵛ) by 'Ser Nicholo del Proposto' is remarkable for the frequency of repeated notes.

del bel gorn' a-pa — — re di-
-sve - glia i chac - ca - tor. Su,
su, su, su ch'e - gli è ten — —
Tos - to che l'al - ba del bel gorn' a -
- po. Al - let - ta li chan; tet -
- pa — — re di - sve - glia i chac - ca -

Both the vocal parts apparently begin with a six-bar instrumental introduction. The canon imposes some strain on the composer's ingenuity, and there is a definite feeling of effort, and occasionally futility, in the supporting instrumental part. The examination of the part-writing of these pieces, however, and indeed the whole subject of the fourteenth-century Italian school, fascinating as it is, lies more without than within the scope of this chapter, which is concerned chiefly with the development of solo song, and only incidentally with the association of two or more voices in parts. In passing we may notice the general attractiveness, superficial though it often is, of the melodies of many of the *caccie*, madrigals, and *ballate* of this period, and regret that their composers were so often induced by inventiveness ill-directed to obscure their original ideas with so much that is merely unnecessary and meaningless. This inventiveness in the upper part of many of the two-part songs leads to a considerable amount of sameness in the lower parts, many of which seem to be compounded of the same obvious formulas. Ascending scales which begin with a repetition of the initial note are common, and the same odd little melodic fragments appear in more than one song. These are the penalties which inventiveness naturally pays. In the more popular style which existed in other countries there is doubtless as much use of *clichés*, but they are less conspicuous because the style of the whole is simpler.

Later Minnesinger and Meistersinger

In Germany the fourteenth century was a time of transition from the Minnesinger to the Meistersinger, from the knightly amateurs to the guild of burghers. We have seen (p. 294) how one of the last of the early Minnesinger, Frauenlob, was responsible for the foundation of a guild of singers at Mainz, and that this example was followed by other towns. In this transition period two names stand out among all this activity on the part of local tradesmen, Hugo von Montfort (1357–1423) and Oswald von Wolkenstein[1] (c. 1377–1445), who were true Minnesinger of noble birth, though they came after the main tide of the Minnesinger movement had passed by. Hugo von Montfort's poems were set to music by Burk Mangolt with a liberal use of introductory *fioriture*, as in the following:

Ex. 37.[2]

[1] Portrait in Kinsky, *Geschichte der Musik in Bildern*, p. 52.
[2] Heidelberg, Univ. Bibl. Pal. germ. 329; facsimile in Wolf, *Musikalische Schrifttafeln*, no. 2.

a - bentz kunst Der nacht wenn sy   her sli - chen

[Instr.]

tut,   3   3   Das ma - chet

als   ir   lieb   ver - nunst   Da - von   so   han   ich

[Instr.]

ho - hen   mut;   Das

ich   ir   gut   solt . .   se - hen   an,   Frowt

[Instr.]

sy   mich nit   die   rain   die   zart,   So

wer   ich   gar   ain   hur - nin   man. . .

* MS. reads

C B C

The transcription of these introductory passages is of necessity conjectural, since the notation of the original is non-mensural.

It is possible that they were sung or played in free time. The initial syllable is in each case placed under the first note of the *melisma*, but it is extremely probable that passages of this kind were instrumental, as definitely instrumental introductions of a similar kind occur in the songs of Oswald von Wolkenstein. In this example the introductory bars seem to be a sort of conventional formula, as there is a very similar passage at the beginning of another of Mangolt's melodies (also a setting of Hugo von Montfort), 'Fraw wilt du wissen':

Ex. 38.

Apart from the problem presented by these *ritornelli*, if they are indeed instrumental,[1] the modal interpretation of these melodies is itself open to some doubt as we are now in a period when the acceptance of the rhythmic modes had ceased to be binding. But as both music and notation copy the methods of the earlier Minnesinger, it is safer to make the transcriptions do the same, even if slight modifications sometimes appear desirable. It is in fact unnecessary to pay too close attention to the precise notation of the smallest details of these melodies. However carefully the conscientious editor may distinguish between ♩♩♩ and ♩♩♩, or ♩ ♪ and ♩. ♩, the practical difference in performance was and will be negligible.

With Oswald von Wolkenstein we are on surer ground. He carries us into the fifteenth century, when the early ambiguities

---

[1] The instrumental accompaniment of these songs is of course well attested. Two songs in Vienna Nationalbibl. 2856, described as 'gut zu blosen', are directed to be accompanied by the *pumhart* (ancestor of the bassoon). In one the instrumental part is written out. It consists mainly of the keynote and fifth. In the other the *pumhart* is to play the keynote (with its octave) throughout. (See Mayer and Rietsch, *Die Mondsee-Wiener Liederhandschrift*, pp. 317 and 321.)

of song-notation had passed away, except among those who, like
the Meistersinger, perversely retained those ambiguities. Like
Guillaume de Machault (see p. 307), Wolkenstein was a composer in the fullest sense as well as a mere song-writer. But
it is with his solo songs that we are here concerned. They are
not all of equal merit. Many of his tunes are bald and gawky
as a result of the very scrappy construction of the words.
The following lacks grace and can only offer as a substitute a
certain rude vigour:

Ex. 39.[1]

[1] Innsbruck MS., fo. 19; facsimile in *Denkmaler der Tonkunst in Österreich*, ix, pt. i, plate vii. Another version with ternary subdivision is in
Vienna, Nationalbibl. 2777, fo. 44; printed by Schatz and Koller, *ibid.*,
no. 68.

Win-der kalt   un - ge - stalt   dein ge - walt   ist ent-spalt
Grü -ner kle   jagt den snee   jar - lang me   in den see

Von den süs-sen lüff - ten.   Liech-ten sum-mer   a - ne kum - mer
Wil-der me - res - flü - te.   Nach - ti - gal - le,   droschel schal - le,

Wil ich tum-mer   als ein frum-mer   Gew-den un - de   güff - ten.
Ler-chen hal - le   uns ge - val - le   Für des o - fens   gü - te.

Those of his melodies which are more pleasing are in style not
unlike the folk-songs of the fifteenth century, of which a large
number have survived in MS. collections such as the *Locheimer
Liederbuch*.[1] They have less in common with the conscious
charm of the best works of the early Minnesinger.

If we turn to the Meistersinger expecting to find a wealth of
delightful melody, we shall be disappointed. They are of comparatively slight importance in the history of song. That
illusions are often harboured about their art is partly due to the
consummate skill with which Wagner in his most human opera
produced so much loveliness from such an unpromising subject.
Their rules, their pedantry, their petty silliness have a fleeting

[1] Published by Arnold in Chrysander's *Jahrbücher für musikalische
Wissenschaft*, vol. ii. One of the songs is by Wolkenstein. The rest are
anonymous *Volkslieder*, some arranged for part-singing. A typical collection of *Spielmann* songs is Vienna, Nationalbibl. 2856 (published by
Mayer and Rietsch). Many of these, e.g. the two-part dialogue entitled 'Ain
enpfahen', are of great charm. Of much the same character are the religious
songs which were popular in the Netherlands in the fifteenth century
(eighty-seven were printed by Bäumker in *Vierteljahrsschrift für Musik-
wissenschaft*, iv, pp. 153 and 287). They dwell mainly on a theme which was
common enough in the homely mysticism of the time—Christ as the
heavenly bridegroom.

interest for the student of social life in the fifteenth century, but for the musician they are more likely to prove a source of irritation than of enlightenment. Their connexion with the Minnesinger is based not only on the foundation of the first guild by Frauenlob but also on their adoption of Minnesinger principles and Minnesinger melodies. The time-honoured system of *Stollen* and *Abgesang* was retained, but instrumental *ritornelli* were abandoned. The Meistersinger composed a certain number of melodies themselves, but a large number were also borrowed from folk-song and from the works of the Minnesinger. Ridiculous names were given to these melodies (which were known as 'tones'[1]) and Minnesinger tunes sometimes appear in very queer and distorted forms. Among the Minnesinger melodies which were appropriated there were four known as *gekrönte Töne* or 'crowned tunes', which were considered the most important. One of these, Müglin's *langer Ton*, is familiar from having been adopted by Wagner:

Ex. 40.[2]

Ge - ne - sis   am neun und zwan - zig - sten uns   be - richt.

The opening may be regarded as a characteristic formula. It appears in melodies by Frauenlob and other Minnesinger (always at the beginning) and in not a few Volkslieder and hymn-tunes, notably 'Wachet auf'.

In spite of their insistence on minute points of detail, the notation of the Meistersinger as exemplified in Adam Puschmann's book[3] is far from clear. These rows of semibreves with

[1] A list is in Staiger, *Benedict von Watt*, pp. 81–107.

[2] From Wagenseil's *Buch von der Meistersinger holdseligen Kunst* (1697).

[3] Puschmann was a pupil of Hans Sachs (see p. 334). His collection, which dates from 1584, is in Breslau, Staatsbibl. 356. Selections have been published by Münzer.

melismata compounded of a huddled crowd of minims do not inspire the reader with confidence.   Still further complications arise from the fact that different scribes had different methods. As in the Minnesinger melodies, the rhythm of the music seems to be dependent on the rhythm of the words.   The words, how- ever, are not regularly constructed and a *Meisterlied* cannot be scanned in the ordinary way.   The accents and stresses change from line to line and from verse to verse in a bewildering fashion. Many of the Meistersinger melodies have a close relation to Gregorian song and may very likely have been sung in free time. Others have more in common with folk-song and fall easily into a humdrum duple rhythm.   But even here a certain licence is necessary where the plain tune has blossomed out into super- fluous ornament (cf. **Ex. 42**).   Sometimes there is the possibility and even the strong suggestion of an alternative rhythm as in the following song, labelled the *kurze Weise* or 'short tune', by Michel Beheim (1416–74):

Ex. 41. [1]

[1] Puschmann's book, nos. 105–6, ii, copied from Heidelberg, Univ. Bibl. 312, fo. 35 (non-mensural notation); printed in duple time by Kühn, *Rhythmik und Melodik Michel Beheims*, p. 156.

Michel Beheim is a late example of a *fahrender Sänger*, a travelling musician who visited courts and noblemen, singing popular songs and among them his own.   He is thus neither a true Minnesinger nor a Meistersinger but a free-lance independent of guilds.   While he preserves the traditions of the Minnesinger he is free of the restrictions which bound their successors. Wagner has given so faithful and life-like a picture of the Meistersinger of Nuremberg at the beginning of the sixteenth century [1] that nothing need be said here of rules and procedure.   It is to be noticed in passing that though secular songs were written the majority were religious or didactic in tone or subject.[2]   The paraphrasing and setting of passages of Scripture was a favourite diversion.   Witness the following version of Romans, chap. v, verses 2–5.   Both words and music are by the celebrated Nuremberg Meister Hans Sachs (1494–1576):

Ex. 42. [3]

Im Rosenton Hans Sachsen.

Das funftt zun Rö - mern aus - er - ko - ren Spricht weil wir
Und thun uns auch der hoff-nung ru-men Der   zu - kunff-

[1] Wagner followed Wagenseil's book, published in 1697, which gives a fairly comprehensive, if diffuse, account of the Meistersinger of the sixteenth century.   See Thompson, *Wagner & Wagenseil* (1927).

[2] Meistersinger melodies were also adapted to sacred songs.   The songs of the Dutch *Rederykers* or 'rhetoricians' (who corresponded to the German Meistersinger) were almost exclusively sacred.

[3] Puschmann's book, fo. 412ᵛ; facsimile in Münzer, facing p. 28.   A curious feature of the notation is the occasional use of a dot to distinguish a radical melody note from its ornamentation, e.g. in this example the notes to 'Durch' in line 4 are written thus in the original:

showing that G A B are unessential notes.

nun ge - recht sint wo — ren, Durch den glau - ben han
- tig herr - li - keit blu — men, Die Gott sol ge - ben

wir da — rumb Fried mitt Gott durch Je - sum Chris - tum, . .
zu der zeit—Nicht a - lein die - ser her - li - keit . .

Durch . . den wir ei - nen zu - gang ha - ben Im glau -
Rü — men wir uns aus die - sen din - gen, Son - dern

- ben zu der gna - den ga - ben. . . . . . .
in trüb - sal zu ver - bring - en . . . . . .

Abgesang.

Weil wir wis - sen aus geis - tes mutt Das trüb - sal ge -

- dult bring - en thutt . . . .

Repeticio des ganzen Stollens.

Gedult aber erfarung bringet,
Erfahrung die hoffnung auffschwinget,
Die niemant wint zu schanden wist
Gottes lieb inn uns gossen ist,
Durch den heyligen Geist im leben
Der uns in unser herz ist geben.

Anno 44. May 20.   H.S.

This exhibits all the normal characteristics of a Meister's song—
the pedantry which includes a reference to the chapter from
which the text is paraphrased, the generally trochaic rhythm,

the repetition of the *Stollen* after the *Abgesang*, and the fondness for little bits of decorative trimming at the end of a phrase.

The Meistersinger undoubtedly had an influence on German art, but how far that influence was artistic may reasonably be doubted. It is more likely that their parochialism helped to foster that intense patriotic passion which finds its most memorable expression in Sachs's address to the masters at the end of *Die Meistersinger*. If the polyphonic composers were affected by external influences, by the music of Italy and the Netherlands, the Meistersinger at any rate were undeniably German, an honest home-grown product, well-meaning and conscientious, but sacrificing inspiration to an over-zealous care for detail and wasting imagination on arid and unprofitable themes.

FIFTEENTH CENTURY—ENGLAND

In England song seems to some extent to have escaped continental influences. The development of polyphony was naturally affected by the works of Machault, the chief exponent of the *Ars Nova*, and there are examples in plenty of motets in the foreign style. But side by side with this imitative work there is much that strikes one as English both in style and in origin. Apart from Dunstable, whose beautiful 'Quam pulcra es'[1] is as melodious and perfect a piece of part-writing as one is likely to find at this period, there are many anonymous compositions of the fifteenth century which seem to have a close connexion with popular song, and in some cases with dance tunes. Songs like 'Ie have so longe kepe schepe' and 'My cares comen ever anew',[2] both of which date from the first quarter of the fifteenth century, not only show traces of having been composed on dance

[1] Printed in Grove (3rd ed.), ii, p. 112.
[2] Stainer, *Early Bodleian Music*, nos. xxi and xxiii. A similar use of repeated notes is found in some of the songs in the Turke MS. (which is of the same period but of less interest), published by L. S. Myers, *Music, Cantilenas, Songs, &c.* (1906).

rhythms, but even suggest (by the use of repeated notes, &c.) that the words were written to be sung to instrumental dance melodies. Many of these pieces, such as the hearty drinking song, 'Tappster, dryngker, fylle another ale',[1] and the Agincourt song, 'Deo gracias anglia'[2] are probably due, in the first place, to popular minstrels, while a more skilled hand has added additional parts. The tune in most of these compositions is in the tenor, as in French contemporary works. It is generally distinguished by being both melodically and rhythmically straightforward, the cadence being formed by the second note of the scale descending to the final, whereas in the upper part the sharpened leading-note—a polyphonic necessity—is habitual. 'Straightforward', indeed, is the epithet which might well be applied generally to these songs, and it is this characteristic which we like to regard, rightly or wrongly, as typically English. The vocal display of the Italians, and the inconsequent flippancy of many French *chansons* are both supposed to be opposed to our national temperament. Technically this straightforwardness is interesting as it often results in melodies which naturally divide themselves into four-bar phrases, as for instance in this little two-part carol:

Ex. 43.[3]

What ty - dynges bryng-est thou, mes - san - ger, Of

[1] Stainer, *op. cit.*, no. xcvi.

[2] *Ibid.*, no. lxvi; see chap. i, p. 6. Another version from the roll in Trinity College, Cambridge, is in Fuller-Maitland, *English Carols of the Fifteenth Century*.

[3] Oxford, Bodleian, Selden B. 26, fo. 15ᵛ (*c.* 1450); facsimile in Stainer, *op. cit.*, no. lxii.   * F in MS.

Cris - tes birthe this ʒe - res day? . .   A

babe   ys   born of   hye   na - ture   Is   prins of

pes   and   euer   shal   be.   Of

This example reminds us that a very large number of these fifteenth-century songs were carols. The word 'carol' does not necessarily imply a Christmas carol, and many May-Day songs might be so called. But even in the restricted sense of Christmas carols there is a rich harvest to be gleaned among these English song MSS. A certain number are in Stainer's *Early Bodleian Music,* and others from a roll in Trinity College, Cambridge, were published by Fuller-Maitland in *English Carols of the Fifteenth Century.* An interesting collection, slightly similar in style, the music of which has not yet been published,[1] is in Brit. Mus. Add. MS. 5665. Slightly earlier is an odd little

---

[1] Apart from some extracts in Stafford Smith's *Musica Antiqua.*

volume (Brit. Mus. Add. MS. 5666) which is said to be in the handwriting of the celebrated Friar John Brakley of Norwich mentioned in the Paston Letters. Whatever the origin of the MS., the fragments of music which it contains are of interest as among the earlier relics of English secular music. Among those which are legible are a two-part carol, 'I saw a swete semly syght', with a refrain, 'Lullay, lullow, lullay', which is not without a certain rough delicacy, and a quaint little piece for one voice, also a carol, consisting of two verses of two lines each, with a refrain:

Ex. 44.

The carols in Brit. Mus. Add. MS. 5665 are of a different quality. They are mostly in two parts with a three-part refrain. Less polished than the songs in the Bodleian MSS., they have none the less a sturdy vigour which seems appropriate to their west-country origin. The tune is sometimes in the tenor, sometimes in the upper part. In the following characteristic example it is in the tenor throughout:

Ex. 45.[1]

[TENOR.]

Have mer - cy of me, Kynge . . .

of . . . blisse, As mu - che as . . . thy .

. . mer - cy . . . . ys . . .

TENOR.

Have mer - cy of me, Kynge . .

[1] Brit. Mus. Add. MS. 5665, fo. 17[v]. The words are printed by Wright in *Specimens of Old English Carols* (Percy Society, vol. iv), p. 55, and by B. Fehr in Herrig's *Archiv für das Studium der neueren Sprachen und Literaturen*, vol. cvi, p. 268.

of . . . blisse,   As   much [-e] as . . . thy .

. . mer - cy . . . . ys . .

Off Ma — ry   Cris - te . .   was   bore

. .   With - ow — te   wem . . . .   of   a - ney .

As in French and Italian songs, there are evidences of instrumental accompaniments and symphonies in these fifteenth-century English songs, and there are several examples of an instrumental *ritornello* neatly rounding off the song after the voice has finished.[1]

---

[1] e.g. 'Now wolde y fayne sum merthis make', in Oxford, Bodleian, Ashmole 191, fo. 191 (c. 1445); facsimile in Stainer, *op. cit.*, no. xxx.

FIFTEENTH CENTURY—FRANCE

To the end of the fifteenth century belong two collections of French songs,[1] apparently for solo voice without accompaniment, but actually, in most cases, melody parts detached from settings for several voices. Several three- and four-part settings of this kind do in fact exist elsewhere in MSS. and later printed collections. In scope these two MSS. are not confined to any one type of song, though it is noticeable that examples of the *rondeau* and *ballade* are rare, and that the *virelai* is particularly common.

The fact of these tunes having been extracted from polyphonic settings detracts but little from their interest, as they are nearly all tenors [2] and so present the melody with the least variation, and that generally at the end of a phrase. If we compare the beautiful melody, 'L'amour de moy si est enclose', as found in these two MSS. with the tenor of two practically identical four-part settings in Paris, Bibl. Nat. fr. 1597, fo. 71ᵛ, and Petrucci's *Harmonice musices odhecaton*, C,[3] fo. 7ᵛ, we find hardly any difference. Indeed the tenor of the four-part setting is a little simpler.

There was nothing new in this use of popular melodies for polyphonic composition, which had been customary from quite early times. The method was now, however, standardized. The piece normally begins with the other voices, which sing either the plain melody with a varied tail-piece or an embroidered version of it. The tune proper enters later, generally in the tenor, but sometimes in the treble, as in Josquin's 'Bergerette savoyenne' (Petrucci, *op. cit.*, A, fo. 12ᵛ). With the adoption of the idea for masses and other church compositions we are not here

[1] Paris, Bibl. Nat. fr. 9346 (the 'Bayeux' MS.), and 12744. The former was published by Gérold in 1921, the latter by Paris and Gevaert in 1875. There are other smaller collections, but they are not of any great importance.
[2] Cf. p. 352.
[3] Venice, 1503–4; a copy is in the Paris Conservatoire, 21775.

concerned, except to remark once again that French taste sees little incongruity in these adaptations. Used as the basis of the polyphonic *chanson*, a popular air of this period takes on a new and delightful character. Nothing could be more captivating than the nonchalant ease with which these tunes are woven into an ingenious polyphonic web by the cleverest composers of the time.

These tunes have more than once been mistakenly attributed to the authors of the four-part settings. Apart from the difficulty which arises when two entirely different tunes bear the same title, it should have been obvious that the basic melody was not the work of the composer, not only on the analogy of the masses on 'L'homme armé', &c., but also from the fact that the same tune occurs in different settings. The reason why the melodies as given in the two MSS. which we are considering are tune parts extracted from polyphonic settings may well be that written copies of the tunes in their original form were not available. The composer of the polyphonic version would introduce the tune as he knew it by ear, and the earnest collector would remove the tune from its setting so that he or others could sing the songs without their polyphonic framework. It is unnecessary to discuss whether these songs were folk-songs or compositions which had become popular. For our purposes there is no distinction to be drawn (cf. pp. 257 and 349). Some of these songs have what is generally termed a 'frankly popular allure', others suggest that they are the work of a skilled musician, and several are cited by Rabelais in *Pantagruel*, v. 33, as being suitable for dancing.

One curious feature of the melodies remains to be noticed. As we have seen, instruments were at this time freely used in supporting the voices in part-songs and in playing little *ritornelli* at the beginning or end of the purely vocal sections, though it is not always very easy to say where these instrumental sections

begin or even where they are necessary. The transcriber of
these MSS., having simply copied the tune as he found it in its
skilled arrangement, naturally copied it faithfully, so that we
have left little odds and ends of instrumental interlude which
have the quaintest air thus removed from their surroundings.
In an example like 'Le poyrier qui charge souvent', there can be
little doubt that the little phrase without words, which occurs
several times, was originally an instrumental interlude:

Ex. 46.[1]

[1] Paris, Bibl. Nat. fr. 9346, fo. 54ᵛ (Gérold, no. liii and facsimile). The
same tune is in fr. 12744, fo. 28ᵛ (Paris and Gevaert, no. 41), with the usual
variants. Some of the tunes in these MSS. are not complete, only the
refrains being given.

Le rous - si - gnol   y est qui

chan - - - - te Et   y prent son es -

- ba - te - ment.

The interest of these songs, some of which still survive in traditional versions, is heightened by their use for some of the earliest *noëls* (or carols) which we possess. In an ugly little MS. of the fifteenth century (Paris, Bibl. Nat. fr. 2506) six out of forty *noëls* have the name of the tune written above the words, and of these tunes three can be traced in the song MSS. One of them, 'Une mousse de Biscaye', is cited by Rabelais. If a tune was used for a *noël*, we can be fairly certain that it was popular at the time, though they are not all easy to trace after the lapse of five centuries. In two black-letter printed collections of *noëls* in the Arsenal Library, Paris,[1] a large number of these tunes are indicated as *timbres*, such as 'Bergerette savoyenne', 'Mon seul plaisir, ma douce joie', 'Que disons nous de ceulx de Saint-Omer?', and many others which survive in these song-books and in four-part or three-part compositions based on the melodies. In spite of the new music-printing which came in with the sixteenth century, it was only rarely that *noëls* were published with their music (apart from four-part settings by Du Caurroy, Costeley, &c.). The habit of printing the *timbre* (or first line of the words of the tune) at the beginning of each

---

[1] B.L. (Rés.) 8013 and 8014.

noël—a habit which derived from very early practice—persisted until modern times and has not yet been abandoned.

POPULAR PART-SONGS

The popular part-music of Italy, Spain, and England in the latter half of the fifteenth and the beginning of the sixteenth century is of a different character from most of the compositions which have hitherto been discussed. Like those compositions, it generally consists of settings for several voices of popular tunes, but all pretence of elaborate contrapuntal ingenuity is thrown aside. All that is aimed at is a simple version in parts of a tune that is already familiar, or an original piece of work in the same style, so that singers may perform them together or one voice may sing them to simple instrumental accompaniment. The difference between these settings and the simple fourteenth-century compositions for voice and instruments is that fifteenth-century part-writing, though it had not attained the complete harmonic ease which was reached after the spread of the *Nuove musiche* in the seventeenth century, nevertheless had in it the beginnings of homophonic composition. The works of Machault and Landini, even when they are composed of the simplest elements, are still polyphonic and hedged about with a certain awkwardness. The works belonging to the turn of the fifteenth century are written with a facility which doubtless owed much to the great polyphonic masters, Josquin and his contemporaries. At the same time as the madrigal was developing, this simpler style was developing too, though the development in the two cases, starting from the same point, lay in almost opposite directions.

The study of song after the troubadours has shown how difficult it is to draw a hard and fast line between what is essentially polyphonic and what is primarily melodic. The same difficulty faces us here. Many early madrigals are so simple as to be indistinguishable from *frottole*, while others are fully as complicated as the *chansons* of the Netherland school. The *frottola*, however, though less obvious than the *villanella*, was, like the Spanish *villancico*, more deliberately popular in appeal than the madrigal. The invention of music-printing which came in with the sixteenth century opened the way for the vulgarization of compositions of this kind. Eleven books of *frottole* were published by Petrucci at the beginning of the century, containing a large number of these pieces, many of which are anonymous. The most usual musical form for the *frottola* is *ab bc ab*, the scheme of the words being *A B A*. But amidst such a host of examples it is naturally not hard to find a number of exceptions to this general formula. Like most music written with a popular intention, very few of these *frottole* retain any interest at the present day. They are more interesting historically as a reaction against the tendencies which were producing the madrigal. The music is generally extremely dull, and the device of repeated notes (which we have already noticed in the fourteenth-century *caccie*) becomes very wearisome. Much the same may be said of the other kindred forms, the *villotte* (of which three books were published by Gardano in the latter half of the sixteenth century), the *villanelle*, the carnival songs, and the *laudi spirituali* (see p. 365). The poetry of these part-songs, like that of the madrigals, was often of a high quality, and Petrarch and Politian were eagerly set.

Similar Spanish songs of the end of the fifteenth century are preserved in the Madrid *Cancionero* (published by Asenjo Barbieri) and the Seville *Cantinelas vulgares*. The same criticism which we have made of the *frottole* is equally applicable to these pieces. Whether arrangements of popular tunes or imitations of the popular style, they are not often convincing. The pretence of artlessness when a competent composer is responsible for it is apt to be unsatisfying. For though we have called these

compositions by the generic term of 'popular part-music', it
must not be supposed that they were popular in the same sense
in which an ordinary folk-tune is popular. They were often the
work of skilled composers (e.g. in Italy, Tromboncino and Heinrich Isaak) who deliberately chose to write in that style. The
songs in the Madrid *Cancionero* appear to be for solo voice with
accompanying instrumental parts, but these additional parts
could equally well be sung. Indeed, this carelessness as to the
manner of performance is conspicuous throughout the sixteenth
century in all branches of composition. Of the composers whose
work is represented in the *Cancionero* the best known is Juan del
Enzina (1469–1534), who, though a priest, devoted himself
entirely to the composition of secular music.[1] Among the
anonymous works may be cited the very expressive 'Yo me
soy la Reina viuda',[2] which is supposed to be sung by the widowed
mother of Queen Isabella. Many are little more than simple
harmonizations of popular tunes, e.g.:

Ex. 47. [3]

[1] Juan del Enzina's very expressive romance on the death of Queen
Isabella (1504)—'Triste España sin ventura'—is printed by Riemann,
Handbuch, ii. 1 (1920), p. 204. For another example see chap. ii, p. 144.
[2] *Cancionero Musical*, no. 324.
[3] *Ibid.*, no. 304; after Asenjo Barbieri.

In England also a number of compositions were written in a style distinct from the polyphonic methods of the Netherland school. Here again these works were produced by skilled composers. William Cornysh (*c.* 1465–1523) was responsible for some elaborate Church compositions in the polyphonic style, but also had the time and inclination to produce a quantity of little part-songs, either settings of popular airs, or pieces in the same manner.[1] These settings, or compositions, are straightforward,

[1] Burney did not know Cornysch's Church music: 'Most of these Musicians seem to have been merely *secular* Composers, as I have met with none of their names, except that of Fayrfax, among those for the Church. Cornyshe, indeed, seems more a secular Composer than the rest ; and, if we may judge of his private character, by the choice of his poetry from Skelton's Ribaldry, he may be supposed a man of no very refined morals, or delicacy of sentiment. His compositions, however, though clumsy and inelegant, if selecting such words be forgiven, are not without variety or ingenuity, for so early a period of Counterpoint. . . . The Music, indeed, of these Ditties, is somewhat uncouth, but it is still better than the poetry.' (ii, p. 551.) Henry VIII himself, a patron of Cornysch, was also a composer. Among his secular compositions the best known is his setting of the ballad 'Pastyme with good companye', printed in Chappell-Wooldridge, vol. i, p. 44 (*q.v.* for contemporary tributes to Henry's gifts).

apart from the songs in the Fayrfax Collection (Brit. Mus. Add.
MS. 5465), which are more in the madrigalian style and introduce a certain amount of imitation.[1] Neither 'Blow thi horne
hunter'[2] nor 'Adew, adew, my hartis lust' (Ex. 48) need much
in the way of commentary. Songs of this kind were known as
'Freemen songs', a corruption of 'three-men songs', meaning
that they were in three parts. If the tune was altered to make it
more suitable for treatment by several voices, it was termed a
'broken plainsong'.

Ex. 48.[3]

A - dew, a - dew,   my har-tis lust,   A - dew,   my joy   and   my   so - lace. Wyth   dow - byl   sor - row com - playn I must   Un - tyl   I   dye, . . .   a - las, a - las.

[1] Two of these are printed in Hawkins, i, pp. 368–72 (1875 ed.).

[2] Printed in Chappell-Wooldridge, p. 40.

[3] Brit. Mus. Add. MS. 31922, fo. 23ᵛ. Of the other composers represented
in this manuscript, Farthing and Cooper are worth mentioning.

It is to be remarked that whereas in the Italian and Spanish part-songs the tune is now in the upper part, in these English songs it is still in the tenor. The word 'tenor' itself has come to have a different meaning. The 'tenor' was originally the lowest of the three vocal parts employed in polyphonic composition, being so called because it 'held' (Lat. *teneo*) the *canto fermo*. The actual voice (or instrument) which performed the part had ordinarily the compass of the modern baritone. The conception of a 'bass' has no place in the polyphonic style, and the 'tenor', though theoretically the lowest part, often crosses the other parts and occasionally becomes the highest of the three. Even when a vocal 'bass' part appears in the compositions of the fifteenth century, it has not yet what might be called the responsibility which belongs to the bass when once the comparatively modern ideas of harmony have become rooted. It has, however, this effect, that the 'tenor' now becomes the middle part in three-part and the third in four-part music, and occasionally, as in Ex. 48, there is a clear feeling for a 'bass' in the modern sense.

Sixteenth Century—Lute Songs and Part-songs

The lute was not by any means a new instrument in the sixteenth century. It is in fact as old as civilization itself and came to Europe from the East. Its name—a corruption of the Arabic *al 'ūd*—indicates its origin. Bearing in mind that Arab influence played a large part (though less than some writers would have us believe) in the formation of Spanish art and civilization, we shall not be surprised to find the Spanish peninsular the most fruitful source from which to draw examples of the new lute-song, an art-form which was widely spread in Italy and France and which eventually reached England at the end of the century. As an accompanying instrument for solo song the lute had been popular as early as the troubadours. It figures in many thirteenth-century miniatures and is frequently mentioned in four-

teenth-century poems. But just as the string accompaniment
was not standardized till the fourteenth century, so it is not till
the opening of the sixteenth century that there is a sufficient
amount of material to enable us to discuss lute music and lute
songs. Lute music appears among the earliest printed music.
As early as 1507 Petrucci had published the first book of the
Intabulatura de Lauto, and two years later followed a collection
of arrangements for voice and lute of four-part songs by Italian
composers. Many *frottole*, including those of Tromboncino, were
arranged and published in this form very soon after their
original publication, and earned a new lease of life. It is unprofitable to discuss which is the earlier art-form, the original
lute-song or the part-song arrangement. It is more than likely
that the idea of arranging part-songs was suggested by the
popularity of original lute-songs which have not survived. The
songs sung by Ugolino in Politian's 'Favola di Orfeo' (*c.* 1480)
may easily have been lute songs of a simple type. At any rate
the craze for lute arrangements spread very rapidly and the
most unlikely compositions were transcribed for this homely
combination.

In addition to the simple transcription of part-music, there
was another method employed by skilled players, which consisted in elaborating the original so as to make it more effective
for the lute. Adrien le Roy's Tutor for the lute [1] which includes
a number of *chansons* transcribed for the lute alone, prints each
example in two forms. The first is straightforward and faithful
to the original, the second is described as 'more finely handled'
and contains a certain amount of virtuoso work of the kind
which competent performers on any instrument have never been
able to resist. There was therefore a definite feeling for the
peculiar genius of the lute side by side with the comparative
carelessness which ignored the obvious unsuitability for tran-

---

[1] An English translation published in 1574 is in the British Museum.

scription of most of the polyphonic music of the period. This comprehension of the possibilities of the lute naturally had more scope in original compositions than in transcriptions, and it is these original compositions which are important in the history of song.

It may appear a contradiction of what was said above (p. 352) to explain that the Spanish lute-songs were not written for the lute but for the *vihuela*. The *vihuela* is, however, nothing more than the Spanish equivalent of the lute, and the style of music written for it is so similar to lute music that it is no grave indiscretion to class both instruments together. The *vihuela de mano*, to give it its full title,[1] was essentially a drawing-room instrument. The instrument of the people was, then as now, the guitar, which had a certain vogue in France and Italy but was nowhere more popular than in Spain. Though the majority of the music which we are now considering was written expressly for the *vihuela*, it can, as it happens, be comfortably performed on the modern guitar owing to the similarity of the tuning.

In 1536 [2] was published at Valencia the *Libro de Musica de vihuela de mano. Intitulado El Maestro* of Luis Milan (*c.* 1500–65). This was one of the many tutors published during the sixteenth century, but unlike many of them it contained a quantity of original compositions. The system of tablature employed by Milan consisted of figures written on the lines of a six-line stave, each line representing one of the strings of the *vihuela*, which was tuned thus:

Ex. 49.

[1] i.e. *vihuela* played by hand. The *vihuela de péndola* was played with a plectrum like the mandoline, and the *vihuela de arco* with a bow like the viol.

[2] The title-page gives 1535, the colophon 1536, so that it must have taken a considerable time to print. The whole work is beautifully executed. A copy is in the British Museum.

Thus a figure 1 on the third line from the bottom would represent
G sharp, a figure 4 on the fifth line G sharp an octave above, and
so on. In Milan's work the first line represents the first string,
but after him the tablature was written the other way up, the
first line standing for the sixth string. The notes to be sung by
the voice were not written in ordinary notation above the
tablature, as was customary later. Instead they were included
in the tablature, but printed in red, so that they stand out clearly
and boldly. This device also gives a very attractive air to the
printed page. The usual practice was to play over the song as it
stood, including the notes in red, to get a general idea of the
effect, and then perform it properly, the voice keeping to the
red notes and the *vihuela* accompanying. It is not clear whether
the red notes should be duplicated in the accompaniment or
not. A good singer would probably prefer that they should not
be included.

Before we go on to consider actual examples of the Spanish
lute song, it may be as well to draw attention to the value of
lute music for the student of the history of music, especially in
solving the eternal problems of *musica ficta*. In music written
in staff notation an accidental was always liable to be omitted,
either through carelessness or because it was supposed (falsely,
as editors have discovered) that no intelligent person would have
any doubt as to which notes should be sharpened or flattened.
In lute tablature, though misprints do sometimes occur, there
is never the same doubt as to whether a note should be F natural
or F sharp. Each note is represented by a separate figure, and
however much an editor's heart may misgive him, he would be
very unwise to attempt to add accidentals in lute music. He
cannot say, 'This figure is 4, but 5 is clearly necessary', because
4 and 5 are typographically not in the least alike and so there
is no justification for correction. In lute music, also, consecutives
are of common occurrence. As they were not adequately sus-

tained, they ceased to be offensive. We gain therefore from lute
music a definite and sometimes surprising idea of the growing
harmonic sense which was developing all through the century,
and which lute music did much to strengthen. In the following
example from Milan's *El Maestro* there are harmonic progressions
which are certainly not unknown in the contemporary polyphonic music, but which strike us more forcibly when set out in
this simple and unpretentious way--tune with accompaniment:

Ex. 50.

Este villancico que se sigue de la manera que aqui esta sonado : el cantor
pue de hazer garganta y la vihuela ha de yr muy a espacio.

A - quel ca - va - lle - ro ma - dre
Su a - mor tan ver - da - de - ro

Que de mi se e - na - mo - ro . .
Me - re - ce que di - ga yo . .

La buelta.

Ma - dre   a - quel   ca - va - lle - ro
Tan - bien   sien - to   sus do - lo - res

Que   va   he - ri - do d'a - mo - res
Por   que   de - llas   mis-mas mue - ro.

[D.S.]

This is typical *villancico* form—*A B a*, and differs little in
style from the earlier four-part *villancicos*. With a little adjustment the *vihuela* part could easily be rewritten for voices. But
as in the other *villancicos* in Milan's book (and the examples in

Le Roy's Tutor) a more elaborate version follows, in which the
player has an opportunity to display his skill:

Ex. 51.

Este mismo villancico de la manera que agora esta sonado : el cantor
ha de cantar muy llano ; y la vihuela ha de yr algo a priessa.

mi se e - na - - mo - - -
ce que di - ga yo . . .

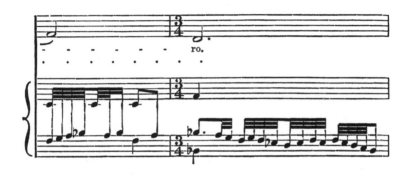

- - - - - - - ro.

Pe - - na el y mue -

[D.S.]

The accompaniments to Milan's romances are written in a similar style. His Portuguese *villancicos* are not strikingly different from the compositions with Spanish words, except that there are examples of a characteristic 6/8 rhythm which is said to recall the rhythm of Galician bagpipe tunes (*ritmo de gaita gallega*). These Portuguese songs were probably written as a compliment to John III of Portugal, to whom *El Maestro* was dedicated.

Those persons who delight to assign parentage would hail Milan as the 'father of Spanish lute-music'. Whether we care to attach this label or not, *El Maestro* is at any rate the first printed collection of lute songs of any importance which we possess, and its value is enhanced by the very thorough instructions given by the author for the playing of the instrument and the performance of the music. There is little that is new in that music beyond a certain harmonic freedom. The method of composition is borrowed from that of the polyphonic *villancicos* and romances, and the only novelty is the variety obtained by writing *bravura* passages for the accompanying instrument. This variety was further exploited by another lutenist, Luis de Narvaez, whose *Seys libros del Delphin de musica* appeared two years after Milan's *El Maestro*. Like Milan, Luis de Narvaez was himself a brilliant performer and is one of those of whom it is related that their playing gave the impression that several voices were singing, so cunningly did they bring out the various contrapuntal parts.

To Narvaez we owe the *diferencia*, the treatment of a theme with variations. The voice repeats the same tune while the *vihuela* varies the accompaniment. Many old ballads and romances, among them the famous 'Conde Claros', were treated in this way by the lutenists of the sixteenth century. A fragment from one of Narvaez's *diferencias* will show the freedom of the accompaniment and give some idea of the agility required by the performer. This style of writing owes little or nothing to vocal technique and is one step further on the road to a conception of vertical harmony based on chords:

Ex. 52. [1]

[1] From 'Con gonzo y tristura' (3rd var.); after Morphy, *Les luthistes espagnols du XVIe siècle*, i, p. 80.

Pieces of the same kind were published by Alonso de Mudarra (including settings of portions of Virgil and Ovid), Enrique Enriquez de Valderrabano, Diego Pisador (including transcriptions of masses by Josquin), and Esteban Daza (including transcriptions of *villancicos* by Vasquez). But the most celebrated of the lutenists after Milan is Miguel de Fuenllana, whose very comprehensive collection of transcriptions and original compositions was published in 1554 with the title *Orphenica Lyra* and a dedication to Philip II of Spain, husband of Mary Tudor. Comic madrigals, Italian *strambotti*, romances, fantasias, all come into Fuenllana's net, and so closely related to part-music are the simpler lute songs of the period that there is no perceptible difference between transcriptions for solo voice and lute of compositions originally written in parts and original lute songs with plain accompaniment. Ex. 53 is an arrangement of a setting of a romance by Morales, no less effective in the new form than in the old. The thirds at the end are even prettier thus than on voices, where the similarity of timbre would tend to make them sound commonplace:

Ex. 53.[1]

De An-te-que-ra sa-le el Mo - ro, De An -

[1] *Orphenica Lyra*, fo. cxlv.

Undoubtedly the easiest pieces to transcribe were those in the so-called 'homophonic' style (though even homophonic music of this time is polyphonic in origin and conception)—plain note-against-note writing. For this reason some of the more straightforward madrigals of composers like Archadelt and Willaert, which are part-songs in all but name, were particularly popular with transcribers. But they also wrestled with the complications of the polyphonic style and transferred to the new medium masses and *chansons* by Josquin and his contemporaries. At the same time as this popularizing of polyphonic music was going on, composers were still writing in the part-song manner, though with the growth of the madrigal on the one hand and of the lute song on the other it was bound to decline in popularity. It should be noted that these compositions were not the work of inferior musicians. In the fifteenth century Heinrich Isaak (*c.* 1450–1517) had composed *villanelle* as well as more serious works, and his example was followed by such well-known composers as Orlandus Lassus (*c.* 1530–94), Orazio Vecchi (1551–1605), Luca Marenzio (*c.* 1560–99), and Hans Leo Hassler (1564–1612). It would not be true to say that compositions of this kind were representative of their authors' work. At the same time they almost always show in themselves that they have been written by men who knew the technique of their art.

The common *villanelle* and *villotte* of the second half of the sixteenth century are so vulgar and tasteless that it is surprising that reputable publishers issued so many. We must suppose that the frequent consecutives, at which contemporary pedants must have been horribly shocked, were not only tolerated by those who sang them, but even enjoyed. The *laudi spirituali* of the time are written in an identical style. Two collections of *laudi* (far different from their fourteenth-century predecessors) were published in the same year at Rome and Venice respectively. They consist for the most part of sacred poems set to popular tunes, which, like the *villanelle*, are fitted with harmonies in the worst possible taste. The words are often parodies of secular songs, and the music is generally in three parts. Of these a writer of the time tells us that fifths were not considered objectionable in this type of composition. In face of this testimony it would perhaps be ungracious to yield further to the temptations of destructive criticism.

German composers not only wrote *villanelle* with Italian words, but also imitated the style in setting verses in their own language. Here a double influence appears, that of the *villanelle* and that of the *Volkslied*, which no true German could avoid. A fair number of pieces in the numerous collections of German songs published in the sixteenth century are definitely polyphonic in style and cannot be discussed here. The most notable of these publications (of which several have been reprinted by Eitner in various volumes of the *Gesellschaft für Musikforschung* series) were Öglin's *Liederbuch* (1512), Heinrich Finck's *Schöne ausserlesene lieder* (1536—his own compositions), and Johannes Ott's two volumes of *Liedlein* (1534 and 1544).

A composer well represented in both the collections published by Ott is Ludwig Senfl (d. *c.* 1555), a Swiss by birth and a pupil of Isaak. His songs are fairly representative of the German homophonic part-song of this time.[1]

The sixteenth century is also a time of great activity on the part of French composers and their publishers. Numerous collections of *chansons* were issued by Attaignant,[2] Susato, and Le Roy and Ballard, containing compositions by Archadelt (*c.* 1514–75), Certon (d. 1572), Clément (d. *c.* 1555), Janequin (d. ?1559), Claudin de Sermisy (*c.* 1490–1562), &c. These are nearly all in the polyphonic style; plain note-against-note pieces are the

---

[1] Other composers who produced part-songs were Matthäus le Maistre (d. *c.* 1577), Antonio Scandello (1517–80), and Jacob Regnart (d. 1600). Regnart should be distinguished from his brother Francis who published a book of settings of poems by Ronsard and his contemporaries. Jacob Regnart is best known from his *Kurtzweilige teutsche Lieder nach Art der Neapolitanen oder welschen Villanellen* (1576–91). In a preface the composer has the decency to apologize for the consecutives which are freely introduced.

[2] A fair selection has been published by Eitner in the *Gesellschaft für Musikforschung* series, Band xxiii (1899).

exception, and when they occur are generally less interesting.[1] These *chansons* are linked up with solo song by the arrangements for voice and lute, which have already been mentioned (p. 365), but, as we have seen, these arrangements themselves are not essentially different in spirit from polyphonic part-music. Printing not only furthered the cause of the skilled composer. It also came to the service of popular melody. In 1576 was published *Le Recueil des plus belles et excellentes chansons en forme de voix de ville, tirées de divers autheurs et Poètes Français, tant anciens que modernes. Auxquelles à esté nouuellement adapté la Musique de leur chant commun, à fin que chacun les puisse chanter en tout endroit qu'il se trouvera, tant de voix que sur les instruments. Par Jean Chardavoine de Beau-fort en Anjou.* This was merely the precursor of a host of similar compilations published by Ballard in the following century. The interest of the volume is that, like many of the Italian collections of *villanelle*, it includes high-class poetry set to popular airs. Among that poetry one is not surprised to find works by Ronsard, who has always appealed to musicians. He had, indeed, an important, though temporary, influence on the composers of his day. Ronsard's ideal, natural enough in the age of humanism, was the perfect union of poetry and music. He was to be the French Pindar. Henceforth music and words would go hand in hand. He would have had more success in realizing this ideal if he had been himself a composer. Heaven, however, had not endowed him with a dual talent, and he had recourse instead to the musicians of his acquaintance. His *Amours* (1552) were published with a musical supplement, containing a small selection of sonnets set in four parts by Goudimel (*c.* 1505–72), Certon, Marc-Antoine Muret, Janequin, and others.[2] These are practically all plain

---

[1] Cf. chap. ii, p. 119.

[2] A copy of this rare work is in the British Museum. The second edition, edited by Muret, does not contain the music. For a modern reprint of the music see *S.I.M.*, iv, pp. 98–128 (supplement to article by Tiersot). For extracts see chap. ii of this volume, p. 120.

note-against-note settings and may well have been arranged
later for voice and lute, as Ronsard often speaks of the lute, and
lute transcriptions were very common at this time. In spite of
ideals, however, the time had not yet come when the subtleties
of poetic rhythm could be successfully translated into song.
For that we must look to the Italian opera composers of the
early part of the seventeenth century. Nor was this aesthetic
wedding likely to be brought about when the same musical
setting, the index of the *Amours* tells us, was to be used for as
many as three, fifty-nine, and even ninety-two different sonnets.

A further attempt to regularize the rhythm of music and
bring it more into accord with the rhythm of the words was
made by Jean-Antoine de Baïf and Thibaut de Courville, who
in 1571 founded the *Académie de musique et de poésie*. The
object of this institution was to put into practice the theory that
French (and Italian) songs should be scanned by quantity in the
same way as Greek and Latin verse. Poetry written in accordance with this principle was known as *vers mesurés à l'antique*,
and examples were already in existence before the foundation
of the Academy. What was new was the application of the
principle to the musical setting. Time, conceived as the regular
succession of notes of the same length grouped into what we now
call bars, was disregarded, and each syllable was set to a note,
proportionate in value to the position of the syllable in the
quantitative scheme. Sometimes the result is not strikingly
different from the regular beat of conventional song, as in the
following example by Jacques Mauduit, where minims represent
longs, and crotchets stand for shorts:

Where the scansion is more complicated, the rhythm becomes much more free:

¹ *Chansonettes mesurées* (1586), no. 4; after Expert, *Les Maîtres musiciens de la Renaissance française*, 10ᵉ livraison, p. 13.

Ex. 55.[1]

[1] *Ibid.*, no. 22; after Expert, *op. cit.*, p. 85. The words of this example are by Baïf.

The system of *chant* and *rechant* was popular with the exponents of the *chanson mesurée*. The *rechant* is the refrain which
precedes each verse (or *chant*) and is sung by itself after the final
verse, something after the fashion of the fourteenth-century
chanson balladée. It may be doubted whether the *chanson
mesurée* would have had much success if it had not been taken
up by men like Mauduit (1557–1627) and Claude le Jeune (1523–
1600). Both these composers produced a number of delightful
compositions in this form, and they were followed by Du Caurroy
and others. The later history of the *air de cour* and its kindred
forms belongs, however, to the seventeenth century. Though it
did not very long survive in the shape of the homophonic part-
song metrically exact and rhythmically free, it laid the foundations of the earliest French operas and may be said to have paved
the way for the French recitative, just as the Italians, working
on somewhat similar though less precise lines, produced the
Italian recitative some years earlier.

English composers of the sixteenth century were on the whole
too occupied in producing masses and madrigals to have much
time to devote to the lighter forms of secular music, unless
indeed a large number of such compositions have perished without leaving any trace. A few songs survive in organ arrangements (without words) in the so-called 'Mulliner Book' (Brit.
Mus. Add. MS. 30513), including the well-known 'In going to
my naked bed' of Richard Edwards (*c.* 1523–66) and one or two

pieces by Thomas Tallis (c. 1505–85), but this is a very small
amount of material to lay beside the mass of true polyphonic
music which was being composed at this time and which gives
this country its surest title to be considered a musical nation.
The part-songs of Thomas Whythorne[1] (1528–c. 1590), published
in 1571, contain a song for solo voice and string accompaniment
—'By new broom'—no new invention, but an early printed
example of the form. Accompanied song was, in fact, becoming
increasingly popular, though it is not till the seventeenth century
that it can be said to have a style of its own. At this time it
differed very little from the madrigal, and the same parts were
written for voices or instruments. In the preface to his *Psalms,
Sonnets and Songs* (1588) Byrd says: 'heere are divers songs,
which being originally made for Instruments to expresse the
harmonie, and one voyce to pronounce the dittie, are now
framed in all parts for voyces to sing the same', and his two
following sets contain examples of the solo song with instrumental accompaniment. There are a few examples of songs with
an accompaniment more definitely instrumental, such as Byrd's
beautiful cradle song, 'My little sweet darlinge', and some of the
songs sung in Elizabethan stage-plays by boy actors, but they
form a very small portion of the vocal music of this period which
has survived.[2] A new style of part-song—the 'fa la' or ballet—
which had been popularized in Italy by Giovanni Gastoldi, was
introduced into England by Thomas Morley (1517–1603), who
followed very closely the Italian model. In this form, which is
free from the vulgarities of the *villanelle*, imitation was employed
in the refrain but not to any extent in the verse. Thomas

[1] It is worth noticing that Whythorne took particular care to insert all
his accidentals and to contradict them where necessary, so that his songs
are of some help in editing the works of others who were less careful.

[2] Examples of accompanied songs of this type are in Brit. Mus. Add.
MSS. 17786–91. Extracts from Elizabethan dramatic songs are printed by
Arkwright, *Musical Antiquary*, i, p. 30, and iv, p. 112.

Weelkes (d. 1623) also published some ballets, but the majority of these are merely madrigals under another name and so not true examples of the form.

If the homophonic part-song was losing its place in the field of secular music, it was none the less firmly established in the offices of the Reformed Church, as the *Choral*, hymn-tune, or metrical psalm. Everywhere where the Reformation had taken root, in Germany, Switzerland, Sweden, England, there had arisen a wealth of sacred song different from anything which the Catholic Church had been able to provide for its devotees. Written by the leading composers of the time—men like Tallis, Goudimel, and Hassler—these hymn-tunes, whether original compositions or harmonizations of melodies already popular, laid the foundations of a tradition of solid and dignified congregational music in the services of the Church. If that tradition has to some extent been lost sight of in this country, it is because we are not conservative enough in things that matter, and while pretending never to lose touch with the past, are in reality like the Athenians, only too ready to welcome any new thing. In the hymn-tune pure note-against-note composition of the highest kind was assured against decay. Not only did it survive, but through the German *Choral* was perfected and beautified by the genius of John Sebastian Bach.

Meanwhile the ever-insistent struggle to preserve melody from the ravages of counterpoint was going on. Hence in Italy we find the new movement which led to the establishment of the modern opera. In England, again, composers turn from the madrigal to the 'ayre', heralded by John Dowland, who published his first collection in 1597. Everywhere initiative and inventiveness were pushing ahead to drive to their ultimate conclusion the lessons which the Renaissance had taught and was still teaching. So we come to the seventeenth century, a time of experiment and earnest endeavour, a time which did not perhaps produce a single really great composer but in which all did their part towards perfecting their art in all its new and ever-wonderful manifestations. Music, a recent writer tells us, does not progress—it only changes. But those changes are not the kaleidoscopic succession of undirected and unco-ordinated impulses. Throughout the history of our art runs the constant desire to catch and preserve in an intelligible form some part of that vision which every musician is bound, if only once, to behold. And no vision is so satisfying, no beauty at once so intelligible and so desirable, as that of the perfect melody which hundreds and thousands of men have aspired to write. The history of song is the story of that endeavour.

CHAPTER VI

INSTRUMENTAL MUSIC

THE history of instrumental music in the Middle Ages is the
most tantalizing of problems. We are overwhelmed with the evidence of its existence. All the other arts bear witness; medieval
literature, painting, and sculpture teem with instruments of
music; Chaucer alone will provide a long list of references, and
any of the great picture-galleries will show a host of lutes,
organs, virginals, recorders; and yet in face of all this we can
only guess vaguely at the nature of the actual music that was
played. Practically nothing has survived in musical notation.
A few fragments here and there are all that we have on which to
base the study of two centuries. Yet, when at last we are able
to see through the mist, we are faced with a well-developed,
independent instrumental style that is obviously no new thing.
The German organ-music of the fifteenth century and the
Italian lute-books of the early sixteenth are evidently the
outcome of a much older tradition, a tradition of extempore
playing that it was not considered necessary to put into
writing. No doubt every master had his own style which he
communicated orally to his pupils, and which they, in their
turn, modified to suit themselves. There was not the same
necessity for writing down music for a single instrument as
there was for vocal music which needed a number of performers,
and it was not until the invention of music-printing gave a new
and commercial impetus that it became necessary to develop a
more definite style and to turn extemporization into musical
composition.

In the case of music for more than one instrument, the viols for instance, the material is just as scant, but for a different reason. The playing or singing of purely contrapuntal music was a matter of indifference. Any voice-part could equally well be played by any instrument with the requisite compass. Purely aesthetic questions of timbre and sonority hardly came into consideration, and it was not until well into the sixteenth century that the two styles, instrumental and vocal, began to take a separate course.

The few glimpses of medieval instrumental music that we are able to obtain are precious, even if the importance of what we find is difficult to assess. One of the oldest documents is a four-teenth-century *chansonnier* in the Bibliothèque Nationale, Paris,[1] in which are a number of *estampies* or dance-tunes of the Troubadour period. These melodies have the characteristic strong rhythms of the Troubadour songs, but their structure is essentially instrumental. Each *estampie* is divided into a number of sections and each section is played twice, first with an 'open' and then with a 'closed' cadence; and furthermore each section ends with the same refrain.

A similar system of repetition with 'open' and 'closed' cadences is to be found in a very important fourteenth-century manuscript known as the Robertsbridge Fragment.[2] This contains in all six pieces which are evidently intended for the organ. The system of notation is much the same as that used by the German organists of the sixteenth century. It is written on one stave, the top voice in notes, the lower in letters. The first three pieces are purely instrumental, the first being incomplete. Each is divided into several sections called *punctus*, a word which survived till the middle of the sixteenth century, for there are several pieces in the Mulliner Organ Book called 'A Point'. These crude pieces have much in common with the style of the

---

[1] Fonds. franç. 844.
[2] Brit. Mus. Add. MS. 28550.

early German organists. Throughout the right hand discants rapidly over the long notes of the bass, though sometimes, but rarely, the two parts move together.

The other three pieces of the Robertsbridge Fragment are transcriptions of motets, two of them taken from the *Roman de Fauvel*. The original motets are in three parts, and these are preserved to some extent in the transcription, the main feature of which is the coloration of the upper voice by splitting it up into notes of smaller value. The following extract is from the second of the three motets—*Tribum quem non abhorruit*.

Ex. 1.[1]

Transcription
(Add. MS. 28550).

Original
(Paris Bibl. Nat. f. fr. 146).

(ru) - e - rit   sci - - - - - - - -

(dic) - ta . . . .

- as   e - - - ti - am

quae . . . .   do - lum

[1] Joh. Wolf, *Geschichte der Mensural-Notation*, Part 3, p. 197.

II   3 C

quid   fruc - tus . . . .

a - cu - - unt . . . .

The original has been transposed a tone higher.

Coloration of the same kind is to be found in a transcription, also for the organ, of a three-part madrigal by Francesco Landino —*Questa Fanciulla*—in a French manuscript in the Bibliothèque Nationale, Paris.[1]   Here the transcription is in two parts, the middle voice being left out altogether.   The coloratura is on the whole more mechanical and rhythmically less interesting than that of the English manuscript.

These few scattered fragments are apparently the only truly instrumental works that have survived in writing from the Middle Ages.   Attempts have been made to trace an instrumental style in the florid Italian madrigals of the *Trecento* and in other music of the same kind, but the matter is by no means clear.   There is more probability in the suggestion that the long-drawn-out tenors of the thirteenth-century motets were played rather than sung, and that the textless introductions and interludes in the music of the Dufay school indicate the presence of instruments either alternating with the voices or playing in unison with them; but, for that matter, there is very little doubt that all through the polyphonic period voices were supported by instruments much more frequently than is generally supposed.

. This material is obviously insufficient for the formation of anything approaching a just estimate of the whole subject, and

---

[1] Fonds, fr., nouv. acq. 6771.

speculation is of very little use without clear confirmation. By piecing together every scrap of obtainable evidence we may arrive at some kind of shadowy conclusion, but no guessing in the world will make up for the disappearance of the music itself. · Our history must begin, therefore, at as early a period as the concrete evidence will allow. In this chapter each of the main countries of Europe is treated separately, a method that appears essential, for in each the values are different. In each there is one particular side of the subject that assumes paramount importance and necessitates a different line of approach. It has unfortunately been impossible to examine the whole mass of existing material, which is scattered among the many European libraries, often in unique examples, but, with one or two exceptions, the most important of these have been accessible. This instrumental music has been undeservedly neglected both by historians and by editors. Much of it is insignificant, but there are also many treasures that deserve a better fate than they have had hitherto.

GERMANY

The earliest signs of an organized school of instrumental composition come from Germany. There have survived several documents, dating from the fifteenth century, which testify to the existence of a highly-developed school of organ-playing at that period, centred apparently round the personality of the blind organist Conrad Paumann. The chief of these are the *Fundamentum Organisandi* (1452) by Paumann himself, which is bound in the same volume as the famous *Locheimer Liederbuch*,[1] and the so-called *Buxheim Organ Book*.[2] The *Fundamentum*, which is the earlier of the two, is divided into

---

[1] Stolberg Lib., Wernigerode. (Codex 3 b 14.)
[2] State Lib., Munich (MS. mus. 3725).

two parts, (i) the *fundamentum* proper, consisting of examples of
free counterpoint on ascending and descending basses, cadence-
formulas, and so on; (ii) a number of organ pieces—arrangements
of melodies mostly taken from the *Locheimer Liederbuch*—and,
at the end, three *preambula* (preambles or preludes). The
arrangement consists in most cases of a free descant according
to the method exemplified in the *fundamentum*, the original
melody being used as *canto fermo*, and sometimes so altered
as to be almost unrecognizable. The arrangement of *Mit gancz-
em Willen wünsch ich dir* illustrates this process admirably.

Ex. 2.
Melody in Locheimer Liederbuch.

Arrangement by Paumann.

Comparison of the original melody with the version used by
Paumann shows what liberties could be taken in altering the
time-values and even the notes themselves; for instance, in the
three bars containing the word *ergeben* Paumann's bass deserts
the original melody altogether, only returning to it at the end
of the phrase.

The *Buxheim Organ Book*, which is evidently a little later in date—about 1470—is a much larger volume, containing some two hundred and fifty pieces as against thirteen in the *Fundamentum*. The connexion between the two MSS. is evident from the fact that the *Buxheim Book* contains no less than four *fundamenta* by Paumann, partly the same as that in the other MS., and several pieces that are common to the two books. A particularly interesting point is that it contains also several arrangements of works by Dunstable (three settings of *O Rosa Bella*), Dufay, and Binchois. Although the technical basis of the two MSS. remains the same, the *Buxheim Book* is in every way a more elaborate production than its predecessor. Apart from its much greater size and wider choice of material, the actual texture of the music is more complex; three-part writing is more common than in the *Fundamentum*, which is mostly in two parts, and the ornamentation is more ingenious. The *fundamenta*, moreover, deal with a more advanced technique. Although the value of these works is historical rather than intrinsic, from that point of view they are of great importance. Not only do they throw light on the practice of an earlier period of which we have no documentary evidence, but they deserve attention as the ancestors of the Chorale Prelude and the Variation-form. The preambles also, slight as they are, are early examples of a free improvisatory form which developed eventually into the Prelude and the Toccata.

More satisfactory from an aesthetic point of view are the dances in the two early song-books, the *Berlin Song Book* [1] and the *Munich (Walther or Schedel) Song Book*.[2] These are scattered about among the vocal compositions, and although they form a very small proportion of the whole (the Berlin book contains thirteen and the Munich book two) they are of great interest.

---

[1] State Lib., Berlin (Mus. MS. 40098).
[2] State Lib., Munich (MS. Mus. 3232).

In form they are not practicable dances but contrapuntal arrangements of dance-tunes, the same tune occurring in more than one setting. They bear curious names, such as *Die Katzen Pfote* (The Cat's Paw), *Der Fochs Schwantz* (The Fox's Tail), *Der Kranich Schnabel* (The Crane's Beak), *Der Pfawen Schwantz* (The Peacock's Tail). This latter, which occurs in three different settings, opens up anew the old question of the origin of the word *pavane*, suggesting that there may after all be something in the discredited notion that it is derived from *pavo* the Latin word for peacock, for it is no great step from *pfawen* to *pavane*, or *pavenne* as Attaignant spells it. Unfortunately, from the three settings which we have here it is impossible to trace the exact form of the original tune, as the time-values seem to have been altered in the process of arrangement.

With the beginning of the sixteenth century we enter upon a new era. The improvement in domestic conditions and the consequent expansion of home life with its festivities and music-making, created a demand which had to be met, while the gradual popularization of printing not only helped to provide the necessary supply, but also affected the nature of that supply in that it encouraged musicians to give a more definite form to their works and to print for the benefit of the world in general what had till then only been communicated orally to their pupils and disciples. Thus there appeared during the first half of the century a number of instruction-books, both theoretical and practical, intended primarily for the use of amateurs. In contrast to the first French and Italian publications of Attaignant and Petrucci, which contain little or no theoretical matter, most of the German books have at least a few pages of instruction for the player.

The earliest of these is Sebastian Virdung's famous *Musica Getutscht* (1511). This is a treatise on instrumental playing, cast, like Galilei's *Fronimo* and Morley's *Introduction*, in the form of a dialogue between master and pupil. It deals first with the various instruments in general use: Clavichord, Virginal, Clavicimbalum, Claviciterium, Vielle (*Lyra*), Lute, Viol (*Gross Geige*), Mandola (*Quintern*), Harp, Dulcimer (*Hackbrett*), Psaltery, Trumpet Marine (*Trumscheit*), Rebec (*Klein Geige*), Shawm, Bumbarde, Tabor (*Schwegel*), Flute (*Zwerchpfeiff*), Recorder, *Ruszpfeiff*, Cromorne (*Krumhorn*), Goat-horn (*Gemsenhorn*), Cornet (*Zincken*), *Platerspiel* (an elementary form of bag-pipe), Bag-pipe, Sackbut (*Busaun*), Military Trumpet (*Felttrumet*), Clarion (*Clareta*), Watchman's Horn (*Thurnerhorn*) '*do mit man den Tag und die Nacht an plaset*', Organ, Positive, Regal, Portative, Cymbals, Bells. Then follow instructions for playing the clavichord, lute, and recorder, which, he says, are sufficient as guides for all the other instruments for ' *was du dann uff der lauten greiffen und zwicken lernest, das hast du leicht uff den harpfen, oder uff dem psalterio oder uff der geigen zu lernen* ' (what you have learnt to play on the lute, you can easily learn also on the harp, psaltery, or viol).

In the following year appeared Arnolt Schlick's *Tabulaturen Etlicher Lobgesang und Lidlein uff die Orgeln und Lauten*,[1] a practical work divided into two parts: the first for the organ, the second for the lute. It is prefaced by a petition from his son, also called Arnolt, begging him to publish his compositions for '*was ist dein kunst, wann niemant weiss was du kanst*' (what is the good of your art if no one knows what you can do). To this Schlick replies in a long *Antwort*, which is really nothing but a violent attack on Virdung, provoked evidently by some rather slighting remarks that Virdung had made in *Musica Getutscht* about Schlick's use of the term *musica ficta* in his *Spiegel der Orgelmacher*, a treatise on organ-building published in the same year, 1511. The first half of the *Tabulaturen Etlicher Lobgesang* contains fourteen compositions for the organ. These are mostly

[1] State Lib., Berlin. Town Lib., Leipzig.

three- or four-part contrapuntal pieces, built on plain-song *canti fermi* (*Salve Regina*, *Ad te clamamus*, &c.), but one or two appear to be ornamented transcriptions of motets. The lute-pieces, on the other hand, are all arrangements of four-part songs from the song-books of Oeglin, Forster, and others. Some of them are arranged for lute and voice, others for lute alone, but the method of arrangement is in every case the same: the original four parts are reduced to three by the omission of the alto part, and in those which are set for lute and voice the voice sings the descant, not the original melody, which is always in the tenor and is left to the lute accompaniment. In the arrangements for lute alone the descant, tenor, and bass remain in their original positions, so that in both cases the principal melody plays a subordinate part. The difference between the organ and lute arrangements can be seen from the two versions of the old hymn *Maria Zart*.

Ex. 3.
Arrangement for Organ.

[Melody in Soprano.]

Arrangement for Lute and Voice.

[Melody in Tenor.]

The arrangement for organ has been transposed a fourth higher.

Schlick says in his preface that he intended to publish another work '*von merern instrumenten und scherffer übung*', and it is a thousand pities that he never did so, for, although the *Tabulaturen Etlicher Lobgesang* shows a decided advance on the achievements of his predecessors, it cannot compare either in technical resource or in diversity of style with the output of the school of the great Viennese organist, Paul Hofhaimer. Although nothing of this was printed, we possess fortunately a number of really representative and carefully-written manuscripts, notably the *Fundamentum* of Hans Buchner of Constance,[1] Leonhard Kleber's organ-book,[2] a short treatise by Oswald Holtzach,[3] and the two volumes copied by Johann Kotter for the humanist, Bonifacius Amerbach of Basle.[4]

Buchner's *Fundamentum* is an exhaustive treatise on organ-playing and composition. The theoretical part is divided into three sections, dealing respectively with fingering and notation,

[1] Univ. Lib., Basle.   [2] State Lib., Berlin.
[3] Univ. Lib., Basle.   [4] Ibid.

arrangement of vocal works, and composition. There follow a number of organ pieces, all founded on sacred *canti fermi,* which are treated in four different fashions: (i) the *canto fermo* in the same voice throughout, (ii) *per mutatio,* the *canto fermo* alternating between the different voices, (iii) the *canto fermo* treated fugally, (iv) free fugal treatment, as in Kleber's *Maria Zart* (see below). Kleber's organ-book, on the other hand, is a purely artistic work. The technical methods are the same as those of Buchner, but there is a much wider choice of material, including several secular melodies and compositions, some of them foreign, and a number of preambles. Here again we have both arrangements and original compositions, the remarkable quality of which may be judged from the following extract from *Maria Zart,* founded on the same melody as that used by Schlick. The words have been added to the *canto fermo* in the bass as a guide to the structure of the piece.

Ex. 4.

[Ma - - - ri - a

zart von ed - ler Art,

Ein   Ros'   ohn'   al   le

Dor - - - - nen

That these books were written essentially for the organ is proved not only by their style but by the specification of certain pieces as *pedaliter* and *manualiter*. Kotter's tablatures, on the other hand, show signs of a distinctive clavier-technique.[1] Besides the usual arrangements of motets and songs they contain a number of dances, whose lively rhythms, frequent repeated

[1] The word *clavier* is used here as the only convenient word embracing harpsichord, virginals, and clavichord.

notes, and harmonic scheme seem to point to the clavier rather than to the organ; this apart from the fact that we know that Amerbach, for whom these books were compiled, possessed and played both the clavichord and the clavicymbal, and that in a later catalogue of his library the bigger of the two MSS. is described as *pro clavicordio*. That the dances were, like those in the *Berlin Song Book*, designed for artistic rather than for practical ends, is evident from the abundant figuration with which they are loaded. The Kotter organ-books contain also several preludes or preambles with various titles—*Prooemium*, *Preludium*, ἀναβολή, *Preambulum*—which all amount to the same thing. Some of them are contrapuntal and more like short fantasias, others are successions of chords bound together by rapid figuration. There is also a *Fantasia*, hardly to be distinguished from the contrapuntal preludes as it develops only one theme.

It is easy to believe that these organ books represent the highest achievements of the school to which they belong, but the same cannot be said of the early German lute-books: Hans Judenkünig's *Utilis et Compendiaria Introductio* (N.D.),[1] and *Ain Schone Kunstliche Underweisung* (1523),[2] Hans Gerle's *Musica Teusch, auf die Instrument der grossen und kleinen Geygen auch Lautten* (1532),[3] and *Tabulatur auff die Laudten* (1533).[4] These are essentially books of instruction for the use of amateurs, and we must beware of attempting to form from them any critical opinion of the artistic level attained by the professional lutenists of that period.

The earliest of these works is Judenkünig's *Utilis et Compendiaria Introductio, qua ut fundamento jacto quam facillime musicum exercitium, instrumentorum et Lutine et quod vulgo Gey-*

---

[1] Royal Lib., Brussels. State Lib., Munich. Nat. Lib., Vienna.
[2] Ibid., and Lib., Brünn.
[3] Brit. Mus., London. Lib., Wolfenbüttel. Second ed. Cons. Lib., Paris.
[4] Heyer Lib., Cologne. State Lib., Berlin. Brit. Mus., London.

gen nominant, addiscitur. . . . There is no date, but it was probably published between 1515 and 1519.   It has a peculiar interest in that it contains *Harmonie super Odis Horatianis secundum
omnia Horatii genera*, a transcription into lute-tablature of the
Horatian Odes composed by Petrus Tritonius for the humanistic
scholar, Conrad Celtis.   These are transcribed after the usual
manner of four-part compositions : only three parts remain, the
alto part being omitted entirely.   The rest of the pieces are of
the most elementary description : two-part transcriptions
(melody and bass) of songs from the collections of Forster,
Oeglin, and others, one *Hoff Dantz*, treated in the same way, and
two three-part arrangements of songs.

Ain Schone Kunstliche Underweisung . . . *leychtlich zu be-
greyffen den rechten grund zu lernen auff der Lautten und Geygen*
shows a technical advance on the earlier book.   The first part
begins with a preface, dealing mainly with the *Applicatz* or
system of left-hand fingering, a matter of great importance in
lute-technique.   After this come six easy pieces in two parts,
then a number of three-part pieces, arranged as groups of exercises for the five *Lagen* or positions of the left hand.   Each group
contains a *Priamell*, and there are four transcriptions of songs
and dances.   The second part, *Das Ander Puechlein*, is entirely
theoretical and is concerned with notation and transcription for
the lute.   The fact that these two books are described as for the
lute or the viols is easily understandable in the light of Virdung's
remark, quoted above, about the similarity of their left-hand
technique: but it only means that their tuning and tablature
were the same.   As regards the right hand, the viols were, of
course, played with a bow, and the lute with the fingers.   It
appears from the end of *Das Ander Puechlein* that Judenkünig
intended to publish another, bigger, book that should be *künstlicher und scherpffer*, but he never did so for he died three years
later, in 1526.

Hans Gerle has a more comprehensive scheme. *Musica Teusch* is divided into five sections, each with rules and examples. The subjects of these are (i) the *Grosse Geygen* or viols, (ii) notation and transcription, (iii) the *Kleine Geygen* or rebecs, (iv) the Lute, (v) transcription into lute-tablature. All the examples for the viols and rebecs are in four parts, in tablature. Most of these are note-for-note transcriptions of four-part songs and dances, but one piece with the title *Das ist ein Fug geen all Stimm auss dem Discant* (this is a fugue; all the voices spring from the descant) is of interest in that it is a strict four-part canon, each voice beginning a fifth below the last.

Ex. 5.

* The clash of E flat against E natural is given as it stands in the original. As the piece is written in tablature, there can be no doubt about the accidentals.

With the exception of two preambles, all the lute pieces are song-arrangements. *Tabulatur auff die Laudten* (1533) is a more purely musical work. The theoretical part consists only of a very short *Underrichtung*, after which comes the music: first five Preambles, then twenty-four *Teutsche Stücklein* followed by eleven *Welsche Stücklein*, and finally nine *Lateinische Stück Psalmen und Muteten*. Here in the *Welsche Stücklein* we find for the first time foreign, in this case French, works grouped together. Judenkünig gives one or two such, notably a *Pavana alla Veneziana* and a *Calata alla Spagnola* taken from Joanambrosio Dalza's *Intabulatura de Lauto*, published by Petrucci in 1508; but here we see for the first time a definite sign of that growing taste for foreign music which was to increase so rapidly during the course of the century. With the exception of the preambles all the pieces in this book are arrangements of vocal works, much more heavily ornamented and more difficult to play than anything in *Musica Teusch*. That even Gerle had to yield to the demand for foreign music is proved by his other two publications, *Musica und Tabulatur auff die Instrument der kleinen und grossen Geygen, auch Lautten* (1546),[1] and *Ein Newes sehr Künstlichs Lautenbuch* (1552).[2] *Musica und Tabulatur* is

[1] Nat. Lib., Vienna. State Lib., Berlin.
[2] State Lib., Berlin. Nat. Lib., Leipzig. Nat. Lib., Vienna.

really a new edition of *Musica Teusch* in so far as the theoretical
part of the work is concerned.   This remains unchanged, but
for the German songs of the earlier edition are substituted transcriptions of French *chansons*, in four parts for the viols and in
three for the lute. *Ein Newes sehr Künstlichs Lautenbuch*, on the
other hand, turns to Italy for its material.   It contains thirty
preambles, and thirty-eight arrangements of dances, chiefly
passamezzos, galliards, and saltarellos, with one or two paduanas
(in triple time), by Joan Maria da Crema, Anthoni Rotta,
Stefano Rosseto, Pietro Paolo Borrono, and others.

Gerle's collections of French and Italian music mark the end
of the old conservative German tradition, the last vestige of the
Middle Ages.   In the lute-books of his successors there is a continual effort to keep up to date, to find new material for transcription. The real prototype of the whole school is Hans Neusidler.   His lute-books are three in number—*Ein Newgeordnet
Künstlich Lautenbuch* (1536),[1] *Ein Newes Lautenbüchlein* (1540),[2]
and the double *Das Erst Buch : Ein Newes Lautenbüchlein—
Das Ander Buch : Ein New Künstlich Lautten Buch für die
anfahrenden Schuler* (1544).[3]   (This last work is not, as might be
imagined from its title, a pastiche of the two earlier books.)
Like the first books of Judenkünig and Gerle, *Ein Newgeordnet
Künstlich Lautenbuch* begins with a short chapter of instructions.
The pieces which complete the first half are graded in difficulty ;
first simple pieces in two parts and three parts with fingering,
then pieces in three parts without fingering.   The second half is
for more advanced players and contains arrangements of all
kinds—*Fantaseyen, Preambeln, Psalmen und Muteten*, including
several by Josquin and Ghiselin.   At the end are a few pieces
mit sonderm Fleis und schönen Laiffen colorirt. Ein Newes Lauten-

[1] State Lib., Berlin. Royal Lib., Brussels. State Lib., Munich, &c.
[2] Nat. Lib., Vienna.
[3] Lib., Karlsruhe. Conservatoire, Paris (1st book only).

büchlein contains no theoretical matter except two short paragraphs about fingering. Like its predecessor, however, it is graded from easy pieces in two parts, *für junge Knaben zu lernen*, to *Welsche Tentz, die sehr gut seind*. The last book, published in 1544, contains two separate books, both graded and containing a large proportion of French and Italian transcriptions, among which are Jannequin's *L'Alouette* and *La Bataille de Marignan*.

The influence of Gerle and Neusidler is evident in the works published by their lesser contemporaries. Rudolf Wyssenbach's *Ein Schön Tabulaturbuch auff die Lauten*, published in 1550,[1] contains a number of *Italianische Dantzlieder*, arranged in groups consisting each of a *Pavana* and three *Spryngerdantz*, and the favourite *Chant des Oiseaux* by Jannequin. The lute-books of Hans Jakob Wecker (1552)[2] and Wolf Heckel (1556)[3] are written, curiously, for two lutes: curiously, because the two lute parts, instead of each being the complement of the other, are so arranged as to be individually complete, a method that leads naturally to a great deal of unison playing. Heckel's book contains a wide selection of German, Latin, French, and Italian transcriptions, and a number of German and other dances. Wecker arranges his dances in the order *passamezzo, saltarello, padoana*. The progress that the technique of transcription had made in a comparatively short space of time is shown in Sebastian Ochsenkhun's *Tabulaturbuch auff die Lauten* (1558).[4] The school of Gerle and Judenkünig adhered rigidly to the traditional method of three-part arrangement, but Ochsenkhun transcribes motets and secular works of four, five, and even six parts, by Josquin, Gregor Petschin, Ludwig Senfl, Arcadelt, Crécquillon, and a number of others.

[1] State Lib., Berlin. Town Lib., Leipzig.
[2] Stolberg Lib., Wernigerode.
[3] Single parts in Berlin, Breslau, and Hamburg. Second ed., 1562, complete in Breslau, Brussels, Dresden, and Vienna. Single part in Berlin.
[4] Brit. Mus., London.

The change that German music underwent during the second half of the century and the widespread influence of Italy and the Netherlands are reflected, as one might expect, in the contemporary lute-tablatures. The most important of these are Bernhard Jobin's *Das Erste Buch Newerlessner Fleissiger ettlicher viel Schöner Lautenstück* (1572)[1] and *Das Ander Buch Newerlessner Künstlicher Lautenstück* (1573);[2] Matthaeus Waissel's *Tabulatura continens insignes et selectissimas quasque Cantiones* (1573),[3] *Tabulatura Allerley Künstlicher Preambuln* (1591),[4] *Lautenbuch* (1592)[5] and *Tabulatura Guter Gemeiner Deudtscher Tentze* (1592);[6] Sixt Kargel's *Novae Elegantissimae Gallicae, item et Italicae Cantilenae Mutetae et Passomezo* (1574)[7] and *Lautenbuch, viler Newerlessner, fleissiger, schöner Lautenstück* (1586);[8] Melchior Neusidler's *Intabolatura di Liuto* (1566)[9] and *Teutsch Lautenbuch* (1574);[10] and Gregor Krengel's *Tabulatura Nova* (1584).[11] Most of these contain transcriptions of motets and madrigals by Lassus, Crécquillon, and others of the Dutch School, together with Italian dances, passamezzos, saltarellos, and so on, while the books of Waissel, Kargel, and Krengel have also a number of *Villanelles* from Jacques Regnart's *Kurtzweilige Teutsche Lieder, zu dreyen Stimmen, nach art der Neapolitanen und Welschen Villanellen* (1576), little three-part songs, whose simple homophonic style and quick tempo made them particularly suitable for literal translation into tablature.

At the same time the style of writing for the lute was chang-

---

[1] State Lib., Berlin. Brit. Mus., London. Nat. Lib., Vienna, &c.
[2] Ibid., except London.
[3] State Lib., Munich. Royal Lib., Brussels. Lib., Wolfenbüttel.
[4] Town Lib., Lübeck. Town Lib., Nuremberg.
[5] State Lib., Berlin. State Lib., Munich, &c.
[6] Lib., Wolfenbüttel.   [7] State Lib., Munich. Lib., Upsala.
[8] State Lib., Berlin. Nat. Lib., Vienna, &c.
[9] Brit. Mus., London. State Lib., Berlin. State Lib., Munich. Lib., Upsala.   [10] State Lib., Munich. Lib., Wolfenbüttel. Lib., Dresden.
[11] State Lib., Munich. Town Lib., Breslau.

ing. The increase of four- and five-part writing in contrast to the earlier rigid tradition of three parts, the transference of the principal voice from the tenor to the treble, and the general quicker tempo, all helped to bring about a style which, while appearing at first sight to be simpler and more chordal than that of the earlier writers, is in reality more complex. For the ornamentation, which served to hide the thin texture of the early style, has given way to a richer, more genuinely contra-puntal style, which perhaps taxes the resources of the instru-ment to the utmost, but which manages nevertheless to keep the separate voices more or less intact.

The highest achievement of the German lutenist school is to be found in a number of anthologies compiled between 1590 and 1625: Adrian Denss's *Florilegium* (1594),[1] Johann Rude's *Flores Musicae* (1600),[2] J. B. Besard's *Thesaurus Harmonicus* (1603)[3] and *Novus Partus* (1617),[4] G. L. Fuhrmann's *Testudo Gallo-Germanica* (1615),[5] Elias Mertel's *Hortus Musicalis Novus* (1615),[6] and J. D. Mylius' *Thesaurus Gratiarum* (1622).[7] In these at last the genuine instrumental forms, apart from dance-movements, appear in something like just proportion, after an almost total eclipse during the preceding fifty years. (Jobin's two books published in 1572 and 1573 contain between them only four fantasias as against eight Italian madrigals, eleven *chansons*, eight *Lieder*, six motets, and fifty-two dances). The proportion of dances is still great even in these later works, but Besard's *Thesaurus Harmonicus* has, at any rate, thirty-seven preludes and forty fantasias, while Mertel's *Hortus Musicalis*

---

[1] Town Lib., Breslau. State Lib., Hamburg. State Lib., Munich. Lib., Wolfenbüttel. Nat. Lib., Vienna.

[2] Town Lib., Breslau. Nat. Lib., Vienna. Lib., Dresden. Lib., Wolfen-büttel.   [3] Brit. Mus., London, and *passim*.

[4] Univ. Lib., Strassburg. State Lib., Munich, &c.

[5] Brit. Mus., London, and *passim*.

[6] Brit. Mus., London. Town Lib., Breslau. Mazarine Lib., Paris.

[7] State Lib., Berlin. Town Lib., Leipzig.

contains nothing but two hundred and thirty-five preludes and one hundred and twenty fantasias and fugues. In the books of Rude, Besard, Fuhrmann, and Mylius, English names appear for the first time, conspicuous among them being that of John Dowland.

An example of the different methods of arrangement adopted by the earlier lutenists can be seen in the versions of *Ach, Elslein, liebes Elslein mein* by Gerle, Neusidler, and Judenkünig. Gerle's arrangement for viols in *Musica Teusch* is in simple four-part harmony, while in *Tabulatur auff die Laudten* the tune is treated fugally and heavily ornamented. Neusidler and Juden-künig, writing for beginners, confine themselves to compara-tively simple ornamentation.

Ex. 6.

1. J. Ott: '121 newe Lieder' (1534).

Ach Els - lein, lieb - es Els - lein mein, wie

2. H. Gerle: 'Musica Teusch' (1532).

3. H. Neusidler: 'Ein Newgeordnet Künstlich Lautenbuch' (1536).

4. H. Judenkünig: 'Ain Schöne Künstliche Underweisung' (1523).

5. Gerle: 'Tabulatur auff die Laudten' (1533).

After the promise shown by the school of Hofhaimer, the key-board music of the second half of the sixteenth century is disappointing indeed. The writers of this period have been nicknamed the 'colourists', and the title is well deserved, as their work consists almost entirely of arrangement and ornamentation of vocal music and dance-tunes. To this school belong Elias Ammerbach (*Orgel oder Instrument Tabulatur*, 1571),[1] Bernhardt Schmid the elder (*Zwey Bücher Einer Neuen Kunstlichen Tabulatur auff Orgel und Instrument*, 1577),[2] Johann

---

[1] Brit. Mus., London. Town Lib., Leipzig. Musikfr., Vienna, &c.
[2] State Lib., Munich. Town Lib., Leipzig. State Lib., Berlin, &c.

Rühling (*Tabulaturbuch Auff Orgeln und Instrument*, 1583),[1] Jacob Paix (*Ein Schön Nutz und Gebreüchlich Orgel Tabulaturbuch*, 1583,[2] *Thesaurus Motetarum*, 1589),[3] Bernhardt Schmid the younger (*Tabulatur Buch*, 1607),[4] Johann Woltz (*Nova Musices Organicae Tabulatura*, 1617),[5] and several others whose works remain in manuscript. These contain large numbers of transcriptions and dances, usually ornamented, but sometimes, as in the case of Woltz's *Nova Musices Organicae Tabulatura*, plain, the ornamentations being left to the taste and discretion of the player. What original organ-music there is in these books is taken chiefly from the works of foreign composers, particularly the Italians, Gabrieli, Merulo, and others. Compared to the output of the preceding period these arrangements are of little intrinsic value. Even the ornamentation, the one sign of independent style, is mechanical and monotonous.

Considering the advance that had been made in the countries under whose influence Germany chiefly came, Italy and the Netherlands, we can only consider the 'colourist' school ridiculously conservative. Considering also the popularity of Dutch and Italian vocal music in Germany, it is rather surprising that until the very end of the century apparently no effort was made to adopt or imitate the foreign styles of instrumental composition. We can perhaps explain this lack of enterprise most easily by saying that the 'colourists' were craftsmen rather than creators, and that the most that they could do by way of innovation was to transfer bodily into German tablature the instrumental works of foreign composers. Naturally enough, when at last a definite step was taken towards a new independent style, it consisted in adopting foreign methods wholesale. The

[1] State Lib., Berlin. State Lib., Munich, &c.
[2] Ibid.
[3] State Lib., Munich.
[4] State Lib., Berlin. State Lib., Munich, &c.
[5] State Lib., Munich. Town Lib., Breslau. Town Lib., Leipzig, &c.

pioneers were Samuel Scheidt in the North and Hans Leo
Hassler in the South. Scheidt, who was a pupil of the Dutch
organist, Sweelinck, published his *Tabulatura Nova* in 1624.[1]
The works of Hassler remained in manuscripts, which have
fortunately survived. Both of these composers show a complete
break with German tradition, in form at any rate. Instead of
arrangements and transcriptions we find fantasias, *ricercari*,
variations, fugues, toccatas, and other independent forms. The
fantasias and fugues of Scheidt show quite clearly his connexion
with his master, Sweelinck; but in other respects he has
a distinct individuality, particularly in his variations, which
resemble those of the English Virginalists. There are several
sets in the *Tabulatura Nova*. The themes are of all kinds, sacred
and secular, including the English tune, *Fortune My Foe*, but
the treatment is usually the same. In each variation the theme
appears whole in one voice or other, usually in long note-values,
but sometimes in dialogue between two voices, and at others
'coloured', that is to say, split up into runs and passages. Round
it is woven a compact web of counterpoint, largely derived from
the theme, and treated with all the usual devices of fugal treatment: imitation, inversion, and so on. These variations, with the
similar 'verses' on the *Magnificat* and other religious themes,
constitute by far the larger proportion of the book. The fantasias are four in number and there are only two fugues. Between these two latter forms it is impossible to draw any real
distinction. The principal theme occurs throughout in both,
while various subsidiary themes are treated contrapuntally in
successive sections. In fact, they have essentially the same
form as the *Ricercare* of Gabrieli, the model used by Hassler.
An interesting comparison can be made between the two fantasias by Scheidt and Hassler on Palestrina's madrigal, *Io son
ferito lasso*. Hassler uses two themes, the first phrase of the

[1] State Lib., Munich. State Lib., Berlin. Nat. Lib., Paris, &c.

madrigal, straightforward and *cancrizans*; Scheidt adds to these a favourite theme of Sweelinck's, the chromatic fourth A, G sharp, G natural, F sharp, F natural, E, descending and ascending, and at the end he brings all four themes together in what he describes as *Concensus et Coagmentatio*. Hassler's *ricercari* are modelled on those of Gabrieli even more closely than the fantasias of Scheidt on those of Sweelinck, but they have nevertheless a character of their own. That they failed to influence the trend of German music as much as might have been expected is due to the overpowering genius of Frescobaldi, the ancestor of J. S. Bach.

If any proof is needed of the vitality of what one may call the German secular tradition at this period, it is to be found in the concerted music. Whatever may have been the origin of music written for single instruments like the lute and organ, there is no doubt that that written for 'consort' was derived from vocal music. In France, Italy, and England, where the contrapuntal forms, the Madrigal and the Motet, held sway, the concerted music developed along the same lines and produced the *Ricercare* and the Fantasia. In Germany the Madrigal was a foreign importation and stood no chance against the indigenous *Tanzlied*, which became the model for the earliest concerted music. In the first half of the seventeenth century vast quantities of dances in four and five parts were published, among which one may look almost in vain for a fantasia or a fugue. But these works are not to be despised because they failed to fulfil a function for which they were never intended. They are symptomatic of one important aspect of the later German Renaissance, of its luxury, its festivities, its shameless, robust joy in life. Although some of the dance-forms are of foreign origin, the music is nevertheless a more characteristically national product than the imitations of foreign models like the *Ricercare* and Fantasia. Some of the tunes, for instance the German and Polish dances in Haussmann's *Venusgarten*, are actual folk-dances, but most of them are the work of German composers, and not transcriptions like the dances in the lute-books.

The multitude of these works prevents any detailed description, but the following names may be mentioned as the most important: Valentin Haussmann, Melchior Franck, J. Chr. Demant, Johann Staden, William Brade, Johann Möller, Thomas Simpson, Johann Schein, Michael Altenburg, Paul Peuerl, Samuel Scheidt. The earliest and one of the most interesting of these is Valentin Haussmann, who published five collections of dances between 1598 and 1604. The first three consist entirely of German and Polish dances. Some are of his own composition, but many are folk-tunes that he had heard played. About half of them have words, but, as he says, these could not be arranged so *zierlich in allen Stimmen* as those that had no text, by which he means that the part-writing for voices must be simpler than that for instruments; but even so he describes the dances in his *Rest von Polnischen und andern Täntzen* (1603)[1] as for the most part simple, and *ohne Fugen*, as is right for viols and other instruments. His other two works are more ambitious: *Neue Intrade* (1604),[2] has, besides nineteen *intrade*, a number of English pavanes and galliards, and a passamezzo with variations and a *represa* in triple rhythm; *Neue Fünff-stimmige Paduane und Galliarde* (1604)[3] contains pavanes and galliards of five parts, and two so-called fugues, which are really fantasias. The second of these takes its themes from one of the pavanes, which bears a strong resemblance to the familiar English tune *Rowland*, or *Lord Willoughby's Welcome Home*. Melchior Franck, a little later than Haussmann, produced as many as eleven books,

---

[1] Rudolfina Lib., Liegnitz. Town Lib., Danzig. Town Lib., Hamburg. Gymnasial Lib., Brieg.
[2] Rudolfina Lib., Liegnitz. Town Lib., Danzig. State Lib., Berlin (incompl.). Gymnasial Lib., Brieg. Town Lib., Bautzen.
[3] Leignitz. Danzig. Bautzen. Town Lib., Hamburg.

not all of which have survived complete. They present a very similar picture to that of Haussmann: pavanes, galliards, *intrade*, and German dances of four and five parts, with one *canzon à* 8.

These two composers with their contemporaries, Demant, Ghro, Fritsch, Staden, Mercker, and Möller are German to the core, but even here the foreigner could not be kept out. Two Englishmen, Thomas Simpson and William Brade, published several works containing not only their own compositions but those of other English musicians such as Dowland, Phillips, Johnson, Farmer, and Tomkins; and with these foreign names came also foreign dance-forms. But the most important of these came, as they did also to England, from France. Michael Praetorius in the preface to his *Terpsichore* (1612),[1] one of a series of works bearing the names of the Muses, says that many of the tunes which he has arranged were communicated to him by Anthoine Emeraud, the French dancing-master of the Duke Friedrich Ulrich of Brunswick and others were composed by another Frenchman, Francisque Caroubel. The dances in question are *branles*, *courantes*, *voltes*, *ballets*, and the already familiar passamezzos and galliards. A summary of this gradual enrichment of the dance *répertoire* is to be seen in an anthology such as Thomas Simpson's *Taffel Consort* (1621),[2] where the following titles occur: *Paduan*, *Intrada*, *Aria*, *Courant*, *Ballet*, *Volta*, *Mascarada*, *Capricio*, *Allmande*, *Ricercar*, and *Canzon*. Here we have the component parts of the Suite, and it is rather curious that the one man who had the originality not only to organize a regular sequence of dances but also to connect them thematically, should have had so little influence on his contemporaries. Schein's *Banchetto Musicale*, published in 1617,[3]

---

[1] Town Lib., Hamburg.
[2] Bass Part: Brit. Mus., London. Other parts: Lib., Wolfenbüttel.
[3] Lib., Kassel.

contains twenty suites of *paduan, galliard, courante, allemande,* and *tripla,* many of them, but not all, derived from one single melody. The following extract will prove this:—

Ex. 7.

But in spite of this it was not till the end of the century that the Suite became an accepted form. In this earlier period, apart from Schein's work, the idea of thematic connexion is confined to occasional pairs, pavane and galliard for instance, which is only an extension, after all, of the much older scheme of *Tantz* and *Nachtanz*.

As to the instruments by which these dances were to be played, the title-pages are more or less unanimous. They are suitable for all kinds of consorts, but particularly for the viols. There are a few curiosities like the *intrada* and *pavane* for four cromornes in Schein's book, but such cases of exact 'casting' are extremely rare. The first sign of the figured bass occurs in Simpson's *Taffel Consort . . . mit vier Stimmen neben einem General Bass*, but though this is the first time that a separate *continuo* part was printed, there is no reason to suppose that up to that date lutes and keyboard instruments were rigidly excluded from the consort because their use was not stipulated in print. In fact, the pictures of musical gatherings on many title-pages and elsewhere show such a mixed collection of instruments playing together that one may well suppose that any and every kind of combination was used, according to the available material.

If we feel bound to deny to this comparatively simple music the intellectual depth and aesthetic beauty of the Italian and English consort schools, we must realize nevertheless that it had its function to fulfil, and that it played a definite part in the cultural advance of the German people. It was meant first and foremost for the many festivities both of public and private life, for banquets at Court, and for wedding parties at home; but it played also a less pompous part in all those private music-makings, which were the foundation of that sturdy musical tradition, which produced in course of time the great German classical composers.

ITALY

The kindly fate which has saved for us so much of the early German organ music deserts us altogether when we turn our attention to Italy. The earliest documents date from the beginning of the sixteenth century, and of their ancestry we know, frankly, nothing. And yet in the two preceding centuries Italian music flourished exceedingly. Much of the vocal music of that period has survived, but we read also of the great Florentine organists, Francesco Landino— ' *nel suo tempo niuno fu migliore modulatore de' dolcissimi canti, d'ogni strumento sonatore e massimamente d'organi*'[1] (in his day none was a better maker of sweet songs, or player of every kind of instrument, and, above all, of the organ)—and Antonio Squarcialupi, '*organa qui docuit doctius arte loqui*'.[2] This absence of documents is all the more exasperating

---

[1] See G. Carducci, *Musica e Poesia nel Secolo XIV* (*Opere*, vol. viii, p. 312).
[2] From an inscription in the Squarcialupi MS. at Florence (Pal. 87). See Wolf, *Geschichte der Mensural-Notation*, vol. i, p. 231.

as the Florentine school was bothsecular and indigenous, whereas the Venetian school of the sixteenth century was overshadowed by the religious influence of the Netherlands.

It was only in the second half of the century that secular music began to regain a place of importance. In 1500 its function was humble enough, but still not without a certain vitality inherited from better days. To the Florentine school belonged the *Caccia*, in which street-cries, hunting-calls, the song of the birds, and other sounds of everyday life were reproduced. The Venetians invented the *Frottola*. About this latter form there is at present much misunderstanding. Grove's Dictionary describes it as 'essentially a popular melody or street-song, treated with a certain amount of contrivance'; but that is putting the cart before the horse. The use of popular tunes in the *frottole* is incidental. In essence they were thoroughly sophisticated little songs of no small musical and literary merit, written by cultured men for a cultured audience; and their use of quotations from popular songs is as cynical as their sentiment. In form they are interesting in that they are written mostly in four parts, the soprano part alone to be sung and the others to be played. Transcriptions exist for voice and lute, and for lute alone.

Slight as they are in substance, the *frottole* are historically of great importance. They form a bridge between two great secular schools. At a time when most serious musicians were in the service of the church, the *frottole* not only kept alive an interest in secular music, but they also effected a balance of musical and literary values which was out of the question in setting to music the established texts of the liturgy. It is this intimate connexion between poetry and music that was the basis of the Italian and English madrigal schools, and of the English Air, a direct descendant of the *Frottola*.

The *frottole* were published in large quantities at the beginning of the sixteenth century by Ottaviano dei Petrucci, who had the monopoly of printing *canto figurato* in Venice. From the same source came a series of lute-books, which are the earliest surviving examples of Italian instrumental music. Of these the first two— *Intabulatura de Lauto. Libro Primo—Secondo*[1] (1507) are by Francesco Spinacino; *Libro Terzo* has apparently disappeared; the next, *Libro Quarto—Padoane diverse—Calate a la spagnola— Calate a la taliana* (sic)—*Tastar de corde con li soi recercar drietro—Frottole* (1508)[2] is by Joanambrosio Dalza; and the last is *Tenori e contrabassi intabulati col sopran in canto figurato per cantar e sonar col lauto. Libro Primo* (1509)[3] by Franciscus Bossinensis. Of the identity of the composers nothing is known.

These four volumes give what one may take to be a comprehensive survey of the different instrumental forms of their period. They comprise transcriptions, dances, and fantasias. Almost all of the transcriptions in the books by Spinacino are of works by famous Dutch and Flemish composers, such as Obrecht, Dufay, Binchois, and Okeghem, taken from *Harmonice Musices Odhecaton*, a collection of sacred and secular music, published by Petrucci in 1501. Some of these are set for two lutes, one playing the melody while the other executes rapid ornamental passages over it. The arrangements in *Tenori e contrabassi*, on the other hand, are, like those in Schlick's *Tablaturen Etlicher Lobgesang*, for solo voice and lute.

The dance-forms represented are the *Pavana* (or *Padoana*), the *Saltarello*, the *Piva*, the *Spingardo*, and the *Calata*. Of these the first four fall into suites: *Pavana alla Venetiana—Saltarello— Piva*, and *Pavana alla Ferrarese—Saltarello—Spingardo*. The *Pavana* has already been dealt with in the section on Germany. The *Saltarello* which follows the *Pavana alla Venetiana* is in triple time and has much in common with the *Galliard*; that which follows the *Pavana alla Ferrarese* is in common time. The

---

[1] State Lib., Berlin.   [2] Royal Lib., Brussels. National Lib., Vienna.
[3] Nat. Lib., Paris. Bibl. Columbina, Seville. Nat. Lib., Vienna.

Piva, in quick triple time, derives its name and its character from the bag-pipes. The *Spingardo* is a jig (*spingare* = to jog the feet). Of the *Calata* there are two types, one in common time and the other in triple. It is interesting to note that there are three dances (a *saltarello*, a *piva*, and a *calata*) arranged for two lutes, one lute playing the melody with variations while the other plays a drone bass. These dances occur in Dalza's book only. A few bars from the first suite of *Pavana alla Venetiana*, *Saltarello*, and *Piva* will serve to show their character.

Ex. 8.
Pavana alla Venetiana.   J. Dalza Intabulatura de Lauto. Lib. IV.

Saltarello.

There remain the fantasias or *ricercari*. There are several interpretations of the title *Ricercare*. Grove's Dictionary, referring to Frescobaldi's *ricercari*, gives '*recherchés* or full of *research*', Riemann's Musik-Lexikon 'a seeking and reseeking for the theme (*suchen* [*das Thema*] *immer wieder aufsuchen*)'; but though these apply quite well to the later developments of the form, neither of them describes the *Ricercare* of Spinacino and Dalza. In this case the word probably means a seeking indeed, but for tonality rather than for a theme. These early *ricercari* are nothing but short improvisations without any thematic development, and were evidently intended to be used as preludes to songs or transcriptions. Many of them, indeed, are so described: *Recercare de Tous Biens* and *Recercare a Juli Amours* both occur in the first book of Spinacino as preludes to transcriptions of the chansons *De Tous Biens* and *Juli Amours* from the *Odhecaton*. That this meaning of the title *Ricercare* was generally accepted right through the sixteenth and seventeenth centuries is proved by its use by contemporary authors: '*Io non voglio aver fatto altro di quel che sogliono i sonatori di liuto, un proemio, come dicevano i Greci, o come noi, una ricercàta*',[1] and '*Fece prima una bella Ricercata con le dita, e di poi cominciò a cantare*'.[2] The terms *ricercare* and *ricercata* are interchangeable.

In spite of a certain similarity of function, the Italian *Ricercare* differs from its German equivalent the *Preambel* in the

---

[1] Danielo Bartoli, *Dell' Ultimo e Beato Fine Dell' Uomo.*
[2] Vincenzo Galilei, *Della Musica Antica e Moderna.*

greater conciseness of its form and in the continuity of its
rhythm.   The following example, taken from the first book of
Spinacino, has no real thematic treatment, but the constantly
recurring figure of four quavers gives it a uniformity which is far
removed from the ramblings of the average *preambel*.

Ex. 9.

The *ricercari* that we have considered so far were all written
for the lute, and many others, written later for that instrument,
conform to the same pattern; but as soon as the form was transferred to the organ it began to take on an independence which
led in a very different direction. This new development is first
found in the works of the two Cavazzonis, Marco Antonio the
father and Girolamo the son. The *ricercari* in Marco Antonio
Cavazzoni's *Recerchari, Motetti, Canzoni* (1523) [1] are still free
improvisations, but they are much longer and more rambling in
form than those written for the lute. Far more interesting are
the two books of Girolamo Cavazzoni, published in 1542 and
1543, [2] for here we meet for the first time the classical type of
Ricercare, with several themes treated fugally in succeeding
sections, which are carefully dovetailed into each other. We
know nothing of the younger Cavazzoni except what can be
gathered from the title-pages of his books, and it would be an exaggeration to describe him as the inventor of the fugal *Ricercare*,
which, as we shall see later, is a logical development rather than
an innovation. But, to judge them on their merits, Cavazzoni's
ricercari are a very remarkable achievement. They are beautifully made. They have none of those stimulating asperities
which come from a highly original and searching mind, but they
flow evenly and sweetly along with an occasional phrase of the
greatest poignancy. They are all too long to be reproduced here,
but one particularly beautiful passage must be quoted.

Ex. 10.

[1] Brit. Mus., London.
[2] Liceo Mus., Bologna.

Of the same type are most of the *ricercari* in the two works of
Jacques Buus—*Recercari di M. Jaques Buus . . . da cantare, &
sonare d'organo & altri stromenti. . . . Libro Primo. A quattro
voci . . . 1547* [1] and *Il secondo Libro di Recercari di M. Jaques Buus
. . . (ditto, ditto) . . . 1549.*[2] Except that they are even longer
than those of Cavazzoni, their plan is in most cases the same.
But there is at least one important exception. No. 1 of the first
book has, instead of several themes, one only, which reappears
throughout the piece in various slightly different forms, but
always easily recognizable. The experiment is not a success.
The absence of fresh material produces a monotony which is not
relieved by any great ingenuity in the treatment of the main
theme, and there is very little rhythmical interest.

The real importance of these books by Buus lies in the light
that they throw on instrumental interpretation. There are in
all three books. The two whose titles have been quoted above

---

[1] Liceo Mus., Bologna. State Lib., Munich. Proske Lib., Regensburg.
[2] Brit. Mus., London. Proske Lib., Regensburg.

are both published in separate parts, although they are described as *da cantare, & sonare d'organo & altri stromenti*. That they should be 'apt for the viols and voices' is not surprising, but the mention of the organ is puzzling, as obviously they could only be played on that instrument from a transcription or from memory. But the third book makes the problem clear. Its title is *Intabolatura d'Organo di Recerchari di M. Giaques Buus... Libro Primo* ... 1549,[1] and it contains four *ricercari* from the other books, transcribed specifically for the organ. The transcription is faithfully carried out, but the simple, flowing lines of the original are heavily ornamented in accordance with the prevailing conception of keyboard style. This explains many of the ambiguous descriptions on the title-pages of later works, and we may take it as a general rule that all such music when played on the organ or the virginals was ornamented in this fashion. The first few bars of one of these *ricercari* in both versions will serve to illustrate the process.

Ex. 11.

Il Secondo Libro di Recercari, 1549.

Intabolatura d'organo ... Libro I, 1549.

[1] Brit. Mus., London.

The changing and indefinite character of the *Ricercare* makes it impossible to draw any real line of distinction between it and the Fantasia, another favourite form in the early sixteenth-century lute-books. It appears for the first time in the works of the 'divine' Francesco of Milan, who published a number of lute-books at this period, sometimes independently, and sometimes in collaboration with his disciples, Pietro Paolo Borrono and Perino of Florence. Francesco's Fantasia is constructed more or less on the same plan as the *Ricercare* of the younger Cavazzoni, making allowances for the limitation of his instrument, while his *Ricercare* is of the non-fugal type of Spinacino. The confusion of the two terms is even more evident in another lute-book: *Intabulatura di Lautto, Libro Quarto, de la Messa di Antonio Fevino sopra Ave Maria . . . con alcuni altri suoi recercari accomodati sopra il tuono di detta messa.* (Venice, 1546),[1] by Marchiore de Barberiis of Padua; for the *ricercari* referred to in the title are called *fantasie* in the body of the book. The two titles appear together in *Fantasie, et Recerchari a tre voci, accomodate da cantare et sonare per ogni instrumento,*[2] published in Venice in 1549 by Giuliano Tiburtino of Tievoli. The thirteen *fantasie* which occupy the first section of the book are not fugal, and are evidently intended primarily as singing exercises, for in each part-book the first few notes have their solmization syllables written under them. The middle part of the book consists of madrigals by Baldassare Donato, Cipriano da Rore, and others, and the final section introduces us, by means of eight *ricercari*, to one of the outstanding figures of this period, Adrian Willaert.

Willaert's influence on Italian vocal music has been discussed in another part of this history, and is beyond the scope of this chapter. Unfortunately, we possess too little of his instrumental compositions to estimate with any certainty his position as

---

[1] Brit. Mus., London. Lib., Wolfenbüttel.
[2] Brit. Mus., London.

a pioneer in this field. The *ricercari* published by Tiburtino are the earliest of his works of that type that have survived; but though they are dated 1549, seven years later than those of Cavazzoni, there can be little doubt that it is to Willaert, and to the Flemish school which he represented, that the ancestry of this fugal type of *Ricercare* must be ascribed. It is a direct off-spring of the Motet. A comparison between the extract given below and any of the motets quoted by Professor Wooldridge in this volume, chapter ii, will show quite clearly the close resemblance of the two types. The connexion is still further emphasized by the fact that, as we know from the title-pages, the *Ricercare* was intended alternatively if not primarily to be sung as a *solfeggio*, and that it had to be transcribed and suitably orna-mented when played on the organ. We must therefore regard the fugal *Ricercare* as just as much a foreign importation as the Motet of the school of Josquin.

The only other publication of Willaert that concerns us, apart from a transcription for voice and lute of the madrigals of Verdelot, is a further collection of *ricercari* with the title *Fantasie, Recercari, Contrapunti a tre voci, di M. Adriano & de altri Autori appropriati per cantare et sonare d'ogni sorte di stromenti* [1] (Venice, 1559). It contains nine *ricercari* by Willaert, three by Antonio Barges, one by Girolamo Cavazzoni, and two anonymous; also two *Regina Coeli* by Willaert and his pupil, Cipriano da Rore. There seems to be no particular significance in the triple title *Fantasie, Recercari, Contrapunti*, unless the *contrapunti* are the two *Regina Coeli*. The *fantasie* and *recercari* are of the same type as those in Tiburtino's book, and add nothing to our knowledge of their composers.

Willaert's real importance lies in the fact that he was the founder of the Venetian school. He was appointed organist of St. Mark's in 1527, and became the first of a long line of great

[1] State Lib., Munich.

organists, including Rore, Zarlino, Croce, Donato, Merulo, Gabrieli, and Monteverdi, to mention only the most important. Venice had long been the chief centre of culture in Italy; by the middle of the sixteenth century it had become the most important musical city in Europe. Musicians flocked to it from all sides to hear and to learn, and Sansovino, writing in 1581, was evidently right when he said that it was '*chiarissima & vera cosa, che la Musica ha la sua propria sede in questa città*' (very clear and true, that Music has its very home in this city).[1] Everything was done to foster music both in and out of church. The priests were even forbidden, on penalty of a fine, to interrupt the organist before he had finished playing. This is significant when compared with an amusing statement in Doni's *Trattati della Musica*: '*Spesso è avvenuto a diversi organisti, e de' migliori, che quando invagati soverchio de' loro contrappunti, hanno fatto certe ricercate troppo lunghe, si è dato loro del campanello per farli tacere*' (It has often happened even to the best organists that they have become so absorbed in their counterpoint that they have made their *ricercari* too long, and that the bell has had to be rung to make them stop).

Under these conditions it is not surprising that music flourished and that rapid progress was made both in the development of the old forms and in the invention of new. With this expansion came a fresh point of view. The old principle by which any single part could be played by any instrument with the requisite compass, gave way to a more exact conception of instrumental timbre. Composers began to give precise indications for the interpretation of their works, and, at the same time, to exploit the sonorities and technical possibilities of different instruments. The *Toccata*, the *Canzone*, and the *Sonata* show in their very names a pre-occupation with tone and technique. Much has been made

---

[1] Fr. Sansovino, *Venetia Città Nobilissima et Singolare. Descritta in XIIII Libri, M.D. LXXXI* (Lib. viii, p. 139).

of the curious mixture of instruments in Monteverdi's orchestra, of his scoring and of his use of tone-colour, but his achievements were only the logical result of the experiments of his predecessors, and the instruments which he used so effectively were only the ordinary instruments in everyday use. Viols, organs, harpsichords, wind and brass instruments, were all catered for by the composers of the late sixteenth century, and Monteverdi's triumph lies not so much in his choice and combination of instruments as in the dramatic possibilities that he found in their use.

Claudio Merulo is known, and justly known, as the father of the Toccata; for he was the first to put into shape, or, at any rate, into notation, a style of playing that had till then been left to the taste and discretion of the player. His two books of *Toccate d'Intavolatura*, published in 1598 and 1604[1] at the end of his life, represent presumably the achievement of many previous years of practice and experiment. But though the development of the Toccata as a musical form must be ascribed to him, in actual fact neither the name nor the idea was new. As early as 1508 the title *Tastar de Corde* appears in the lute-book of Dalza, and Toccata is to be found in Casteliono's *Intabolatura de Leuto de diversi autori* (1536).[2] The *Tastar de Corde* is musically quite insignificant. It is only a short succession of chords and scale passages without any intelligible form, and was evidently intended, as the name suggests, to be played as an exercise or a prelude. But still, like the *Touch* which is found in English lute-books, it is a kind of miniature toccata, for both *tastare* and *toccare* mean 'to touch'.

It is a long step from the little *Tastar de Corde* of Dalza to the long, rambling toccatas of Merulo. To modern ears these may

[1] Brit. Mus., London.   State Lib., Berlin.   State Lib., Munich.   Royal Lib., Brussels.   Liceo Mus., Bologna, &c.
[2] Nat. Lib., Vienna.   Nat. Lib., Paris.

sound dry and formless. But, nevertheless, at their best they have a certain sonorous beauty and dignity. They contain all the germs of the greater toccatas of Frescobaldi and Bach: alternations of rapid and slow sections, brilliant ornamentation, occasional melodic beauty, and flowing, if rather monotonous harmony; but, above all things, they are real keyboard music, and one can well imagine the grand effect that they must have made when Merulo played them on the organ of St. Mark's.

A long and exhaustive account of Merulo's style and technique is to be found in *Il Transilvano*, written by his pupil Girolamo Diruta. This work was published in two parts, the first in 1597 [1] (possibly there was an earlier edition in 1593), and the second in 1609.[2] It is a complete treatise in dialogue form on the technique of organ-playing and ornamentation, and of transcription for the organ, as taught and practised by Merulo. It contains also, by way of illustration, a number of toccatas and *ricercari* by the most famous composers of the day: the Gabrielis, Merulo, Luzzaschi, Guami, Banchieri, the author himself, and others. There are many interesting things in it. The directions for a dignified attitude at the organ, the difference in technique between playing the organ and the harpsichord, the exercise of good taste in transcription, and the directions for playing ornaments are indispensable to all who would play the works of Merulo. There are good things, too, among the musical examples. Some of the toccatas, which are little more than studies of velocity, are dull; but others are worthy to rank with Merulo's, particularly one by Luzzasco Luzzaschi, and the *ricercari* are often beautiful. As an antidote Burney's description of the book is worth quoting. 'It contains instructions for playing the organ and other keyed

[1] Brit. Mus., London. Liceo Mus., Bologna. Later eds. passim.
[2] State Lib., Berlin. Lib., Augsburg. Conserv., Paris. Second ed., Wolfenbüttel, Glasgow, Bologna.

instruments, with preludes by most of the celebrated organists of Italy at the time: but in these no keys are used but those of the church, and all the passages consist of running up and down the scale with both hands, alternately, without other intention than to exercise the fingers in the most obvious and vulgar divisions then in use.' 'Divisions' was the English word for *coloratura*.

Among the works of Merulo there exists also a volume with tne title: *Canzoni d'Intavolatura d'Organo di Claudio Merulo da Correggio, a quattro voci, fatte alla Francese* . . . 1592.[1] The *Canzone alla Francese* is an exact parallel to the *Ricercare*, being modelled on the Motet. But while the great virtue of the *Ricercare* lies in the careful manner in which its uniformity is preserved by the careful dovetailing of the sections, the *Canzone* relies for its effect on those very qualities that are so studiously avoided in the other. Sharp contrasts of texture and mood emphasize its secular nature as opposed to the semi-religious character of the *Ricercare*.

Although the instrumental *Canzone*—the *Canzone per Sonar*—belongs to a later generation than the *Ricercare*, its origin is not really any more recent. They both originated in the custom of playing music written for voices, and a glance at the index of the *Odhecaton* will show that the *Chanson* was just as popular at the beginning of the century as the Motet. But long after the *Ricercare* had become an independent instrumental form, the *Canzone* still remained undeveloped. The title is found in Cavazzoni's *Intavolatura, Libro Primo* of 1542 [2]—*Canzone sopra Il et bel et bon* and *Canzone sopra Falt d'Argens*—but these are hardly more than transcriptions, as are also the innumerable *canzoni francesi* to be found in every lute-book published in the middle of the century.

[1] University Lib., Basle.
[2] Liceo Mus., Bologna.

The reason for the sudden popularity of the *Canzone* is due, in part at any rate, to the change that came over the *Chanson* itself. The characteristics which have been described above belong not to the earlier *chansons* of the *Odhecaton*, but to those of the school of Jannequin, whose works first appeared in France in 1529. Twenty-five books of these were published by Attaignant between 1535 and 1549, and they soon found their way into the Italian lute-books. From these came the *Canzoni alla Francese* of which those published by Merulo seem to be the first. Many others are to be found in the works of Adriano Banchieri (the famous author of *L'Organo Suonarino*), Giovanni Cavaccio (organist of Santa Maria Maggiore in Bergamo), Francesco Stivori (a pupil of Merulo), Giuseppe Guami (second organist of St. Mark's from 1588 to 1591), Vincenzo Pellegrini, and Giovanni Trabaci of Naples.

But all these composers are of secondary importance by the side of the one real genius of the period, Giovanni Gabrieli. There were two Gabrielis, who must not be confused. Andrea, the elder, was born in 1510. He was a pupil of Willaert, and succeeded Annibale of Padua at the second organ of St. Mark's in 1556. He died in 1586. The younger, Giovanni, born in 1557, was nephew and pupil of Andrea. He too played the organ in St. Mark's, being appointed successor to Merulo at the first organ in 1584. He died in 1612.

The following is a full list of the instrumental works of the Gabrielis:

1589 *Madrigali et Ricercari di Andrea Gabrieli, a quattro voci.*[1]

1593 *Intonationi d'Organo di Andrea Gabrieli, et di Giovanni suo nepote, . . . Composte sopra tutti li dodeci Toni della Musica.*[2]

---

[1] Univ. Lib., Basle (complete). Separate parts in London, Berlin, Bologna, and Wolfenbüttel.

[2] Univ. Lib., Basle. Liceo Mus., Bologna.

1595 *Ricercari di Andrea Gabrieli, . . . Composti et tabulati per
ogni sorte di Stromenti de Tasti, Libro Secondo.*[1]

1596 *Terzo Libro de Recercari di Andrea Gabrieli, . . . Insieme uno
Motetto, Dui Madrigaletti, & uno Capriccio sopra il Pass' e
mezo Antico, in cinque modi variati, et Tabulati per ogni sorte
di Stromenti da Tasti.*[2]

1597 *Sacrae Symphoniae Ioannis Gabrielii . . . Senis, 7, 8, 10, 12,
14, 15, and 16, Tam vocibus quam Instrumentis.*[3]

1605 *Canzoni alla Francese et Ricercari Ariosi, Tabulate per sonar
sopra Istrumenti da Tasti, dall Eccell. Andrea Gabrieli . . .
Libro quinto.*[4]

1605 *Canzoni alla Francese per sonar sopra istromenti da
tasti, Tabulate dall' Eccellentiss. Andrea Gabrieli . . . Libro
Sesto.*[5]

1615 *Canzoni et Sonate del signor Giovanni Gabrieli, à 3, 5, 6, 7, 8,
10, 12, 14, 15 & 22 voci, per sonar con ogni sorte de Instru-
menti. Con il Basso per l'organo.*[6]

It is noticeable that all these works were published posthumously, except Giovanni's share of *Intonationi d'Organo* (1593)
and *Sacrae Symphoniae* (1597). The latter is the date of the
second edition, the first having been lost.

The elder Gabrieli need not detain us long. In general his
music keeps to the traditional paths. His *ricercari* are mostly
built round a single theme, and his *canzoni alla francese* are
transcriptions of or fantasias on madrigals by Lasso, Jannequin,
and Crécquillon. His music is thoroughly sound and workmanlike, but, however well wrought, it says nothing that had not
been said before.

[1] Ibid.
[2] Ibid.
[3] State Lib., Berlin. Nat. Lib., Vienna. Proske Lib., Regensburg. Incomplete in London and Augsburg.
[4] Lib., Augsburg.
[5] Liceo Mus., Bologna.
[6] Lib., Kassel. State Lib., Berlin (13 pts.). Lib., Augsburg (18 pts.).

With Giovanni Gabrieli we are on new territory, with a completely fresh and objective outlook. The earlier writers wrote in the abstract, without any clear conception of effect or contrast of tone-colour. Giovanni Gabrieli was the first to see some of the possibilities in those enticing but dangerous playthings. He experimented with combinations of instrumental timbres, with contrasts of quality and intensity, and, above all, with the effects produced by two choirs answering one another. In contrast to the contrapuntal complexity of his predecessors, his music is conceived in a simpler, more harmonic idiom, and aims at bold effects rather than delicacy of texture. In fact, he wrote definitely for an audience. Fortunately, his musical genius was sufficient to save him from the obvious pitfalls of such an attitude, and even to justify a course which might well have proved a dead end.

One of the best known of his works is the *Sonata Pian e Forte* from *Sacrae Symphoniae* (1597). This is written for two 'choirs', consisting of a cornetto and three trombones. These answer one another with continual alternation between loud and soft.

Particularly charming is the opening of the *Canzon Primi Toin* from the same source. In this case the instruments are not specified, but they are again divided into two choirs.

Ex. 13.

In *Canzoni et Sonate* (1615) there is a *canzone* à 6 that is exceedingly interesting as an experiment both in form and in
scoring. It is written for two violins, two cornetti, and tenor and
bass trombones, in a form which would be best described as
'verse and refrain'. In the verses the instruments answer one
another, usually in pairs, and in the last verse each instrument
has its own say.

Ex. 14.

The *Canzone* and the *Sonata* are the forms most frequently found in the works of the younger Gabrieli. The *Canzone* has already been dealt with, but the *Sonata* is new. It differs from the *Canzone* in being continuous instead of divided into sections. Like the Toccata it is a true instrumental form—a piece to be played by instruments, just as the Toccata was a piece to be 'touched' on the organ or the harpsichord. It has, of course, no connexion with the classical Sonata, being quite free in form. It was the ideal form for a writer such as Gabrieli, who wished to experiment with sounds rather than with shapes, and, although in his published works the *canzoni* far outnumber the *sonate*, it is in the latter that some of his most original ideas are to be found. The *Sonata Pian e Forte* has already been discussed, but at the end of *Canzoni et Sonate* there is a *Sonata con Tre Violini* which served as a model for many later sonatas. Unfortunately, it is too long to quote here, but it can be found in more than one modern reprint.

After the turn of the century (it must be remembered that Gabrieli's works were written long before they were published) things began to move very quickly. The development of the

Opera, of accompanied song, and of figured bass, mark the beginnings of a new epoch which soon eclipsed the more modest achievements of the preceding century. Among the music that has been discussed in this chapter there is little that can compare with the work of the great masters of the seventeenth and eighteenth centuries, but there are nevertheless a number of things worth rescuing, for their own sakes, from the oblivion into which they have vanished. The exquisite sweetness of Cavazzoni and the vigorous originality of Gabrieli stand out from the rest; but even among the works of the less important composers there are, here and there, real treasures to be discovered.

SPAIN

Until recent years the music of the Spanish School of Lutenists was completely unknown. Their rediscovery is due to the labours of Count Morphy, who devoted a lifetime to their study, and whose great work, *Les Luthistes espagnols du xvie siècle*, was published posthumously in 1902. Another eminent scholar, Felipe Pedrel, rendered the same service to the organist, Antonio de Cabezon, whose entire works he transcribed and published in his *Hispaniae Scholae Musica Sacra*. Through the labours of these men came to light the produce of a whole school of composers, whose music is not only of great importance historically, but also of the finest quality, judged on its own merits.

There are not many books of lute music: Luis Milan's *El Maestro* (1535), Luis de Narvaez's *Los seys libros del Delphin de musica* (1538), Alonso de Mudarra's *Tres Libros de Musica en cifras* (1546), Enrique Enriquez de Valderrabano's *Silva de Sirenas* (1546), Diego Pisador's *Libro de musica de vihuela* (1552), Miguel de Fuenllana's *Orphenica Lyra* (1554), Esteban Daza's *Parnaso* (1576); but their size and quality are some compensation for their small number.

The description 'lute-book' is useful but inaccurate. The

instrument in question is not the ordinary lute, such as was used in the rest of Europe, but the vihuela da mano, a cross between the lute and the guitar. It had the flat back and incurved sides of the guitar with a comparatively short, broad neck, more like that of the lute. It had six strings (five single and one double) tuned the same as those of the lute

The Spanish guitar, on the other hand, started with only four strings, to which a fifth was added in the sixteenth century, and a sixth only of recent years.

The pioneer of this school of vihuelists was Luis Milan, whose chief work, *El Maestro*, was published in 1535,[1] barely thirty years after the earliest Italian lute-book, Spinacino's *Intabolatura de Lauto* (1507). The comparison of dates is significant, for it is to Italy that we must look for the origin of Milan's style. It is not certain whether Milan himself ever visited Italy, but he came into close contact with the art and culture of that country through his position at the court of Valencia, where the *Vicereine*, Germaine de Foix, had married in 1525, as her third husband, the Duke of Calabria, son of Don Fadrique of Aragon, King of Naples.

Like all the other books for the vihuela, *El Maestro* consists partly of music for that instrument alone, and partly for accompanied songs, and it must be confessed immediately that the most interesting music is to be found in the songs, which are of extraordinary beauty and strength. There is a special reason for this, for Spain more than any other country in Europe, founded its song-literature on its folk-lore. It was extremely rich

[1] Brit. Mus., London.   Nat. Lib., Madrid.   Nat. Lib., Paris.

in traditional poetry and music, much of which was of Moorish descent, and many of the finest ballads and romances were set for the voice and vihuela. This fact helps also to explain some of the peculiarities of the purely instrumental music. Traces of a traditional style of extemporization are even more evident than they are in the Italian music, particularly in the sets of *diferencias*, which will be described later.

Milan's instrumental music is simpler and more Italian in style. *El Maestro* contains as many as forty fantasias and four *tentos*. The fantasias lie half-way between the two styles of Italian *ricercare*; they are longer than the earliest *ricercari* written for the lute, and less solid and less fugal than those of Girolamo Cavazzoni. They contain a certain amount of thematic treatment, but the contrapuntal flow is constantly interrupted by successions of chords. The *tentos* are even more chordal, approaching more nearly to the early Toccata or *Tastar de Corde*. Apart from these, the only other instrumental pieces are six pavanes of real beauty, two of which are admittedly of Italian origin. The following is No. 4:—

Ex. 15.

The note values have been halved.

Luis de Narvaez's *Los seys libros del Delphin de musica*[1] was published in 1538, three years later than *El Maestro*. Narvaez's fantasias, though perhaps more academic than those of Milan, are much more fully worked out as regards fugal treatment, and the joins between the sections are more carefully hidden. It is in the *Delphin de musica* that the *diferencias* make their first appearance. The idea of composing variations on a tune seems to have arisen, in Spain at any rate, from the necessity of varying the accompaniment to the many verses of a long romance. Narvaez gives several compositions of this kind in which the accompaniment becomes more interesting and more florid as the song proceeds. The instrumental variations are rather different in texture, for it is the harmonies, not the tune, that supply the material for variation. Instead of merely adding a counterpoint to the tune, the instrument skips nimbly through the whole compass of treble and bass, giving a kind of rapid sketch of the harmony implied. The following extracts from the variations on *Guardame las vacas* will explain this:—

Ex. 16.

---

[1] Brit. Mus., London.   Nat. Lib., Madrid.   Prov. Lib., Toledo.

The note values have been halved.

Mudarra, in *Tres Libros de Musica en cifras*[1], also has *diferencias* on *Guardame las vacas* and on another famous tune, *Conde Claros*, rather more complicated than those of Narvaez but much the same in style. Here it is the bass that remains constant, a method often used later by the English virginalists. In some of the variations of *Conde Claros* the tune disappears entirely, leaving the bass as a kind of ground. Among the other instrumental pieces are some pavanes, a galliard, and a very curious fantasia written apparently in imitation of the harp, as well as a number of transcriptions of motets by Josquin.

The only distinctive feature in Valderrabano's *Silva de Sirenas*[2] is the introduction of transcriptions of vocal works for two lutes, an idea already carried out in the lute-book of Spinacino. It is interesting to note in passing that the two lute-parts are printed on opposite pages, so arranged that the players could sit opposite to one another with the book between them, just as the singers could when singing Elizabethan airs. Valderrabano's arrangements and variations (both *Guardame las vacas* and *Conde Claros* are included) are about equal to those of his contemporaries.

[1] Nat. Lib., and Escurial, Madrid.
[2] Brit. Mus., London. Nat. Lib., Madrid. Lib., Modena. Nat. Lib., Vienna.

In Pisador's *Libro de musica de vihuela* [1] the fashion for transcription is carried further. He gives as many as fifteen transcriptions of Masses by Josquin, as well as a number of motets. The inevitable variations on *Guardame las vacas* and *Conde Claros* are at the beginning of the book, as well as a pavane ' *muy llana para tañer* ' (very easy to play).

Many Masses and motets are also to be found in Fuenllana's *Orphenica Lyra* (1554),[2] but even they are outnumbered by the fantasias, of which there are as many as eighty-eight. These are, of course, modelled, like all the other Spanish fantasias, on the Italian *Ricercare*, and written very smoothly and with a technical skill which rather belies the author's modest description, 'para desemboltura de mano' (for the loosening of the hand). These transcriptions and fantasias make up the entire bulk of the purely instrumental music in the book, of which the most interesting part is the fifth section, composed of songs of various kinds, romances, *villancicos*, *sonetos*, and *strambotes*.

The other outstanding figure of the Spanish school besides Luis Milan is the blind organist Antonio de Cabezon, who died in 1566. His one great work, *Obras de musica para tecla* (keyboard) *arpa y vihuela*,[3] was published posthumously by his son Hernando in 1577. Cabezon was organist to the Emperor Charles V and to his successor Philip II, the husband of Queen Mary of England. It has even been suggested that he visited England with his royal master, but no substantiation of this has been forthcoming. The greater part of Cabezon's work consists of 'verses' and other short pieces such as were used during the celebration of the Mass. These show a richness of invention and an expressiveness that place them on the same level as the best work of his Italian contemporaries, if not even higher. Still better are the variations,

[1] Brit. Mus., London. Nat. Lib., Madrid. Nat. Lib., Paris.
[2] Brit. Mus., London. Nat. Lib., Berlin. Nat. Lib., Paris, &c.
[3] Nat. Lib., Berlin. Proske Lib., Regensburg. Roy. Lib., Brussels, &c.

of which there are several sets. Cabezon's method of variation differs essentially from that of Narvaez, for the melody is kept more or less intact, passing from one voice to another in the manner of a passacaglia, while the other voices weave new figures round it. The third variation of the *Canto del Caballero*, with the tune in the tenor, is one of the best:—

Ex. 17.

The possibility that the English school of virginalists came under the influence of this small group of Spanish composers has been put forward as a theory, and indeed there is a certain amount of prima facie evidence in support of it. During the first half of the century England was much in touch with Spain, especially during the reign of Queen Mary, and even if Cabezon himself was absent there is no doubt that Spanish musicians of some kind must have been in the train of Philip II; and again, looking at the music itself, there is much in common between the two schools, particularly between Cabezon's variations and those of the virginalists. It is this one point that lends more probability to the theory than any other. The variation form was by no means common in the other schools of Europe, indeed before the end of the century it was only the Dutchman Sweelinck who really developed the form, and it is hardly necessary to underline the close connexion between Spain and the Netherlands. More than this it is not possible to say. Whatever part Spain and the Netherlands may have played in the development of the English style, there is no doubt that both England and Spain derived their first impulse from Italy, but there is food for thought in the fact that the Italian *Ricercare*, the father of all fantasias, originally came from the Motet of the Netherlandish school. Thus the wheel comes full circle.

FRANCE AND THE NETHERLANDS

It is hard to deal justly with the French instrumental music of this period. Considering the achievements of French musicians in other branches of the art, it is astonishing to find in the whole course of the sixteenth century hardly one who did anything to raise instrumental composition above the level of mere mechanics. The books of music for the viols, lute, organ, and virginals, that have survived, are nearly all anthologies of arrangements, ably done it is true, but the work of able craftsmen rather than of artists. The outstanding personalities are not musicians but printers and publishers who relied, no doubt, on the custom of fashionable amateurs, especially ladies, for in France above all other countries the virginals and lute were women's instruments. The books that they produced were easy collections of dances and *chansons* arranged for the instrument in question in most cases by unknown hands, perhaps by the publisher himself or by some 'hack' musician in his employment.

The first and the most productive of these printer-musicians was Pierre Attaignant, *demourant en la rue de la Harpe, pre leglise Saint Cosme*. The list of books printed by him from 1528 onwards and, after his death, by his widow, is a long one. Like Petrucci in Italy, he was the first French printer to use movable metal type. His books for lute, organ, and viols cover the entire ground of the instrumental music of his day: dances, *chansons* transcribed and ornamented, 'verses' for the organ, books of instruction. All these are anonymous except the *Livres de Danceries* where the names of Claude Gervaise, '*scavant musicien*', and Estienne du Tertre are mentioned.

Among all this mass of notes the only music that has any real vitality or significance is in the dances. The transcriptions of *chansons* are of the florid type already familiar in German and Italian music. There are many of them: *Très brève et familière introduction* (1529)[1] for the lute, *Dixneuf chansons musicales* (1530),[2] *Vingt et cinq chansons musicales* (1530),[3] *Vingt et six chansons musicales* (1530)[4] for the '*Orgues, Espinettes, Mani-*

---

[1] State Lib., Berlin.　　[2] State Lib., Munich.　　[3] Ibid.　　[4] Ibid.

cordions, et telz semblables instruments musicaulx.' The most
interesting of these are in the lute-book, where twenty-five out
of the thirty-nine songs are given in two versions, one for the
lute and voice, the other for the lute alone.

The two books of sacred music, *Tablature pour le jeu d'orgues* [1]
and *Magnificat sur les huit tons* [2] have very little intrinsic merit,
and cannot compare in any way with their Italian counterparts.
They contain two long preludes and a number of those 'verses'
which it was customary for the organist to play between the
sections of the Mass.

Far better are the dances of which Attaignant printed in all
ten books; one for the lute, *Dixhuit Basses Dances* (1529),[3] one
for the virginals, *Quatorze Gaillardes &c.* (1530),[4] and eight for
viols or other instruments, *Six Gaillardes et six Pavanes* (1529),[5]
Neuf Basses Dances (1530),[6] *Second, Troisième, Quart, Cinquième,
Sixième, Septième Livre de Danceries* (1547–57).[7] The third,
fourth, fifth, and sixth books of these latter are by Claude Gervaise, and the seventh by Etienne du Tertre, otherwise no composers are mentioned. There are a number of good things in
these *Livres de Danceries*. Not all the tunes are of equal quality
and the four-part setting is of the simplest, but they have far
more strength and vitality than any of the other music produced
by Attaignant.

The best source of technical information about the dances for
which this music was written is the *Orchésographie* [8] of Thoinot
Arbeau. This treatise was not published till 1588, but like most
text-books it is reactionary and describes the dances that the
author knew in his youth. (He was sixty-nine years old when
the book was published.) The difference in date between
Attaignant and Arbeau is therefore less than it seems to be.

[1] State Lib., Munich.   [2] Nat. Lib., Paris.   [3] State Lib., Berlin.
[4] State Lib., Munich.   [5] Ibid., and Stolberg Lib., Wernigerode.
[6] State Lib., Munich.   Second ed., Nat. Lib., Vienna.
[7] Nat. Lib., Paris.   [8] Brit. Mus., London.

Arbeau's dances tally exactly with those that we find in Attaignant's books: *Pavane, Basse-Danse, Gaillarde, Volte, Courante, Allemande,* and the many varieties of the *Branle.* In fact, Arbeau says: 'You will find a sufficiently large number of them (pavanes and *basses-danses*) in the books of dances printed by the late M. Attaignant, who resided near the church of Saint Cosmo at Paris, and in the books of the late Master Nicolas du Chemin, printer at Paris at the sign of the Silver Lion. All the same you will have to rearrange in triple time all the *Basses-Danses* which are set in duple time.' [1]

The slowest and most stately of these was the Pavane—'It is used by kings, princes and great lords, to display themselves on some day of solemn festival with their fine mantles and robes of ceremony; and then the queens and the princesses and the great ladies accompany them with the long trains of their dresses let down and trailing behind them, or sometimes carried by damsels.' None of Attaignant's pavanes is the equal of the exquisite *Belle qui tiens ma vie,* quoted by Arbeau, but the following, written or arranged by Claude Gervaise, is one of the best:—

Ex. 18.

In 1588 the *Basse-Danse*, once so popular, had already been out
of fashion for some forty or fifty years, 'but,' says Arbeau, 'I for-
see that wise and decorous matrons will restore them to favour
as being a manner of dancing full of honour and modesty'.
Naturally enough, wise and decorous matrons did nothing of the
sort and the *Basse-Danse* disappeared. As its name indicates, it
was danced 'low', that is to say, with the feet kept close to the
ground, a style of dancing that was thrown into disfavour by the
leaps and caprioles of the Galliard and *Volte*.

Ex. 19.   Basse-Danse, 'La Roque.'

Both the *Basse-Danse* and the Pavane had its *Nachtanz*: the *Basse-Danse* was followed by the *Tordion*, and the Pavane, as in other countries, by the Galliard. Arbeau gives very intricate directions for the steps of these, and says that there is very little difference between them, except that the *Tordion* is danced 'low' in a light, quick tempo, while the Galliard is danced with high steps to a slower measure.

The *Volte* is described as 'a kind of Galliard familiar to the people of Provence, which, like the *Tordion*, is danced in triple time'. It was a sprightly measure ending in a quick whirl of both dancers together—'After having turned for as many cadences as it pleases you, restore the damsel to her place, when she will feel, whatever good face she puts upon it, her brain confused, her head full of giddy whirlings, and you cannot feel in much better case.

I leave you to consider if it be a proper thing for a young girl to make such large steps and separations of the legs; and whether in the *Volte* both honour and health are not concerned and threatened.'

The *Courante* and the *Allemande* are both familiar to us through the suites of Bach and the Fitzwilliam Virginal Book. The *Courante* was quick and '*sauté*', the *Allemande* was 'a plain dance of a certain gravity, familiar to the Germans'. Of *Branles* there were all kinds—*Branle Simple, Branle Double, Branle Gai, Branle de Bourgogne, Branle de Poitou, Branle d'Ecosse, Branle de Champagne*. Among all these there are a great many dull tunes, but there are a few that are really quite exquisite, like the following *Branle de Champagne* arranged by Claude Gervaise:—

Ex. 20.

Another man of just the same kind as Attaignant, half artist, half merchant, was Adrian Le Roy. Attaignant died about 1553, and in 1552 Le Roy and his brother-in-law, Robert Ballard, joined partnership and obtained a patent as sole printers to the king, Henri II. The list of their publications is long and important. In it are to be found Masses, *chansons à quatre parties*, *chansons en forme de vaudeville*, tablatures for the lute and guitar, a book of instruction for the lute, and many other things. The names of all the foremost French composers of the day are to be found in these anthologies, and of not a few foreigners also, notably Orlando di Lasso, who was entertained at Le Roy's house on his visit to Paris in 1571 and subsequently published several works through this firm.

The guitar tablatures are interesting not so much for the music they contain as for the fact that they are the oldest books of music for that instrument published in France. There are five volumes dated between 1551 and 1554. Just about that time the guitar became exceedingly popular in France. The anonymous author of *La Manière de bien et justement entoucher les lucs* (*luths*) *et guiternes. A l'imprimerie d'Enguilbert de Marne, 1556*, says that whereas in his youth the lute was more in use than the guitar, '*depuis douze ou quinze ans de ça, tout notre monde s'est mis a guitarer, le luth presque mis en oubli, pour être en la guitare je ne sais quelle musique, et icelle beaucoup plus aisé que celle-la des luths, comme vous disent les Grecs:*

> *Les choses tant plus que sont belles*
> *Plus a les avoir coutent elles.*'

The music of these guitar tablatures is much the same as that of the lute-books: *Premier Livre de Tabulature de Guiterre, contenant plusieurs Chansons, Fantasies, Pavanes, Gaillardes, Almandes, Branles, tant simples qu'autres,*[1]—*Tiers Livre de Tabulature de Guiterre, contenant plusieurs Préludes, Chansons, Basse-dances,*

[1] Mazarine Lib., Paris. Brit. Mus., London.

Tourdions, Pavanes, Gaillardes, Almandes, Bransles, tant doubles que simples,[1]—easy pieces for delicate, aristocratic fingers. The ladies took to the guitar and the troublesome lute was left to the greater skill of professional players, many of them foreigners, for the two Hedintons came from Scotland, 'Jacob' from Poland, and Alberto da Ripa from Mantua.

Alberto was lutenist to François I and Henri I. During his lifetime he achieved great fame as a virtuoso and was made Sieur de Carois; when he died in 1551 of the stone, poets competed in doing him honour. Mellin de Saint-Gelais wrote an epitaph in Latin, J. Dorat wrote another which was imitated in French by Jean-Antoine de Baif, and Ronsard wrote a poem in the form of a dialogue between a priest and a passer-by, from which we learn that Alberto died of 'une pierre qui vint lui boucher la vessie'. None of his music seems to have been published during his lifetime, but after his death his pupil Guillaume Morlaye collected his works and issued them in six volumes.

Morlaye also published some lute-books of his own: three volumes '*contenant plusieurs chansons, fantasies, motetz, pavanes, et gaillardes, composés par Maistre Guillaume Morlaye, et autres bons autheurs*',[2] and an arrangement of Certon's Psalms.[3]

Another lute-book, *Le Trésor d'Orphée*[4] by Antoine Francisque, has become well known through a recently published transcription, but there is nothing in it to distinguish it from others of the same kind. All but the first six pieces and two short preludes towards the end are dance-tunes—pavanes, passamezzos, galliards, courantes, voltes, and *branles* of all sorts—with no particular quality to make them worthy of more than passing attention.

Unless other books of the kind have vanished completely, the only serious attempt on the part of a French musician of this

[1] Ibid.
[2] State Lib., Munich. Royal Lib., Brussels.
[3] Ibid.
[4] Nat. Lib., Paris.

period to write consort music is Eustache du Caurroy's *Fantaisies à 3, 4, 5, & 6, parties*[1], published as late as 1610, after the composer's death. Indeed, apart from the *Livres de Danceries* of Attaignant and Jean d'Estrées and one or two fantasias by Claude Lejeune, there is no other music at all for the viols. Du Caurroy's *fantaisies* are neither very beautiful nor very original, but in the absence of all rivals they are worth consideration. They are written skilfully enough, but they have neither the lyrical beauty of the Italian fantasias nor the rhythmical sprightliness of the English. Some of them are free, others are written on a *canto fermo* from the plain-song. The latter type is the more interesting. The twentieth *fantaisie*, for instance, is written on the following theme, played by the alto:—

Ex. 21.

There is a good deal of ingenuity in the way in which the threads that are woven round the main theme all spring from the same source. Phrases such as these appear, obviously derived from the main theme:—

Ex. 22.

[1] St. Gen. Lib., Nat. Lib., Paris.

The real fault of these fantasias is their monotony. They have no contrasting sections, they never work up to a climax, they do not even make use of triple time, that classical device of the sixteenth century for increasing intensity. They run no risks and consequently they never rise above a certain respectable level that shows no trace of really original, inventive genius. The great days of French instrumental music were yet to come; but the sixteenth century was a beginning, for the little dances of the lute-books led to the ballets of Rameau and the *ordres* of Couperin.

A little later in date than Attaignant and earlier than Le Roy is Pierre Phalèse of Louvain, who was born about 1510 and died in 1573 or 1574. His books of lute and consort music are of just the same type as those of his two French contemporaries. For the lute he published five volumes of *Chansons . . . réduitz en tabulature de luc* (1545–8),[1] *Hortus Musarum* (1552),[2] *Luculentum Theatrum Musicum* (1568),[3] *Hortulus Cytharae* (1570),[4] and *Theatrum Musicum* (1571);[5] for the viols or other instruments *Liber primus leviorum carminum* (1571),[6] and *Chorearum molliorum collectanea* (1583).[7]

The first book of *Chansons réduitz en tabulature de luc* contains many arrangements of French *chansons* and a few Dutch popular songs, such as *Die lusteljeke mey* and *En vrolick wesen*; the second book is much the same, but in addition it has nine fantasias, Jannequin's *Battle*, and one or two Spanish pieces; the third book has French *chansons* and Latin motets, and the fourth book is entirely Italian, with fantasias by Francesco da Milano and P. P. Borrono, paduanas, passamezzos, and other dances. The fifth book is a collection of transcriptions by Francesco da Milano, Antoni Rotta, Joan Maria de Crema, and others.

---

[1] State Lib., Vienna. Hirsch Lib., Frankfurt.   [2] Lib., Dunquerque.
[3] Nat. Lib., Vienna. Univ. Lib., Rostock.   [4] Univ. Lib., Rostock.
[5] State Lib., Berlin. State Lib., Munich. Lib., Karlsruhe.
[6] Gymn. Lib., Heilbronn.   [7] State Lib., Munich. Univ. Lib., Upsala.

The first book of *Hortus Musarum* is divided into two parts. The first has fantasias by Rotta, Gintzler, and Francesco da Milano, with a large number of transcriptions for one lute; the second part is for two lutes. The second volume of the *Hortus* consists of transcriptions for voice and lute of vocal music by Crécquillon, Josquin, Clemens non Papa, and others.

The *Theatrum Musicum* is a huge collection. It begins with thirty-three fantasias by Paul Baron, Francesco da Milano, Sixt Kargel, and Neusidler; the next ninety-four numbers are transcriptions from the works of Crécquillon, Bacfarc, Orlando di Lasso, Cipriano da Rore, and Clemens non Papa, then some madrigals of five and six parts and motets of four, five, and six parts. The next section has a few dances arranged for two lutes, and the last section is all dances with Jannequin's *Battle* to end up with. Phalèse's two books for the viols contain nothing but dances; in fact, they bear the French sub-titles *Livre de Danseries* and *Recueil de Danseries*.

Other anthologies worth mentioning are the third volume of Tielman Susato's *Musyck Boexken* (1551),[1] which contains a large number of dances of all kinds, and two books of lute music by Emmanuel Andriaensen—*Pratum Musicum* (1584)[2] and *Novum Pratum Musicum* (1592)[3]—but none of these is of primary importance. The only really great instrumental composer produced by the Netherlands is Jan Pieterszoon Sweelinck, a full account of whose works will be found in the next volume of this history.

ENGLAND

When Henry VII died, a worn-out and disillusioned man, at the age of fifty-two, he left the country in a state of prosperity

[1] State Lib., Berlin.
[2] State Lib., Berlin. Second ed., Brussels, Copenhagen, London.
[3] State Lib., Hamburg. Brit. Mus., London. Maz. Lib., Paris.

such as it had not known for a very long time. Twenty-four
years of constant toil and thrift had done much to repair the
damages of the preceding century. The state coffers were full,
the country was at peace, and the new spirit of the Renaissance
had set foot in England in the shape of one of its greatest
scholars, Erasmus. But as far as the Arts were concerned England was still deep in the Middle Ages. The king was a hard-
headed business man who cared for nothing but practical
matters, and his private life at Court was as austere and
economical as his public policy.

When Henry VIII came to the throne he set to to profit by
his father's thriftiness, and by indulging his natural taste for all
the Arts he let in the full flood of the Renaissance, its music, its
literature, its painting, and, above all, its luxury. His Court
was as rich and magnificent as his father's was poor and meagre,
as gay and worldly as that other was gloomy and ascetic. He
flung wide his gates, and artists from every country in Europe
flocked in. No one who had anything to offer was turned away.
The young king himself was no mean adept in the Arts, according to the description given of him by the Venetian Magnifico,
Piero Pasqualigo, who accompanied the more famous Giustiniani
to England in 1515. 'His Majesty is the handsomest potentate
I ever set eyes on; above the usual height, with an extremely
fine calf to his leg, his complection very fair and bright, with
auburn hair combed straight and short, in the French fashion,
and a round face so very beautiful, that it would become a
pretty woman, his throat being rather long and thick. He was
born on the 28th of June, 1491, so he will enter his twenty-fifth
year the month after next. He speaks French, English, and
Latin, and a little Italian, plays well on the lute and harpsichord, sings from book at sight, draws the bow with greater
strength than any man in England, and jousts marvellously.
Believe me he is in every respect a most accomplished Prince;

and I, who have now seen all the sovereigns in Christendom, and last of all these two of France and England in such great state, might well rest content, and with sufficient reason have it said to me, "abi viator, sat tuis oculis debes".'[1]

Fortunately, the dispatches sent by Giustiniani to the Signory of Venice have been preserved, for they give a very full and illuminating account of the English Court, and tell us certain things about musical conditions of which we should otherwise be ignorant. In a letter from Giustiniani's secretary, Nicolo Sagudino, dated May 3rd, 1515, the writer gives an interesting description of the May Day festivities at Greenwich Palace, where he was made to perform himself. 'The King then went to dinner, and, by his Majesty's order, the ambassadors, and we likewise, dined in his palace, with the chief nobility of this land. After dinner the ambassadors were taken into certain chambers containing a number of organs and harpsichords and flutes, and other instruments, and where the prelates and chief nobles were assembled to see the joust which was then in preparation; and in the mean while the ambassadors told some of these grandees that I was a proficient on some of these instruments; so they asked me to play, and knowing that I could not refuse, I did so for a long while, both on the harpsichords and organs, and really bore myself bravely, and was listened to with great attention. Among the listeners was a Brescian, to whom this King gives 800 ducats annually for playing the lute, and this man took up his instrument and played a few things with me; and afterwards two musicians, who are also in his Majesty's service, played the organ, but very ill forsooth: they kept bad time, and their touch was feeble, neither was their execution good, so that my performance was deemed not much worse than theirs. The prelates who were present told me that the King would certainly

---

[1] From *Four Years at the Court of Henry VIII*, a translation by Rawdon Brown of the dispatches written by Sebastiano Giustiniani.

choose to hear me, as his Majesty practises on these instruments day and night, and that he will very much like my playing. So I shall prepare, and hope not to disgrace myself if called upon, and will give you notice of the result; and pray send me some compositions of Zuane Maria's, as I vaunt him to everyone for what he is, and thus they have requested me to send for some of his music, promising me some of theirs in return; and I should also wish to receive a few new ballads (*frottole*)'.[1]

The great musical personality at Court, though Giustiniani's letters would naturally be prejudiced in favour of another Venetian, seems to have been Fra Dionisio Memo one of the organists of St. Mark's, who arrived in England in September 1516, and made such an impression that the king contrived to keep him in this country. 'Friar Dionisius Memo the organist of St. Mark's, arrived here a few days ago with a most excellent instrument of his, which he has brought hither with much pains and cost. I presented him in the first place to the Cardinal, telling him that when your Highness heard of his wanting to quit Venice for the purpose of coming to his Majesty, you gave him gracious leave, which you would not have done, had he intended going to anyone else. His lordship chose to hear him in the presence of many lords and *virtuosi*, who were as pleased as possible with him; after which his right reverend lordship told him to go to the King, who would see him very willingly, employing many words of flattering commendation. He afterwards went to his Majesty, who, knowing he was there, sent for him immediately after dinner, and made him play before a great number of lords and all his virtuosi. He played not merely to the satisfaction, but to the incredible admiration and pleasure of everybody, and especially of his Majesty, who is extremely skilled in music, and of the two Queens (Catherine of Aragon and Margaret of Scotland). My secretary was also present, who

[1] See note 1, p. 458.

highly extolled the performance, and told the King many things in his praise as it went on, mentioning how much favour he enjoyed with your Highness and all Venice, which had been content to deprive itself for the satisfaction of his Majesty, with many other very suitable words, so that said Majesty has included him among his instrumental musicians, nay, has appointed him their chief, and says he will write to Rome to have him unfrocked out of his monastic weeds, so that he may merely retain holy orders, and that he will make him his chaplain.'[1]

This plan seems to have been carried out, for Memo remained in England for some years, enjoying the king's utmost favour. When the French ambassadors arrived in July 1517, they were made to listen to 'the instrumental music of the reverend Master Dionysius Memo, his chaplain, which lasted during four consecutive hours, to the so great admiration of all the audience, and with such marks of delight from his Majesty aforesaid, as to defy exaggeration.'[1] When the king retired to Windsor to escape from an outbreak of the plague he took with him only his physician, three of his favourite gentlemen, and Master Dionysius Memo. In the following year the king sealed his reputation with the remark 'Per Deum, iste est honestissimus vir et unus carissimus, nullus unquam servivit mihi fidelius et melius illo, scribaris Domino vestro quod habeat ipsum commendatum'.[1]

It is a pity that none of Memo's organ music has survived, as it would have helped to establish more clearly the musical link between England and Italy. But we can make a fairly safe guess at its character. The elder Cavazzoni's *Recerchari, Motetti, Canzoni* (1523) is a good sample of the earliest Venetian organ music, and we may take it for granted that Memo's music followed more or less the same lines. But if Italian models are lacking, we have several manuscript volumes from which we can gauge the repertoire of the average English organist at the

[1] See note 1, p. 458.

beginning of the century. One of the most important of these is
a volume in the British Museum (Add. MS. 30513), a collection
of organ music in the hand of Thomas Mulliner, Master of the
Choir of St. Paul's. Though it bears no date it seems to have
been written either in Queen Mary's reign or at the beginning of
Elizabeth's, but much of the music is earlier than that. The
composers' names mentioned are Nicholas Carleton, Thomas
Tallis (*c.* 1510–85), Newman (?), Richard Alwood, Farrant (probably Richard), William Blitheman (d. 1591), John Shepherd 'of
the Queen's Chapel' (d. *c.* 1563), John Redford (*c.* 1485–*c.* 1545),
William Shelby, John Taverner (*c.* 1495–1545), Robert Johnson,
Richard Edwards, Christopher Tye (*c.* 1500–72), Heathe,
William (?) Mundy. Some of the leaves at the beginning of the
book are missing, and some of the music has been added by a
later hand; but even so, there are over one hundred pieces of
organ music of various kinds. Some of these are straightforward
transcriptions of motets and madrigals, among them Edwards's
famous *In going to my naked bed*; others are compositions on the
plain-song. How many of these latter are original and how many
transcriptions it is impossible to say until all the music of this
period, vocal and instrumental, has been collated and catalogued.
Some of them, that have a florid descant over a plain-song bass
or vice versa, are obviously original, but many follow the vocal
style so closely that it is impossible to distinguish one from the
other without more facts than are at present at our disposal.
One type of plain-song composition, however, is definitely
original—the *In Nomine.*

The career of the *In Nomine* is one of the most curious episodes
in English musical history. So far no satisfactory reason has
been found why the one particular phrase of plain-song which is
its invariable *canto fermo* should have been chosen rather than
any other; but the fact remains that it exercised the ingenuity
of practically every eminent composer of instrumental music,

and of many obscure ones too, from Taverner at the beginning
of the sixteenth century to Purcell at the end of the seventeenth.
In Nomines are to be found in almost every book of organ, virginal, or viol music, and in such numbers that it is usually
possible to find at least two copies of each.   Even Purcell wrote
one among his Fantasias, and Roger North, at the beginning of
the eighteenth century, mentions them in his *Memoirs of Music*;
'But that which was styled *In nomine* was yet more remarkable,
for it was onely descanting upon the eight notes with which the
syllables (*In nomine domini*) agreed.   And of this kind I have
seen whole volumes, of many parts, with the severall authors
names inscribed.   And if the study, contrivance, and ingenuity
of these compositions, to fill the harmony, carry on fuges, and
interspers discords, may pass in the account of skill, no other
sort whatsoever may pretend so more.   And it is some conforma-
tion that in two or three ages last bygone the best private music,
as was esteemed, consisted of these.'   The plain-song melody of
the *In Nomine* is always the same (one may safely say that the
very few *In Nomines* written on other *canti fermi* are misnamed).
It is that of the first psalm-antiphon of the First Vespers for
Trinity Sunday:—

Ex. 23.

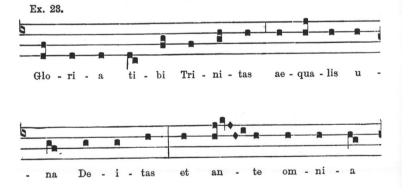

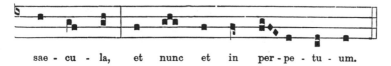

sae - cu - la,   et   nunc   et   in   per - pe - tu - um.

What then can be the meaning of the title of *In Nomine*, for it is obviously not a quotation from the text of the antiphon? There can be no doubt of the identity of the tune used in the *In Nomine* with the *Gloria Tibi Trinitas*. Taverner used it both for his Mass, *Gloria Tibi Trinitas*, and for his *In Nomine*, and in the Fitzwilliam Virginal Book Bull uses both titles for pieces on this same theme. What can be the explanation of its title and of its extraordinary vogue in England? Why should this one phrase of plain-song have been promoted to a unique position? Whatever the reason may be it must be bound up with some national tradition, for outside England the *In Nomine* was unknown. There must have been some very cogent reason why almost every English composer of the sixteenth century who wrote any instrumental music at all should have tried his hand at the same thing. Byrd, Bull, both Ferraboscos, Parsley, Tallis, Taverner, Tomkins, Tye, Whyte, Alwood, Blytheman, Ives, Strogers, Gibbons, William Lawes, and even Purcell all carried on this curious tradition, the explanation of which still remains a mystery.

In the Mulliner Book there are five *In Nomines*, one each by 'Master Newman', Alwood, Taverner, Johnson, and an anonymous composer. Taverner's is interesting as being one of the earliest of all. There are several other copies of it: another for organ in a manuscript at Christ Church, Oxford, one in five parts for viols in a volume at the British Museum which will be referred to later, and a version for lute which is probably only a lute-part for consort use. The four-part version in Mulliner's book is apparently the original; the fifth part, which appears in the arrangement for viols, seems, judging by internal evidence, to be a later edition.

Taverner starts by using the first notes of the plain-song thematically:—

Ex. 24.

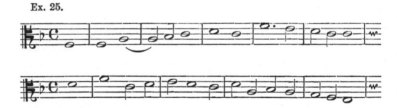

From this germ most of the other material is taken. Themes such as these appear:—

Ex. 25.

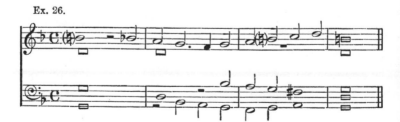

The unexpected cadence on G is particularly noteworthy:—

Ex. 26.

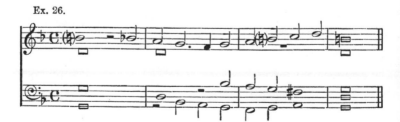

Among other things in this manuscript are several short pieces called either *A Point* or *Versus*. These are the counterparts of the *versi* found in so many Italian organ-books. The following by Shepherd is typical:—

Ex. 27.

Earlier in date than the Mulliner Book are two thin volumes from the Royal Collection, Appendices 58 and 59. These contain all kinds of music: songs, organ or virginal pieces, lute-tablatures, and so on. Among them is the famous *Hornpipe* by Hugh Aston. There is so much confusion about the identity of Aston that it is very difficult to date this piece. The probability is that the composer was not the same man as the priest who was Archdeacon of York and Canon of St. Stephen's, and who died in 1522. It seems incredible that it could have been written

II 3 o

before that date. Its whole style and technique seem to deny
it. It is not written on a ground bass, as has been sometimes
stated, but on a kind of drone bass over which the right hand
scurries up and down, making occasionally some very big leaps
—in one case of an octave and a sixth. There are some very
good antiphonal passages and some lively cross-rhythms. In the
same book is another piece, also written on a drone bass, *My
Lady Carey's Dump*. This is even more improbable in the
matter of date, as it is written in variation form. Certainly
there is nothing else like it in the music of the first half of the
century.

In dealing with consort music we are on less safe ground than
with keyboard music. The mere absence of text is not sufficient
proof that the music was meant exclusively for instruments.
Of course, everything that could be sung could also be played on
any instruments having the necessary compass, but what we
are looking for is real instrumental music, and it is this broad
belt of common territory that makes the task so hard.

A big book of such music is in the British Museum, Additional
MS. 31390. It bears the title *A booke of In Nomines and other
Solfaing songes of v, vi, vii and viii parts, for voyces or instruments*.
In it is a huge collection of all kinds of music, including about
forty *In Nomines*. It must have been compiled towards the end
of the century, but much of the music is by earlier composers:
Tye, Taverner, Shepherd, and others. Some of these earlier
works look as if they had been touched up by the addition of
extra parts, as in the case, already mentioned, of Taverner's *In
Nomine*; for this is the volume referred to in that connexion.

Nineteen of the *In Nomines* are by Christopher Tye, and most
of these have curious, apparently irrelevant sub-titles, such as
Free from all : *I come* : *My death* : *Follow me* : *Rachel weeping* :
Weep no more, Rachel. There are no vocal compositions by Tye
that tally with any of these, and it seems unlikely that these

rather meaningless phrases should have been chosen arbitrarily, on the analogy of East's *Fancies* and Tobias Hume's pieces for *viola da gamba*. Can it be that they are not titles at all but 'cues' from some of the choir-boy plays such as were acted by the Children of the Chapel Royal? It is not inconceivable that these *In Nomines* were used as incidental music, perhaps to accompany some of the more high-flown speeches. The point is at any rate worthy of investigation even if it does not point to the ultimate solution of the problem of the *In Nomine*.

A volume of much earlier date than the one just described is Add. MS. 31922, a big, bulky book, exquisitely written and illuminated on vellum in the reign of Henry VIII. It is well known as the source of a number of compositions supposed to have been written by the king himself, but the ascription is rather doubtful. It is founded on the fact that the king's name appears on the top of several pages, but, as all the other composers' names are carefully written at the end of their compositions, it seems more likely that the royal name means no more than that the king was the owner of the book, unless it was written purposely at the top of the page to distinguish him from all the others.

Many of the pieces have no text, but only one or two at the end seem to be definitely instrumental. One of these has for its subject the Flemish folk-song *T'Andernacken op dem Rhein*, which was used by any number of German composers and even by Spinacino in his lute-book. The history of this tune which formed a common basis for so many styles is a fit subject for a separate study.

The use of popular tunes as a basis for musical composition is one of the familiar characteristics of the Renaissance. They crop up in all kinds of shapes, whether as the ground bass of a Mass or as the refrain of a *frottola*, and no doubt the essential characteristics of the folk-music of different countries influenced the various methods of handling them. The long-drawn-out, almost unrecognizable tunes of the Masses are of course a wilful exception, but the stocky squareness of the German songs and the vulgarity of the Italian street-ditties are reflected in the music derived from them.

England is no exception to the rule, but, as has happened at other times, English composers, while content to accept foreign models, yet contrived to make of them something new. The influence of folk-songs runs through the music of the Elizabethan age like a coloured thread, tingeing everything and sometimes gleaming out in the most unexpected places—in a fantasy by Byrd, in a song of Dowland's. It leavens the whole lump instead of lying like lead at the bottom or frothing on the top.

The father of Elizabethan music is William Byrd. After three centuries of neglect his name has at last won the position that it deserves. The details of his life have been traced and the bulk of his music has been transcribed, published, and performed. The personality that has emerged is of the richest. The quality of his very large output is in just proportion to its scope. He covers the whole field with equal success: his anthems, services, Masses, and madrigals do not concern us here, but even so it is impossible in so short a space to do justice to his rich store of instrumental music.

There are about one hundred and twenty-five compositions for organ or virginals, found in *Parthenia*, the Fitzwilliam Virginal Book, the Virginal Books of Benjamin Cosyns and Will Foster, and other lesser manuscripts. These fall roughly under four headings: dances, fantasias, grounds and variations, and pieces of no set form. The dances are pavanes and galliards (joined or separate), almans, jigs, voltas, and corantos. The most important and the most beautiful of these are the pavanes and galliards, which go for the most part in pairs. They are no mere dance music; indeed, it is improbable that they were meant to be danced to at all unless the ornamented *reprises* which follow each section were left out for practical purposes. It is likely that the dances were originally written for viols and transcribed for the virginals, the *reprises* being added in the process of transcription. These latter are done in such a masterly fashion that they heighten the beauty of the melodies instead of smothering them in a mass of mechanical coloratura.

Not all the pavanes and galliards are of equal merit, but the best, *Pavana Bray* for example, have a tender, lyrical beauty both of harmony and of melody that is unsurpassed in virginal music. The variations, on the other hand, make for brilliance. All the usual devices are employed, rapid scale-passages, leaps, ornaments, intricate cross-rhythms with a big, cumulative effect towards the end. The melody is always kept in the right hand, but it usually passes to the alto part in the last or penultimate variation.

One of Byrd's most famous virginal pieces is *The Battle.* Descriptive pieces of this kind are by no means an unfamiliar feature in the music of the sixteenth century. The most famous are the four *chansons* of Jannequin—*Le Chant des Oiseaux, La Guerre, La Chasse,* and *L'Alouette. La Guerre* is the famous *Battle of Marignan* which appears in so many German, French, and Italian lute-books. Byrd's *Battle* is obviously modelled on this latter piece. It contains all the same rather childish imitations of warlike noises, trumpets, fifes and drums, and so on, but even here he cannot resist a good tune. The *Irish March* may possibly be a folk-tune, but in any case it has a really beautiful melody which comes as a relief from the crudities of the rest. The idea of using musically the familiar sounds of everyday life—and one may almost describe war as part of the everyday life of that Age—was not new. It seems to go back almost to the beginning of musical history. The song of the cuckoo appears in *Sumer is icumen in,* and all the noises of the countryside are in the *caccie* of the early Florentine school. In England there is an exact parallel to these in the 'cries' of Gibbons and Deering, in which the familiar cries of street-vendors are echoed; but there are other compositions in which the same method is put to more poetical use. There is, for instance, a *Knell* for five viols, by Robert Johnson, in which the following phrase:—

Ex. 28.

is used passacaglia-wise, passing throughout the piece from one part to another without interruption. Another piece of the same kind is *The Bells* by Byrd, which is written in the form of a ground on the following bass:—

Ex. 29.

All its nine variations are vividly illustrative of the pealing of bells, big and small.

Byrd's consort music consists of one *In Nomine* of seven parts, and several à 5 and à 4, three fantasias à 6, three à 4, and two à 3, a pavane and galliard à 6, two preludes à 5, and a set of variations on the ground, *The leaves be green.* The most important of these are the fantasias. The typical English Fantasia of the sixteenth century is modelled fairly closely on the Italian *Ricercare.* Like the latter, it develops fugally a number of themes, making rather for a cumulative effect than for any vivid contrast between the sections. The rhythmical interest is usually heightened by a section in triple time, either at the end

or near to it. There are hundreds of fantasias by English composers modelled on these lines, and so also are some of those by
Byrd, but there are, at any rate, two that are highly original
both in form and in texture. One of these in six parts comes
from *Psalms, Songs and Sonnets* (1611).[1] It starts fugally in the
usual manner but about half-way through this merry, jig-like
tune breaks in and forms a whole section in 6/4 time:—

Ex. 30.

This in its turns leads, after a cadence on G, to another rather
slower dance-like section in 3/2:—

Ex. 31.

Here fugal treatment disappears altogether, and the phrases of
the tune are tossed from one instrument to another in dialogue
with a simple harmonic accompaniment. The final section in
common time is only eight semibreves long and just serves to
give a dignified ending to the work.

[1] Brit. Mus., London.

Another six-part fantasia, from Additional MSS. 17786/91 in the British Museum, also has a long and complete section in triple rhythm with this tune:—

Ex. 32.

Here the melody is shared chiefly by the cantus and quintus parts in dialogue, a method that is used also in the earlier part of the work, where the quintus, altus, and tenor are answered by the tenor, sextus, and bassus. This antiphonal scheme is very reminiscent of the *canzoni* of Giovanni Gabrieli. It is common enough, too, in English vocal music, particularly in the homophonic canzonets and ballets; but the melodies quoted above have a different and essentially instrumental cast. The tune in the fantasia from *Psalms, Songs, and Sonnets* (Ex. 30) might quite well be a folk-tune, but the others are much more like the pseudo-dance-tunes of the suites of Lawes and Locke.

All Byrd's consort music is written for whole consort, a term which was used to describe any family of the same instrument, in this case viols. A mixed collection of instruments was known as a broken consort. Although it is evident from contemporary pictures and literature that viols, lutes, recorders, and so forth must continually have been used together in consort, very little music, either English or otherwise, was actually scored. Instruments are mentioned in some of the later Italian books from Gabrieli onwards, but most of these belong to a later period. Two collections of music for broken consort were published in the first years of the seventeenth century, but, by a stroke of great misfortune, neither has survived complete. They are *The*

First Book of Consort Lessons by Thomas Morley (1611) and *Lessons for Consort* by Philip Rosseter (1609). Morley's book is for 'the treble lute, the pandora, the citterne, the base-violl, the flute, and the treble violl'. Of these, the parts for pandora, citterne, flute, and treble viol have survived; the treble lute and bass-viol parts have disappeared altogether, and the parts that have survived are scattered. It is even worse in the case of Rosseter's *Lessons*, for of these only the citterne part exists. Interesting as it would be to have complete copies of these works, their value must not be overrated. It is not to be imagined that they contain anything comparable with the fantasias for viols of Byrd, or indeed with any of the best English viol music. From what has survived it is evident that the short pieces of which they consist are all simple arrangements of popular tunes, and it is in the choice of instruments and in the scoring that the interest would lie rather than in the music itself. On the other hand, it is a thousand pities that we should not be able to hear the results of these early experiments in instrumentation.

Morley's other instrumental work consists chiefly of virginal music, of which there is a certain amount in the Fitzwilliam Virginal Book—a fantasia, two pavanes and galliards, an almand, and two sets of variations. One of the pavanes has frequently been described as a setting of Dowland's *Lachrimae*, but in fact it is not so, although the first few notes are the same. There are, however, two real settings of *Lachrimae* in the Fitzwilliam Book by Byrd and Farnaby. The popularity of this melody is really remarkable. It appears in all sorts of forms—as a song with lute accompaniment, as a solo for lute in innumerable arrangements, as a piece for viols, arranged for the virginals and for broken consort in Morley's Consort Lessons. It is impossible to say which of these was the original form. Dowland was first and foremost a writer of tunes, and he cared little into what form he cast them, for the same tunes occur frequently in his

works in different guises. *Lachrimae* is certainly among the
most beautiful of these, and it is also one of the most tragic and
the most despairing. 'Happy, happy they that in Hell feel not
the world's despite' are the final lines of the words that he wrote
for it. The extreme popularity of such a piece puts, surely, a
different complexion on the traditional conception of Merry
England. There are many references to *Lachrimae* in contemporary literature. It occurs, for instance, in *The Knight of the
Burning Pestle* at the end of the second act:

> *Citizen*. 'You musicians, play Baloo!'
> *Wife*. 'No, good George, let's ha' Lachrymae!'
> *Citizen*. 'Why, this is it, cony.'
> *Wife*. 'It's all the better, George.'

So popular did it become that Dowland set it himself for five
viols and added six more *Pavanes*, all beginning with the same
descending phrase:—

Ex. 33.

To the original *Lachrimae* he gave the title *Lachrimae Antiquae*,
and to the others the titles of *Lachrimae Antiquae Novae*,
Lachrimae Gementes, *Lachrimae Tristes*, *Lachrimae Coactae*,
Lachrimae Amantis, and *Lachrimae Verae*. These seven pavanes
were published with a number of other pavanes, galliards, and
almands in 1605 in a book with the title *Lachrimae, or Seaven
Teares figured in Seaven Passionate Pavans, with divers other
Pavans, Galiards, and Almands, set forth for the Lute, Viols, or
Violons, in five parts*.[1] This is Dowland's finest achievement in
instrumental writing. There is perhaps nothing in the book
that is quite so original or so beautiful as the best of the songs.

[1] Brit. Mus., London.

The wonderful elegiac quality and the rhythmic freedom of these cannot, of course, have full play in the more formal dance measures, but within their limitations the pavanes in particular are as fine as anything of their kind in Elizabethan music.

The seven *Lachrimae Pavanes* and the two others that follow them—*Semper Dowland Semper Dolens* and *Sir Henry Umpton's Funerall*—are all essentially instrumental music, and do not exist in any other form, but several of the galliards appeared also as songs. *Diggorie Piper's Galliard*, for instance, is the same as *If my complaints could passions move*, and *The Earl of Essex His Galliard* is the same as *Can she excuse my wrongs?* The simpler, more melodic shape of the galliard, with its characteristic alternation between 3/2 and 6/4 time, lends itself more easily to the adaptation of words than the slow phrases and intricate harmonies of the pavane. The two almands which occur at the end of the book are much inferior to the rest, and indeed Dowland never seems to have been at his best in a quick measure. In all his songs there are very few that go fast. His own word-play *Semper Dowland Semper Dolens* describes exactly his emotional outlook and, one may presume, his reputation. One may look in vain through his works for that lively, folkish strain that is so noticeable in the works of his contemporaries. But one very curious instance may be noted in the accompaniment to *Can she excuse my wrongs?* in which a snatch of the tune *The woods so wild* suddenly occurs. It must surely be intentional, as at that moment the voice part is subordinate to it.

Dowland's other instrumental works consist of a mass of short pieces for the lute and for the viols, to be found in innumerable manuscripts and printed collections, the latter mostly of foreign origin. It is impossible to tell which of these are original and which arrangements. Dowland travelled much, and it is likely that many of the pieces ascribed to him in foreign lute-books are no more than the editors' versions of what they had heard him play. Every lutenist had his own style and his own technique, and that would explain why hardly any two versions of the same piece agree in detail. The only works, therefore, that we can regard as authentic, apart from *Lachrimae*, are the few pieces scattered among his lute-books and in his son Robert's *Varietie of Lute-lessons* (1610).[1]

To give a complete account of all the music written for viols, virginals, and lute in Elizabethan England would need a separate treatise, even supposing that all the original research needed had already been done, which is far from the case; for there is an enormous quantity of material still unexplored. In the lute-books in the University Library at Cambridge alone there are many hundreds of pieces. Not everything is worth reviving, but exploration is bound to produce a certain amount of treasure among a lot of rubbish. The following little piece, attributed in Besard's *Thesaurus Harmonicus* to Dowland and in one of the Cambridge lute-books, in a slightly different setting with reprises, to Daniel Bachelor, is surely worthy of preservation:—

Ex. 34.

[1] Brit. Mus., London. Bodl. Lib., Oxford.

A great deal of the music in the five famous virginal books—the Fitzwilliam, Cosyn's, Forster's, Lady Neville's, and Parthenia —belongs to a later date than the period with which we are concerned, and therefore does not come within the scope of this chapter. It is exhaustively treated in the next volume, the music of the seventeenth century, by Sir Hubert H. Parry. The many excellent reprints that have been issued of late years have gained for it a remarkable degree of prominence and popularity; but only when the same has been done for the lute and viol music shall we see all three in just proportion, and only then shall we be able to assess the debt of each to the other.

It is not easy to draw any definite line between the true Elizabethan period and that which followed. The turn of the century is no milestone, for the lives of most of the chief Elizabethan composers pass it. In point of time, England was many years behind the rest of Europe, and the school that was eventually formed was slow to disappear. The French influences of Charles the First's reign failed to destroy the older tradition of viol playing which continued to flourish, modified but unimpeded, almost to the end of the century, when it eventually succumbed to the country from which it first sprang—Italy. There is a world of difference between Byrd and Purcell, but the difference is the outcome of a gradual logical development, not of any sudden change. When Purcell, in his early years, sat down to write fantasias and *In Nomines* he was obeying a tradition that had preserved its essential characteristics for well over a century.

INDEX

TO VOLUMES I AND II

488   INDEX TO VOLS. I AND II

498   INDEX TO VOLS. I AND II

Terpsichore, ii. 406.
TERTRE, Estienne du, ii. 446, 447.
Terzo libro dei madrigali nov. di Archadelt, &c., ii. 124.
Testudo Gallo-Germanica, ii. 399.
Tetrachord, i. 13, 23, 28, 29.
Teutsch Lautenbuch, ii. 398.
Théâtres Lyriques, ii. 262.
Theatrum Musicum, ii. 455, 456.
Thesaurus Gratiarum, ii. 399.
Thesaurus Harmonicus, ii. 399, 476.
Thesaurus Motetarum, ii. 402.
Thesmophoriazusae, ii. 256.
THIBAULT, Geneviève, ii. 265, 310.
THIBAUT DE CHAMPAGNE, ii. 264, 277.
THORLEY, William, ii. 12.
TIBURTINO, Giuliano, ii. 420.
TIERSOT, Julien, ii. 281.
Timbre, ii. 346.
Time signatures, i. 235.
TINCTORIS, i. 316; ii. 1, 95, 157.
Toccata, ii. 423.
Toccate d'Intavolatura, ii. 423.
TOMKINS, Thomas, ii. 215, 216, 406, 463.
Τὸν πρωκτὸν κυνός, ii. 256.
Tones (of Meistersinger), ii. 332.
Tordion, ii. 450.
TORRENTES, Andrés, ii. 149, 150.
Tosto che l'alba, ii. 320, 324.
Tournai MS., i. 238 sqq., 242, 244.
TRABACI, Giovanni, ii. 426.
Tractatus de Consonantiis Musicalibus, i. 63.
Transcriptions, ii. 353, 363, 364 sqq., 367, 377 sqq. *V.* chapter VI, *passim*.
Transilvano, Il, ii. 424.
Trattati della Musica, ii. 422.
Treble-sight, i. 331.
TRÉBOR, i. 254.
TREND, J. B., ii. 148, 298, 302.
Trent, Council of, ii. 243.
Trent MS. *See* Vienna.
Très brève et familière introduction, ii. 446.
Tres Libros de Musica en cifras, ii. 437, 442.
Trésor d'Orphée, Le, ii. 453.
Triad, ii. 115.
Tribum quem non abhorruit, ii. 377.

Tripla, ii. 408.
Tripla (Magna tripla), i. 127.
Triplum, i. 86, 201, 203, 208, 212, 238, 331. *See* Organum Triplum.
Triste España sin ventura, ii. 349.
Triste plaisir, ii. 46.
Tristezas me matan, ii. 151.
Tritone, i. 12, 13, 15 sqq., 22, 24, 43, 84; ii. 280. *See* Chromatic alteration.
Triumphs of Oriana, ii. 219.
TROMBONCINO, ii. 349, 353.
Trombone, ii. 428, 431.
Trope, i. 45, 195, 196.
Troper (Winchester MS.), i. 34, 49, 52.
Troubadour, i. 74, 243; ii. 263 sqq., 289, 290, 352. *See* chapter V, *passim*.
— MSS., ii. 268.
Troubadours, The, ii. 277.
Trouvères, i. 2, 42; ii. 263 sqq., 290, 307, 309. *See* Troubadour.
Trouvères et Troubadours, ii. 282.
Tu che l'opera d'altrui, i. 261.
TUDOR, ii. 162.
Tudor Church Music, ii. 167 sqq., 181, 193, 210.
TUNSTEDE, Simon, i. 111, 317.
Tu patris sempiternus, i. 11, 15, 16.
TURGES, ii. 162.
Turke MS., ii. 336.
TYE, Christopher, ii. 172 sqq., 176, 187, 188 sqq., 192, 206, 215, 461, 463, 466.
TYES, ii. 11.
TYPP, ii. 11.

UMBRIA, ii. 303.
Un bel sparver, ii. 318.
Une mousse de Biscaye, ii. 346.
Upsala (University Library), ii. 147.
URSPRUNG, O., ii. 142.
Ursprung des Motetts, i. 202.
Utilis et Compendiaria Introductio, ii. 391.
Ut queant laxis, i. 280.
Ut tuo propitiatus, i. 51, 55.

VAILLANT, Jean, i. 254.
VALDERRABANO, Enrique Enriquez de, ii. 363, 437, 442.

PRINTED IN GREAT BRITAIN AT THE UNIVERSITY PRESS, OXFORD
BY JOHN JOHNSON, PRINTER TO THE UNIVERSITY